The Short Victorious War

Also by David Walder

Fiction
Bags of Swank
The Short List
The House Party
The Fair Ladies of Salamanca

History
The Chanak Affair

The Short Victorious War

The Russo-Japanese Conflict 1904-5

DAVID WALDER

1817

HARPER & ROW, PUBLISHERS

NEW YORK, EVANSTON, SAN FRANCISCO, LONDON

FIRST U.S. EDITION

Library of Congress Cataloging in Publication Data

Walder, David
  The short victorious war.
  Bibliography: p.
  1. Russo-Japanese War, 1904–1905. I. Title.
DS517.W34   1974   952.03'1   74-801
ISBN 0-06-014516-1

CONTENTS

Photographs follow page 162.

All illustrations are reproduced by courtesy of the Radio Times Hulton Picture Library except for 'The MIKASA, Togo's flagship, completed in 1902 by Vickers' which is reproduced by courtesy of Vickers Ltd., and 'Admiral Vitgeft', 'The Tsar blessing his troops', 'The TSAREVICH, French-built, completed in 1904 and destroyed at Port Arthur', 'Japanese battleship SHIKISHIMA, completed in 1900 on Clydebank', 'The crew of the ASAMA', 'The crew of a Russian battleship' which are taken from the author's collection.

MAPS

PREFACE

This is a history of the first, and in its result, the most surprising war of the twentieth century. It was also the most observed, chronicled and discussed conflict until the First World War. Many of the military observers, such as Ian Hamilton, Max Hoffman and John Pershing, were to hold high command in their own armies a decade later, and one, Douglas MacArthur, was to exercise both military and political power after the Second World War.

This is however not a purely military history, and the reader who desires further detailed and specialised information is recommended to the Official Histories and their Appendices set out in my source notes.

The diplomatic background to the defeat of one of the European Great Powers by a rising Asiatic nation is equally well documented and extensively covered, especially as the war and its results were seen at the time to cast shadows forward to both the 1914–18 World War and the Russian Revolution.

The possible sources of information and comment, and the potential bibliography, both military and political, are therefore almost infinite. In consequence I owe a considerable debt of gratitude to the Librarians and staff of a number of institutions and libraries in Great Britain and the United States. In Britain the libraries of the House of Commons, the Ministry of Defence (War Office), Royal United Services Institution, the British Museum Reading Room, the Admiralty Library and the London Library. In the U.S.A., the Library of Congress, the U.S. National Archives, the U.S. Army War College at Carlisle, Pennsylvania, and the Library and the History Society of Portsmouth, New Hampshire.

Transcripts of the Crown-copyright records in the Public Record Office appear by permission of the Controller of Her Majesty's Stationery Office.

As on a previous occasion, I should like to thank Mrs. Joan St. George Saunders for invaluable research work, Captain A. B. C. Reynolds for the loan of books and Brigadier John Stephenson for bringing to my attention material which I might otherwise have missed. Throughout the writing of this book, as with *The Chanak Affair*, I have been assisted by Lady Paulina Pepys, without whose research and industry this work would simply not have been possible. Needless to say, none of the individuals or institutions mentioned are in any way responsible for any of the judgments, opinions and prejudices expressed, nor for any errors committed. They are my own.

Finally, I should like to thank the Arts Council of Great Britain for its assistance which enabled me to carry out researches in the U.S.A., and the Government of the People's Republic of China for their hospitality in their country where the story of 'the last imperialist war' began and ended.

D. W.

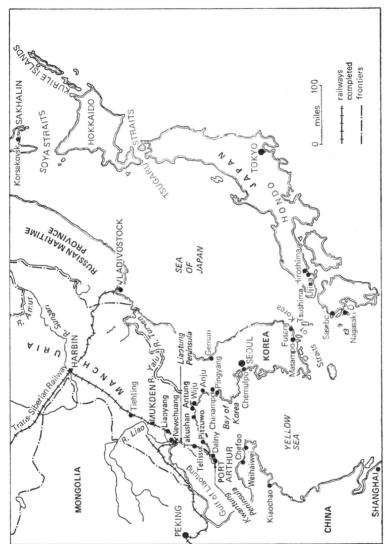

Theatre of War

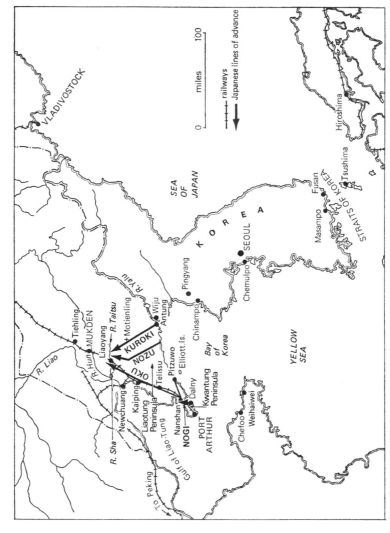

Area of Operations 1904–5

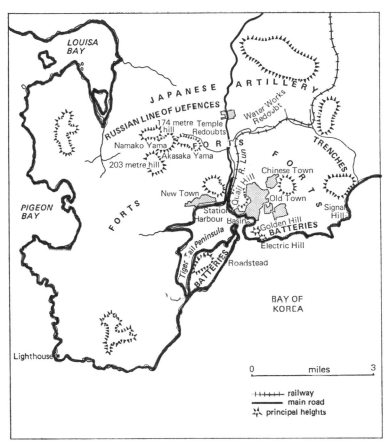

Port Arthur

*'What this country needs is a short
victorious war to stem the tide of revolution'*
V. K. PLEHVE, Russian Minister of
the Interior, to General A. N. Kuropatkin,
Minister of War, 1903

ONE

'The noodles have had a lucid interval'

KAISER WILHELM II

On August 28th, 1900, in the ancient walled city of Peking eight foreign nations, Britain, the U.S.A., Russia, France, Germany, Austria-Hungary, Italy and Japan, held a victory parade.

For fifty-five days the foreign legations had been besieged by fanatical members of 'the Society of the Fists of Righteous Harmony'. For much of that time the Boxers, to give them their more familiar name, had been assisted by regular troops of Tzu Hsi, Dowager Empress of China. The declared aim of the Boxers had been the extermination of the 'foreign devils' on the soil of China and all Chinese who had been converted to Christianity.

Now, however, the Boxer Rebellion was over, the various contingents of the International Relief Force occupied the Forbidden City and the 64-year-old Empress had left Peking, disavowing the Boxers who were soon being beheaded in large numbers on her orders as the price of failure. The dying Manchu Empire had produced its last convulsive and characteristic gesture of independence.

As a matter of fact, the parade, organised to demonstrate allied solidarity and the unity of the civilised world, wasn't much of a success. The commander of the relief force, Alfred, Count von Waldersee, recently promoted Field-Marshal and jockeyed into the position by the Kaiser, had unfortunately not yet arrived in China. So General Linievich, with the Cross of St. George from the Tsar, the Japanese Order of the Rising Sun and ten trunks of loot to his credit, now argued that he was the senior general present and therefore entitled to take the salute.

Having won his protocol victory it is doubtful if the Russian commander enjoyed it much. Hardly one contingent marched at the same pace as any other. The Russian military band produced a cacophonous and inaccurate rendering of the Japanese national anthem, saluted the Italians with the Marseillaise and then lost out in competition with the pipe band of the 1st Sikh Regiment. The Japanese in formal blue moved like marionettes, the tiny Tonkinese who made up most of the French force trudged by in torn and dirty uniforms, the solemn goose step of the straw-hatted Germans provoked giggles from the spectators. Also present, leading his diplomatic colleagues, was Sir Claude MacDonald, the British Minister. On the basis of seniority and active service with the Highland Light Infantry in his youth, he had taken charge of the defence operations during the siege and was now the hero of the hour. However, he did not look like a hero: to grace Linievich's triumph he wore not his gold-braided diplomatic uniform and his medals, but shabby civilian clothes topped by a floppy Panama hat.

After the parade the jealousies and the rivalries between the nations continued and increased. Indeed when von Waldersee at last arrived in October both his small store of tact and his scarcely acknowledged authority had to be exercised to the utmost to prevent open conflict between the armed forces of the notionally co-operating Powers.

It was not really the fault of the naval and military officers gathered together in Peking, nor of their diplomatic colleagues who both encouraged and supported them. For the situation in the Chinese capital was but a microcosm of a worldwide pattern. In the first year of the new century Europe was still the centre of the world and Europe was divided into two armed camps so that rivalries and dissensions were repeated wherever Europeans set their feet on the face of the globe.

Europe had been at peace for thirty years and now, seventy years and two world wars later, sentimental hindsight paints a picture of the turn of the century as a golden age of peace and prosperity, order and tranquillity. In fact this was an iron age of strident nationalism and imperialism, militarism and monarchism, devious diplomacy, espionage, unrest and crisis. Nearly all the major European Powers, whose contingents paraded in Peking in 1900, were members of one military alliance or another, pledged to different degrees of obligation, admittedly, but committed in varying sets of circumstances to war.

There was only one exception – Great Britain. Proud of the fact that she was not a member of any warlike alliance or understanding, she was the only nation represented in China which was actually engaged in fighting a war.

Just before the Boxers had commenced their siege Sir Claude MacDonald had been congratulated by his fellow diplomats on the good news from South Africa. Mafeking had been relieved. With what sincerity they did so it is impossible to say, for Britain, involved in a none too successful war with sharp-shooting Boer farmers, was without doubt the most unpopular nation in Europe. Not that anyone in Paris, Berlin or St. Petersburg cared a damn about the Boers as such. There were however rumours of the formation of a Continental League to take advantage of Britain's predicament. Admittedly in Vienna the old Emperor Franz Josef had said to the British Ambassador, 'In this war I am decidedly on the side of the British', but his lone support only emphasised the British isolation.

In fact the Continental League never materialised because Britain had the largest navy in the world, and so could do what she liked in South Africa. At the same time however there could be no doubt that Germans, Frenchmen and Russians, as well as Belgians and Dutchmen, derived a special pleasure from the fact that Britain's present embarrassment arose from her colonial empire. For that empire was larger than that of the Romans, larger than the former dominions of the Spanish kings: over 13 million square miles of territory stretching into five continents; a population, as far as it could be estimated, of 437 millions. Indeed it came as a surprise to Queen Victoria when it was pointed out to her that she ruled over nearly a quarter of the population of the world. The statistics were overpowering and the vast areas of red on the map, which the British accepted with anything from pride to near indifference, were to many Europeans in 1900 an affront and a challenge and a permanent nagging source of jealousy.

Britain's possession of the largest empire in the world protected by the most powerful navy insulated her from the rivalries of Europe where Germans allied to Austro-Hungarians and
Italians faced Frenchmen allied to Russians. In the 1880's and
1890's however a new element entered into those rivalries when
the nations of Europe became themselves empire minded. There
had of course always been other empires besides the British, the
Portuguese, the Dutch and the French but in the 1870's the
opening up of the interior of Africa gave new impetus to the
colonial urge. Missionary zeal, scientific curiosity, desire for
trade and plain covetousness all combined as original motives,
but soon the drive for 'a place in the sun', in the Kaiser's phrase,
became a prestige race between the nations, an extension of the
power struggle already existing in Europe. Unfortunately,
though, for British popularity, Britain seemed once again to
have acquired the lion's share. That the Biblical principle that
'unto he that hath shall more be given' appeared to operate in
the colonial sphere was of no consolation to Europeans who
hankered after the goldfields and diamond mines of South
Africa, and who resented the fact that the British Empire,
already large, had become even larger and was protected by a
fleet built deliberately stronger than that of any two possible
rivals combined.

In 1896 in the Canadian House of Commons Sir George
Eulas Foster had talked of 'these somewhat troublesome days
when the Great Mother Empire stands splendidly isolated in
Europe'. A month later George Goschen, the British Chancellor
of the Exchequer, took up the phrase 'splendid isolation' and
used it with approval to describe his country's situation.

The expression has been much used since to give title to a
myth: that the chosen foreign policy of Lord Salisbury, who
was Prime Minister until July 1902, was complete and contented indifference to all that happened in Europe and that the
effect of Britain's unpopularity, demonstrated in the South
African War, was so traumatic that as soon as Salisbury had
retired his successor, A. J. Balfour, was anxious to join an alliance,
any alliance, as soon as possible.

The facts do not support the myth. Britain, so long as neither
her Empire nor her naval supremacy were threatened, had no

need of a binding European military alliance. Nevertheless both Salisbury and Balfour well realised that in 'troublesome days' isolation, however splendid, was not a desirable situation.

For instance, from November 1899 to January 1902, there were intermittent but serious negotiations between Britain and Germany for what Joseph Chamberlain called 'the natural alliance'. When the negotiations came to nothing the Kaiser, Wilhelm II, was confirmed in his view that the British Ministers were 'a set of unmitigated noodles'. Lord Lansdowne, the Foreign Secretary, reflected that 'one thing is certain and that is that Wilhelm II would have been almost unbearable as an ally'.

Yet there was more to the Anglo-German conversations than a clash of personalities. For they revealed both Britain's limitations as a European ally and her fears.

They came to nothing because the two countries each sought a different kind of agreement. The British would have liked some sort of understanding which cleared up a number of difficulties, in Africa, in the Pacific and in China. The Germans wanted a military alliance with definite objectives. Britain was not prepared to commit herself in Europe to Germany and to Germany's moribund partner Austria-Hungary as well. Germany was not prepared to pledge her general co-operation to future developments in the British Empire. As Salisbury had written to Balfour in 1898, 'I imagine what really pre-occupies German statesmen is not the cutting up of China but the cutting up of Austria and how can we help him [the Kaiser] there?'

This was the essential difficulty in Britain's dealings with any European power, not only Germany. Each nation on the continent was bound to a military alliance, each one could look across a frontier and view a potential enemy. All were vulnerable to invasion. Britain had none of these problems, she had no land frontiers, the last successful invasion had been in 1066. Her war scares were far from home, in Africa, in Egypt and the Sudan, on the borders of Afghanistan and in Persia, on the farthermost limits of her Empire and her still spreading spheres of influence.

This basic fact many Europeans seemed unable or unwilling to comprehend, the Germans, 'the natural ally', least of all.

The second point of significance lay, despite their failure, in the arguments advanced by the Germans to persuade the

British into an alliance. In this respect the inhabitants of the
Ballhausplatz saw very clearly indeed. The strongest bargaining
factor for the Germans, and it became a threat in their heavy
hands, was that if Britain was not prepared to bind herself to
the Triple Alliance then Germany would have to look elsewhere for a friend, and it was obvious in which direction – *closer
to Russia.* The Kaiser, though admitting to Lansdowne that he
had no high opinion of the Tsar, who was 'only fit to live in a
country house and grow turnips', felt confident that the Franco-
Russian alliance could not last. The implications were obvious.
The Kaiser was known to be in constant touch with the Tsar.
There was a strong pro-German element at the Russian Court.
Perhaps the Russians could be seduced away from their French
ally, perhaps the old Reinsurance Treaty between Russia and
Germany could be revived.

In fact the threat didn't work. The cautious, suspicious
British were not to be stampeded into an alliance, but it is
nevertheless surprising that they didn't yield, for fear of
Russian designs had been the mainspring of British foreign
policy for nearly a century. Suspicion of Russia's intentions to
dismember the Ottoman Empire had brought Britain, with
France as her principal ally, to war in the Crimea in 1854.
Twenty-four years later for the same cause Disraeli moved the
Mediterranean Squadron into Besika Bay as a counter to a
Russian army at the gates of Constantinople, and the two
countries had been on the brink of war. At the same time the
acceptance of a Russian diplomatic mission by Sher Ali, the
Amur of Afghanistan, provoked the 2nd Afghan War which resulted in a virtual British protectorate over the mountain kingdom. By the 1880's Britain had lost interest in protecting the
Turks, and the scene of Anglo-Russian confrontation had
shifted decisively to Turkestan on Afghanistan's northern
frontier. In April 1885 the Russians clashed with Afghan troops
at Penjdeh and the British Cabinet, led by the pacific Glad-
stone, actually drafted a declaration of war. Only British isolation in Europe, and German support for Russia, prevented the
outbreak of hostilities.

Almost immediately after the settlement of the Penjdeh crisis
Russian penetration further westwards into northern Persia had

again provoked British apprehension and antagonism. Spheres of influence in Persia were not in fact settled until 1907, but at the turn of the century once again the scene of Anglo-Russian rivalry shifted, this time to the shores washed by the South China Sea, the Yellow Sea and the Sea of Japan.

The explanation of this century of friction was in essence geographical, although in their political attitudes and their patriotic mystiques Britain and Russia were well-matched rivals. The Russians despised the British preoccupation with trade and their democratic processes. The British regarded the Russians as a nation of backward peasants ruled by tyrannical autocrats obsessed by military glory. Britain was the home of parliamentary government, Russia was in Karl Marx's phrase 'the gendarme of Europe'. The British were convinced that they had special skills in dealing with native peoples whose territories and destinies they held 'in trust' for the future. The Russians talked of their 'civilising mission' in Asia. Britain's power rested on her powerful navy, Russian might lay in her vast army. The 'Great White Queen' stalemated the 'Great White Tsar'.

In the nineteenth century, Britain had steadily acquired more and more territory in India until she was brought to the borders of Afghanistan, Persia, Nepal and Tibet. Upper Burma had been occupied in 1886. From Singapore British influence had spread to the Malay States, Sarawak and North Borneo. Hong Kong was a British possession after 1841, and Kowloon on the mainland after 1860; a series of rather disreputable wars had ensured that Britain acquired through the Treaty Ports along the coast the bulk of Chinese trade.

While the British Empire had expanded by sea the Russian Empire had grown overland. In the late eighteenth and early nineteenth centuries large areas of eastern Europe and Asia were absorbed into the Russian dominions. Poland and Finland were both Russian ruled and in the east settlers and soldiers moved across the wastes of Siberia towards the Pacific and into the regions of the Caucasus. After the reverse of the Crimean War the Russians began to penetrate into Turkestan both to fill a power vacuum and to assuage their wounded pride. Against brave but ill-equipped and indisciplined adversaries a number of generals made their reputations: in Russia for military skill, and on the scene of their easy triumphs, for ruthless cruelty. Chimkent in 1864, Tashkent in 1865 and Samarkand in 1868 fell to Generals Tcherniaeff and Kaufmann. In the latter year the Amir of Bokhara finally recognised the suzerainty of the Tsar. In the 1870's Khokand surrendered and Kaufmann perpetrated a massacre at Khiva. In 1881 at Geok Tepe the last resistance of the wild hard-riding Turkoman tribesmen was finally crushed by Skobeleff, 'the White General', and his lieutenants, Kuropatkin and Linievich, in a battle which was deliberately allowed by the victors to degenerate into a massacre. By 1884 the Russians were at Merv, a stone's throw from the Afghan frontier and the British Cabinet began to suffer from 'mervousness' as the Duke of Argyll put it. The Penjdeh crisis followed a year later.

There were no trading opportunities nor financial advantages in these inhospitable sparsely populated uplands, but Russia had at last gained some recompense for her humiliation in the Crimea. As the violent anglophobe Skobeleff remarked, 'the stronger Russia is in Central Asia, the weaker England is in India, and the more conciliatory she will be in Europe'.

Consequently it was Russian policy on the spot, and by directive from far-off St. Petersburg, deliberately to reduce the area of neutrality between herself and Britain.

One of the few British travellers in the Russian-controlled area was the Hon. George Curzon, then a rising young Conservative M.P., but destined one day to be Viceroy of India. In his *Russia in Central Asia*, published in 1889, he remarked 'only a few giddy subalterns in St. Petersburg think seriously of the conquest of India'. Nevertheless, throughout the rest of his book he cannot help drawing attention to the anti-British sentiments of Russian generals and administrators, to Russian journalists who wrote of 'the road to India', and to the strategic threat presented by the troop-carrying potential of the Trans-Caspian Railway. The author is roused to alternate scorn and anger by the common Russian (and French) misconception that upon the arrival of the first *sotnya* of Cossacks at the head of the

Khyber Pass the whole of India would rise up to exchange British masters for Russian.

It was not only in Central Asia though that Russian and British expansion had produced a situation where the spheres of influence of the two Empires were so contiguous that if either stirred they were bound to collide. In 1860 the Russians reached Vladivostock and, although the port was by no means ice-free throughout the year, established a naval base. It was a culminating stage in what had been a steady march to the Pacific. Once again the Russians had had to cross no frontiers nor seas to increase the Tsar's domains. Peasants hungry for land at two roubles an acre, time-expired soldiers, ne'er-do-wells and adventurers, opponents of the regime and common criminals, the latter frequently forcibly married to prostitutes, were all encouraged or coerced into occupation and settlement of the vast regions of Siberia which stretched from the river Ob to the sea of Okpotsk. It was in essence a military settlement, the total Russian population in this inhospitable area never exceeded a third of a million people. Nevertheless, this time without firing a shot or facing any enemy save distance, terrain and climate, the Russians found themselves once again in a part of the world where Britain considered her own interests paramount. The Trans-Siberian Railway, opened in 1901, could prove itself as much of a military threat as the Trans-Caspian. The Russians were soon casting covetous eyes south of the Amur river at the Chinese province of Manchuria and the Liaotung Peninsula with its southernmost tip, Port Arthur, an ice-free port on the Pacific.

In his letter to Balfour Lord Salisbury had referred to 'the cutting up of China'. The idea was not peculiar to Lord Salisbury. Before the outbreak of the Boxer Rebellion the internal chaos of the Manchu Empire had led many European statesmen to wonder if China might not go the same way as Africa. Inevitably they began to speculate how it might be divided up into colonies or at least spheres of influence.

Superficially the partition of the Pacific in the 90's had much in common with that of Africa in the 80's. Australia and New Zealand were of course part of the British Empire. The Germans, French and British had snapped up the little chains

of islands which stretched from New Guinea to Pitcairn. In the
north the Russians, who had sold Alaska to the U.S.A. in 1867
primarily to prevent it becoming British, were stretching down
to the mainland of Japan. Sakhalin, where Anton Tchekoff
worked as a doctor in the criminal settlements, had been ceded
by the Japanese in exchange for the Kurile islands in 1875. A
newcomer to the race was the U.S.A., in possession of Wake,
Midway, Honolulu and Hawaii, and in 1898 accepting the
cession of the Philippines from Spain.

The Boxer Rebellion in 1900, provoked by European penetration, demonstrated the disadvantages of China as a colonial
proposition. The Chinese were a nation, and prepared to offer
armed resistance to foreigners. The sheer size and inaccessibility
of the Celestial Empire, the vast distances to be covered and the
magnitude of its population also deterred those powers which
had previously thought of the mainland as an area ripe for
occupation and exploitation.

After the suppression of the rebellion and the departure of
the International Force, the lists were cleared for those powers
both able and willing to concern themselves with Chinese affairs
and prepared to maintain a presence and sustain their interest in
the area. After 1901 only interested parties remained but their
interests differed. Russia, both before and after the Boxer
Rebellion, was much concerned with Manchuria and the protection of her railway development to the east. The U.S.A. was
also naturally concerned but with no desire, as the Philippines
were proving troublesome enough, to acquire further possessions. Britain, with the largest commercial stake in China, was
determined once again to resist what she saw as more Russian
expansion. In the centre, and vitally concerned with the changes
in the balance of power on her doorstep, was Japan.

On the periphery was France. Possessed of an Empire in
Indo-China but one which always took second place to her
African possessions. Concerned with Chinese trade but not to
the same extent as Britain, allied to Russia but for European
rather than Asian reasons. Perhaps because of her position at
one remove from the situation developing in and around
China, Japan and Korea, France saw more clearly than her
Russian ally. In 1901 Delcassé, the French Foreign Minister,

remarked that 'we must prevent England from finding in the Far East in Japan the soldier that she lacks'.

Japan itself was an unknown quantity. Almost as little was known about the collection of offshore islands ruled by an Emperor reputedly descended from the Sun God as was known about China. In 1853 Commodore Perry of the United States Navy had sailed into Yedo Bay to be met on shore by an armoured array of feudal war lords as if he had travelled backwards in time to early Tudor England. Japan, like China, had stood still for more than 300 years. Now it was understood that Japan, unlike China, had decided to meet the challenge of Europe and the U.S.A. by the sincerest form of flattery, imitation. Great progress had been made in the processes of modernisation in the last fifty years. The French and then the Germans had trained her army, the British her navy. In 1895 she had fought China over Korea and had gained Formosa, and the Liaotung Peninsula and Port Arthur. The Treaty of Shimonseki which recognised these gains aroused the displeasure of Germany, Russia and France who by joint action and in the most peremptory manner compelled Japan to return the Liaotung Peninsula to China.

Almost immediately afterwards, and to the fury of the Japanese, Russia forced a long-term lease of Port Arthur from the Chinese with permission to connect it by rail to Mukden, the Germans established a naval base at Kiaochow and the French obtained Kwangchanwan. On the insistence of Curzon, now an Under-Secretary of Foreign Affairs, Britain, as a counter-stroke, established a small base at Weihaiwei in 1898.

The rivalries of the Powers were following a familiar pattern and it seemed apparent that the European Powers were not prepared to allow an Oriental nation equal opportunities in the competition. With one exception – significantly Britain had not been a party to the joint policy of coercion and in consequence her influence in the area seemed to have waned. It came therefore as more of a surprise to the world when in February 1902 there were presented to both Houses of Parliament in London copies of a document which had already been forwarded to Sir Claude MacDonald, now the Minister in Tokyo, by which

Britain entered into her first full-scale alliance for nearly a century – with Japan.

'The noodles have had a lucid interval', observed the Kaiser. Britain had found her soldier in the Far East.

TWO

'Gallant little Japs'

HAROLD MACMILLAN

The outcome of the negotiations secretly carried out in London between Lord Lansdowne, the Foreign Secretary, and Baron Hayashi, his country's ambassador, was a relatively simple treaty.

In scope it was confined to the Far East. Britain and Japan recognised the independence of China and Korea, but at the same time authorised each other to intervene in either territory if their own 'special interests' were threatened by another Power or by internal disorder. If the defence of such interests resulted in war with another Power then the obligation upon each partner to the alliance was benevolent neutrality. If however Japan or Britain became involved in war with two Powers then each was bound to come to the other's assistance.

On the same day, February 13th, 1902, the alliance was debated in both Houses of Parliament, Lords and Commons. In the Lords Lansdowne defended his own handiwork and in the Commons the duty fell upon Arthur Balfour, soon to be Prime Minister.

In both Houses Britain's emergence from isolation was received with the most cautious sort of optimism. Lords Spencer and Rosebery were both anxious about Britain's obligations and sought some definition of the circumstances in which she would be obliged to wage war. Needless to say, Lansdowne did not give either of them a precise answer, but took refuge in rather cloudy generalities and some curious reasoning:

'I may say at once that, in our view, this compact is one which concerns no other Power. I do not think it can be said for an instant that any other Power has interests in the Far East at all comparable to those of Great Britain and Japan.'

Later on, however, he did say,

'What do we see on all sides? We observe a tendency on the part of great Powers to form groups. We observe a tendency to ever-increasing naval and military armaments. . . . There is also this – that in these days war breaks out with a suddenness which was unknown in former days when nations were not, as they are now, armed to the teeth and ready to enter on hostilities at any moment.'

None of Lord Lansdowne's fellow peers disagreed with that, indeed it was the very fact that Britain was now with Japan forming yet another group that worried them. Presumably to allay their fears the Foreign Secretary went on to state what were, in his view, the three objects of the alliance. The maintenance of the *status quo* in the Far East, of the 'open door' to Chinese trade and, of course, the common form of every alliance, the preservation of peace. 'It was however our policy to support Japan, to protect Japan against the danger of a coalition of other Powers.'

It says much for the traditional good manners of the House of Lords that no one in Lansdowne's noble audience asked him who these Powers might be, and if one were Russia, had she not 'interests' in the Far East as well?

In the House of Commons there was, as usual, a more robust atmosphere. Mr. Norman, the Liberal Member for South Wolverhampton, suffered from none of their lordships' inhibitions. The agreement itself, he said, 'came like a bolt from the blue' and he wanted to know 'what kind of situation is here envisaged in which England may be called upon to take up arms?' Obligingly he answered his own question. 'If Japan, of its own independent, free, unfettered decision, which according to this text we cannot control, considers Russia to be taking aggressive action in Korea or Manchuria, Japan may take up the quarrel and call upon us to keep the other Powers out of the dispute.'

'Everyone knew,' said Mr. Norman, 'that Japan and Russia have been preparing for war for a considerable period.' He himself was well disposed towards Japan, but he would have liked to see better relations with Russia as well. For with France, Russia's ally, Britain was now 'on cordial terms'. Yet, 'it was quite useless to deny that this treaty is aimed at Russia'.

Surprisingly, after so much outspokenness, the Member for Wolverhampton ended rather tamely. Apparently he did not condemn the treaty after all, but merely wished to put two questions to the Government. Is it wise? Is it necessary?

Not entirely surprisingly, Lord Cranborne, an Under-Secretary for Foreign Affairs, who replied, was convinced that it was both of these things. His answer took the form of an historical sketch which told his hearers little that they did not know already save perhaps when he said that he 'had no doubt that in this agreement we shall command the full approval of the Government of the United States'.

Like Lord Lansdowne in the Lords he talked of Britain's interests, 'we own, I think, roughly 60% of all the shipping which trades with China, we own about one-half of all the commerce which goes to and comes from China'. Japan's interests were also extensive, said Cranborne, and he went on to describe them at some length, but he forbore to mention those of Russia.

Sir Henry Campbell-Bannerman, the Leader of the Liberal Opposition, was not satisfied and said so. 'Why this sudden step?' he asked. 'Seeing that things were established on so satisfactory a basis, why take this step? Does it involve some danger of interfering with the present satisfactory position by arousing some new jealousies and suspicions among the Powers themselves?'

Unfortunately in replying Cranborne only succeeded in getting into an argument with Sir Henry. Eventually Balfour had to rise to pour oil on troubled waters.

Peace was his theme. Certainly Britain could not allow Japan to be crushed by two Powers, but that situation would not arise now that the treaty was signed. The agreement itself was not 'unfriendly to other nations'. 'The Government is most anxious to be friendly with Russia – the dangers which this treaty guards against are the dangers of an adventurous policy, of which His Majesty's Government are very far from suspecting the Russian Government in the Far East.'

That of course was the precise reverse of the truth, but Balfour went blandly on to recommend the treaty to the House and the country in almost the same terms as Lansdowne had used in the Lords. When he sat down most of the steam had gone out of the debate, although a number of Liberals who followed him stressed the dangers of international complications and the possibility of conflict with Russia. Conservatives, supporting their Government, countered by extolling the virtues of the Japanese. As one speaker said towards the end of the debate, 'We are allying ourselves to one of the pluckiest little nations in the world.'

That particular sentiment just about epitomised the general public reaction in Britain to the new-found friend. It was also very nearly the sum total of knowledge as well. Never had the British known so little about an ally.

The Japanese were small in stature, yellow of skin, and lived crowded together on an island, or rather four islands, and they were physically tough and courageous. Little else was known save by those who had lived or travelled in the Far East. Before the alliance the average Englishman came to the Japanese through the medium of Gilbert and Sullivan's 7-year-old comic opera, 'The Mikado'. Naturally enough the newspapers valiantly attempted to fill the gaps in their readers' knowledge. In the process some curious images emerged: 'The gallant island race' was the favourite expression and a number of purple passages suggested that the Japanese were really very like the British, industrious, patriotic seafarers on the other side of the world, differing only from their allies in trifling matters of appearance, race, language and religion. *The Times* excelled itself by suggesting a very close parallel between 'bushido', the warrior code of the samurai, and the ideals of mediaeval Christian chivalry.

In every paper the Japanese regard for their family and ancestors was stressed, and at the same time no columnist failed to praise the tremendous processes of modernisation which had taken place in the last forty years. Wooden shoes and fans, samurai swords and hari-kari, the divinity of the Emperor and ancestor-worship, but at the same time an efficient German-trained army, a powerful British-trained fleet and a modern merchant marine, a parliament and a compulsory education system plus up-to-date commercial and industrial development.

No doubt many readers in Britain were justifiably a trifle confused and wondered which version to accept. Yet the papers had done their task of reporting faithfully, for the two apparently conflicting aspects of Japanese life and society did in fact exist side by side.

When Commodore Perry, 'Old Bruin' to his subordinates in the U.S. Navy, sailed his squadron of 'black ships' out of Yedo Bay in 1853 with the promise to return the next year with a larger force, the Japanese had been left with the problem of their future relationship with the outside world to be solved. Were they to attempt to resist the inevitable encroachments of powerful foreigners or modernise their whole society in imitation so that one day they might compete as equals?

The next year Perry did return as promised and soon an agreement was reached by which Shimoda and Hakodate were opened to U.S. vessels. Close behind the Americans came the British, the Dutch and the Russians, also demanding and obtaining harbour facilities. At first sight it looked as if Japan was going the way of China: an anachronistic society forced, step by step, to yield economic and political advantage to the hated and despised, but more efficient and powerful, 'Western barbarians'.

However, the character of the oligarchs who ruled Japan was very different from that of their Chinese equivalents. The Chinese despised the foreigners and were indifferent to their civilisation, the achievements and products of which they dismissed as being of no account. The Japanese, on the other hand, albeit often apprehensively and reluctantly, were prepared to compromise and imitate as the price of survival. In consequence, in fifty years of turbulent history, they accelerated through stages of development which had occupied the most advanced European nations for more than five centuries. It was as if England had moved from the Wars of the Roses to the reign of Victoria in the lifetime of one adult.

The Japan of Perry's day was an Oriental feudalism which had hardly changed in over 400 years. At the lowest level of society existed the Eta and Hinin, the latter meaning literally 'not human'. These were akin to the untouchables of the Hindu caste system who carried out the tasks regarded by the rest of society as repugnant or degrading. Immediately above them were the three classes of citizens: in order of superiority, No, Ko and Sho – farmers, artisans and traders. In turn immeasurably above them, the majority of the people, were the first class of society, the Samurai. The rank and file of this upper caste had no economic significance whatsoever, they were warriors pure and simple, their two swords the outward symbol of their exclusive right to bear and use arms. Divided up into clans of military retainers in the service of the Daimo (literally 'great names') or feudal chiefs, they spent their time, as did the mediaeval knight, in military exercises and muscular sports in preparation for war.

The Daimo themselves were the great territorial nobles, ruling virtually as independent sovereigns. In the 1850's Japan consisted of nearly 250 of their territories, as if the system of land tenure of mediaeval Europe had survived untouched for five centuries. There were other similarities as well, just as in mediaeval Europe central government tended to be virtually powerless in the face of mighty feudatories, so also in Japan, but with an added Oriental complexity.

The real ruler of Japan was not the Emperor, power was in the hands of the Shogun. As far back as 1192 the then Emperor had handed over control to Minamoto Yonitomo, his most powerful general, and given him the title of Shogun or generalissimo. From that point onwards real power was increasingly exercised by the Shoguns, with the Emperors as mere figures of ceremonial and religious reverence. In time the Shogunate itself became hereditary within certain clans and families which also provided the members of the Government. By the 1860's the office of Shogun had been held by a dynasty of the Tokugawa family for 260 years.

In 1866 the then Shogun, Iemochi, well advanced in years, died in Osaka and was succeeded by Hitotsubashi Keiki. The next year, on February 3rd, the old Emperor Komei died, to be succeeded by the young Mutsuhito known to posterity simply as the Meiji Emperor.

At the time of the death of these two representatives of the old order, Katsu Awa, of the Tokugawa clan, had written,

'From the day of Perry's arrival for more than ten years our country was in a state of indescribable confusion. The government was weak, and irresolute, without power of decision.'

In fact, even without Perry, Japan was approaching a climacteric. The Shogunate, like many another monarchy based on personal qualities alone, was in decline. Keiki proved to be the last of his line.

The treaties with the U.S.A. in March 1854, with Great Britain in October of the same year, with Russia in February 1855 and with Holland in the November, marked a point of no return. The intelligentsia were challenging the powers of the Shoguns and were anxious for Western knowledge, practical men were curious about Western techniques. The Japanese, restless and energetic by nature, and far less susceptible to the attractions of contemplative inaction than other Oriental Buddhists, were ready for a change. In November 1867 Keiki, genuinely in failing health, resigned and with him disappeared the powers of the Tokugawas. A year later the Shogunate itself was abolished and after a brief bout of civil disturbance the whole country submitted to the young Emperor who had become the focus for the forces of modernisation and progress.

Japan now embarked on a wholesale process of Westernisation. It would be wrong, however, to think that the Japanese at the same time adopted what are conventionally called 'Western' ideals or attitudes of mind. The British press in 1902 naturally enough concentrated on those superficial aspects of modernisation which seemed to bring Japan closer to her ally, industrialisation, education, parliamentary government and the like, but the realities were significantly different. The Japanese were still an hierarchical people more concerned with national prestige than the creation of a model system of democracy.

Certainly there were among them individuals who thought in terms of both modernisation and libertarian reform, but the Marquis Ito on a fact-finding mission in Europe found himself most attracted to the authoritarian system as practised in Germany. In his conversations with Bismarck and Lorenz von Stein he found their views on monarchy, political parties and the armed services acceptable because Japanese sentiments and ambitions with regard to these subjects were already very close to those of the Prussianised ruling *élite* in Germany. Similarly, in the field of education, he favoured a patriotic system which would inculcate loyalty and discipline. Significantly enough one of the first Japanese 'reforms' was the 1870 Conscription Law which was the means by which Yamagata Aritomo (later Marshal Prince Yamataga) created a modern standing army by 1873. Before 1870 training had been in the hands of invited French officers. After the defeat of France in that year by the Germans, the victors took over. The British, who had no serious rivals, remained as instructors to the navy.

In 1877 Japan endured a crisis which both illustrated the difficulties and limits of change. In that year Saigo Takamori, head of the Satsuma clan, rebelled on behalf of the old order and for six months a bloody civil war raged, 65,000 government troops fighting 40,000 Samurai rebels. Casualties were high, over 6,000 dead and more than 10,000 wounded on each side. When victory for the Emperor was no longer in doubt the wounded Saigo had himself decapitated by a friend. A national army had beaten a force of clan retainers, it was the end of military feudalism but not of the social system engendered by it. Members of the samurai caste had fought in considerable numbers on both sides, but after the suppression of the rebellion the majority of government officials and officers of the army and navy still came from the Satsuma and Choshu clans.

After the blood letting of 1877 the independent power of the samurai had disappeared, many of their number being absorbed, according to status, into the ranks of the army, navy and the police. Internally Japan's development was thereafter peaceable. The first general election was held in 1890.

In many ways it too demonstrated some of the inner paradoxes of Japan. Certainly for the first time in psephological history, and perhaps for the last, there was a rehearsal before the actual event to ensure that everything went smoothly and in an orderly and peaceful fashion.

Only a very small proportion of the population voted because of the high and stringently applied property and residential qualifications for inclusion on the voting roll. Nevertheless, by these means a Diet or Lower House was elected, but even forgetting the fact that only about four or five people in every 100 voted the procedure did not provide Japan with a parliamentary democracy, only its facade.

For Ministers were not chosen from, nor were in any real sense answerable to, the Diet. The elected members could criticise, but could not influence policy or legislation. Even then the real rulers of Japan were not necessarily the Ministers, but the inner council of Genro or elder statesmen who actually advised the Emperor who was himself beyond criticism.

All that the 1890 general election did was to create a sort of stylised opposition of the most limited scope and powers. So far as real power was concerned Japan remained what it had been before 1890, an absolute monarchy run by oligarchs.

Side by side with their natural urge for economic and legal parity with the European and American nations marched Japan's interests and ambitions with regard to her own more immediate neighbours, especially Formosa and Korea, and China, still technically the suzerain of both. Both Formosans and Koreans were thorns in the flesh of the Japanese, but for widely different reasons. Formosa was inhabited by a number of savage tribes whose favourite sport was the murdering of visitors and shipwrecked mariners. The Koreans, on the other hand, although certainly more civilised and pacific than the wild Bhotans of Formosa, had in effect withdrawn themselves from the world into a remote and infuriating seclusion. 'The hermit kingdom', as it was known, still paid some lip service to the idea of Chinese overlordship, but so far as the activities of any other nation, European or Oriental, were concerned, it was contemptuously and ridiculously indifferent.

The Formosan problem was quickly solved, the combination of a punitive expedition and the diplomacy of the skilled and scholarly Soyejima, then Foreign Minister, extracted from Peking a grudging acceptance of Japan's acquisition of the Riuku islands as a police post midway between Japan and Formosa. Korea, however, was to pose a problem which beset the Japanese for twenty-five years and twice led them to war.

If a parallel could be found in English history, Korea was Japan's Belgium and Egypt rolled into one. No Japanese Government could be indifferent to the possibility of a powerful rival occupying Korea which would then become, in the words of a Japanese statesman, 'an arrow pointed at the heart of Japan'. Equally, no Japanese Government could fail to be tempted to interfere in the internal affairs of 'the hermit kingdom', technically subject to a dying empire, ruled by corrupt incompetents, its finances in chaos, incapable of either self-government or self-defence. The Japanese themselves spoke of 'the Korean affairs' of 1882, 1884, 1894 and 1902 as if in some way they grew up of themselves and the fault lay on the side of the Koreans. This, perhaps needless to say, was very far from the truth. There was always a 'war party' in Tokyo eager to solve the Korean problem in the shortest, sharpest way, by invasion and occupation. The only restraint in the councils of the Emperor was the fear that such a policy might provoke intervention by the Great Powers with interests in the Far East, especially Russia who had shown herself, in 1875, in the matter of Sakhalin, quite willing to use the threat of superior force.

Accordingly, peaceful penetration was decided upon. In the wake of the newly established diplomatic legation there followed a whole train of Japanese traders and merchants and a large number of unscrupulous adventurers, many ex-samurai seeking a return to their former occupation. In the event, and not entirely to the regret of the Japanese, the penetration became anything but peaceful. For the Koreans, described by an English traveller in these words – 'the prevailing impression among the people is one of intense inertia, an absolute lack of interest in anything, coupled with a strong distaste for novelty' – did possess one powerful emotion – hatred of the Japanese.

In 1882 unpaid and mutinous Korean soldiers inspired by the Tai Won Kun (father of the King and leader of the pro-Chinese party) burnt down the Japanese legation. Smoked out, the Minister and his staff formed square and fought their way through the streets to the protection of a British warship, H.M.S. *Flying Fish*. A strong Japanese land and sea force arrived in Korea, ostensibly to accept the formal Korean apology with something like good grace.

Two years later it was the turn of the so-called Progressives in Korea. This was a court party opposed to the continuation of Chinese influence and therefore prepared to use the Japanese but only for their own purposes. Pro-Chinese Ministers were murdered, but Chinese occupation forces soon gained control. Once more however there were anti-Japanese riots, again the Japanese legation was burnt down, once more a Japanese Minister with his staff and legation guards had to fight his way to the coast.

The demands for war were growing not only in government circles in Tokyo, but in Peking as well. Passions cooled however, and in April 1885 the Marquis Ito and the Chinese Viceroy, Li Hung Chang, signed the Tientsin Convention by which both countries agreed to withdraw all their troops from Korea. In addition, both Japan and China agreed to inform each other if either should find it necessary to intervene with troops in future and to allow the other party to the agreement to despatch an equal number.

For nine years there was constant friction between Koreans and Japanese, but there was peace. Then in 1894 another rebellion broke out against the oppressive and corrupt Korean Government, this time spreading well beyond the bounds of Seoul, the capital.

Everywhere the King's troops were in retreat from the rebels and the Chinese again came to the rescue, sending a force of 2,000 soldiers to Seoul. The Japanese were informed and immediately a mixed brigade of their marines and soldiers arrived on the scene.

The rebellion was at an end, put down by the Chinese, but Japan's patience was exhausted. Her troops would not be withdrawn until there was some positive assurance of peace and order. The Chinese denied the Japanese right to demand such an undertaking. The diplomatic exchanges before war broke out were curt, the Chinese were contemptuous of Japan's strength, the Japanese were determined on a final settlement.

It took eight months, from September 15th, 1894, until March 30th, 1895, for the Chinese to learn just how mistaken they had been. The land battle opened at Pingyang, two days later the remnants of the Chinese fleet were dispersed southwest of the Yalu river. Simultaneously Japanese armies invaded Manchuria and the Liaotung Peninsula. On November 21st Port Arthur fell, to a furious assault led by General Oyama. By March, after the battle of Tien chuang tai, on the right bank of the Liao, the Chinese were defeated, or in disorderly retreat on every front and sued for an armistice. By the Treaty of Shimonoseki China recognised 'the full and complete independence of Korea' and ceded the Liaotung Peninsula, Formosa and the Pescadores to Japan, and agreed to pay £25 million by way of war indemnity.

The manner in which Russia, France and Germany combined to deprive Japan of her gains on the mainland has already been related. Ostensibly, the Japanese Emperor,

yielded to the dictates of magnanimity and accepted the advice of the three Powers . . . out of regard for peace,

but it was not likely to be a lasting peace.

In Korea Japan had rid herself of one rival only to find herself faced by another, more anxious and more competent than China to take advantage of the continuing state of Korean unrest. The situation was still explosive and complicated. The Tai Won Kun had returned from an enforced exile in China and now found himself in rivalry with his daughter-in-law, the Queen, a woman of great strength of character and determined views.

In October 1895 again the rival factions in Seoul erupted into violence. The royal palace was stormed and the Queen and her female attendants brutally murdered. It was Koreans who carried out the dead, but the Japanese were seriously and closely implicated as accessories. There can be no doubt that the Japanese Minister was himself a prime mover in the plot, but it recoiled upon his own head. As a direct result of the confusion and bloodshed in his capital the King of Korea, claiming protection, took refuge in the Russian delegation.

For two years the titular ruler of Korea remained behind Russian defended walls and the Japanese were forced to watch in fury while Russian influence replaced Chinese in a land which in their view they could no longer afford to see controlled by a rival. Unfortunately, also, from the Japanese viewpoint, the Russians appeared to be considerably luckier in their dealings with the Chinese than they were. Count Cassini, the Russian Minister in Peking, was able to extract a secret convention from Li Hung Chang which promised among other things Chinese assistance with Russian railway building in Manchuria. In 1896 Li Hung Chang represented his country in St. Petersburg at the coronation of Nicholas II, the new Tsar. Prince Lobanoff, the Foreign Minister, was most attentive to the Chinese Viceroy, Cassini's good work was improved on, and Li left the Russian capital, his benevolence reinforced by a substantial bribe. The next year the Germans, taking advantage of the murder of two of their missionaries, occupied the harbour of Kiaochow.

The Russians soon opened negotiations at Peking for permission to winter their fleet at Port Arthur. On March 15th, 1898, they were granted a 25-year lease of the port and its surrounding territory. The Russian delight at obtaining a warm-water port at last was only equalled by the chagrin of the Japanese at seeing what they had captured by force of arms possessed by their most dangerous rival.

The next move in the drama came with the slowly gathering momentum of the Boxer Rebellion, provoked by increased foreign intervention following the conclusion of the Sino-Japanese war. In 1899 the first incidents were being reported, by June of 1900 the legations were under siege.

Naturally enough the nations first able to take action were those with naval or military forces near at hand, Britain, Russia and Japan, closely followed by the U.S.A. Among these the Japanese were first off the mark, operating with the advantage of a home base, and brigades of their short stocky infantrymen and marines were soon moving rapidly towards Peking. Less efficiently and more slowly large bodies of Russian troops began to move south into Manchuria. A contingent was also despatched northwards from Port Arthur. There can be little doubt that even at this stage both nations saw more significance in their operations than the mere relief of the diplomatic colony in the Chinese capital.

Certainly the Japanese were conscious and confident of their growing strength on which their participation in a minor war alongside Europeans had put the seal of respectability. The contrast between their own present status and that of the Chinese enemy, a few years ago their equals, was certainly not lost on them.

The French, their minds sharpened unpleasantly by the fact

that in the days of the Second Empire their diplomatic stake had been on the moribund Shogunate as against the 'new men' gathering round the young Emperor, were perhaps the first but not the only nation to observe the rise of a new power to be reckoned with in the Far East. The Germans were certainly not unaware of the quality of the nation whose army they had trained. The British often in friendly diplomatic contact with the Japanese in the early days had trained the navy and built many of its ships. In common with the Americans, who adopted a kind of collective responsibility for the actions of the prime mover Commodore Perry, they now had an almost paternal attitude to what Harold Macmillan remembered were called in his childhood 'gallant little Japs'. In the competitive military atmosphere inevitably existing in Peking at the turn of the century the appearance and conduct of the Japanese contingent confirmed this view. Everyone's eyes seemed to have been opened save those of the Russians.

Even when two years later the Japanese took the next step to full Great Power status with their alliance with Great Britain Russian eyes still seemed closed. It would have seemed elementary for the Russians, now that the Japanese had obtained a powerful friend, to be doubly on their guard, but, alone apparently, they refused to take the Japanese seriously. Perhaps the incompetent and hopelessly inaccurate reports of their naval and military attachés on the state and size of the Japanese armed forces reassured them. In any event Russian penetration into Korea and Manchuria continued unabated.

In the former country, despite the presence of numbers of Japanese immigrants and traders Russia had succeeded in largely replacing the now defunct Chinese influence by her own. The King, as has been seen, had taken refuge in the Russian legation. On his emergence Russian civil servants virtually took over the various administrative departments and Russian officers began to be employed to train the Korean army and everywhere the old Korean conservative (and anti-Japanese) party was in the ascendant.

In Manchuria at the beginning of the Boxer Rebellion strong detachments of Russian troops had taken over the protection of the railway and the formation of a buffer to protect neighbouring Russian territory from both Boxer bands and Hunhutsus, the local bandits. When the danger from the Boxers had disappeared the troops remained. Negotiations with China to end what was in effect a Russian occupation seemed designed to come to no conclusion. No doubt as a piece of window-dressing to impress other European powers Russia announced in April 1903 that the beginning of troop evacuation would commence in October and would be completed within the year. As an accompaniment a draft treaty was proposed to be negotiated with the Chinese whereby other foreign nations were to be excluded from commercial and mining rights in Manchuria and Mongolia, leaving the field clear to the Russians themselves.

April, May and June of 1903 passed and there was no discernible diminution of Russian troops in the area. In July the Japanese ambassador in St. Petersburg, Komira, put forward a set of proposals: first, both Japan and Russia were to recognise the independence of China and Korea. However, both nations were then to recognise the other's preponderance, Japanese in Korea balanced by Russian in Manchuria. Both were to recall their troops from their respective areas of influence – as soon as possible – in the interim Russians would protect the railways in Manchuria and the Japanese do the same in Korea. No reinforcements were to be sent in either case. Russia would have an open door for her commercial ventures and enterprises in Manchuria, Japan for hers in Korea.

In essence it was a carve-up but not an inequitable one. The proposals were met with a fantastic front of official procrastination on the part of the Russians.

Meanwhile it came to the notice of the Japanese that the Russians were building up their naval and military forces in the Far East. Troops were being moved, not only into Manchuria but into Northern Korea as well. The Russian Korean Bank which had been formed in 1897 was stepping up its operations whereby Russians acquired property and land concessions in Korea. A Russian combine acquired a 25-year monopoly on timber cutting on the Yalu and Tumen rivers and in April 1903 it began its operations and demobilised troops began to follow in the wake of the foresters and engineers as security guards.

It became obvious to the Japanese that the Russians had no

intention of relinquishing their hold on Manchuria and Korea, nevertheless the negotiations for a settlement continued in St. Petersburg until January 1904. Between October 16th, 1903 and January 13th, 1904 six drafts of agreement were exchanged. On New Year's Day, 1904, at his reception for the diplomatic corps, the Tsar was seen to be speaking (in his own words) 'very earnestly and sternly' to the Japanese Minister. Nicholas said that Russia was 'quite conscious of her strength' and that there was also a limit to her patience.

Finally, on January 13th, the Japanese Minister presented to Count Lamsdorff, the Foreign Minister, his last proposal, accompanied by a request for a speedy reply. More Russian reinforcements were still moving to the Far East. By February 4th no reply had been received and Japanese patience ran out. On February 6th their Minister informed Lamsdorff that he had been ordered to sever diplomatic relations and leave St. Petersburg. On February 10th – four days later – both nations produced formal declarations of war, but by then operations had already commenced.

THREE

'An armed clash with Japan would be a great disaster for us'

SERGIUS WITTE

The nation which Japan defied was both in population and area the largest in Europe. The total of the Tsar's subjects was somewhere above 130 million, his army comprised a million men, supported by nearly twice that number of reservists. The Imperial Navy was the third largest in the world, with bases on the Baltic, the Black Sea and in the Far East.

It was also a nation like no other in Europe. In 1814 Princess Lieven had said, 'Russia is not in Europe, nor indeed will it ever be', but it was more than geographic position and ethnographic origins which separated the Russians from their neighbours and contemporaries.

For Russia was an absolutism, pure and simple. As the Russians said, 'Above the Tsar there is only God, and he is far away.' All other European monarchs in 1904 – the constitutional Edward VII of Great Britain, old Franz Josef in Vienna now in the fifty-sixth year of his reign, the posturing militarist Wilhelm II of Germany and all the cousins and relations occupying thrones from Scandinavia to Greece – all shared power and influence to different degrees with parliaments, advisers and aristocracies. Each and every one had limitations placed upon him both by men and institutions. Not so the Tsar. Article I of the Fundamental Laws of the Russian Empire allowed no such possibility: 'To the Emperor of all the Russias belongs the supreme autocratic and unlimited power. Not only fear, but also conscience commanded by God himself, is the basis of obedience to this power.'

This was no ceremonial verbal flourish such as might appear in a coronation oath, but the truth and the practice, accepted and acted upon implicitly.

In the preceding century Russia had been ruled by five Emperors and it is highly significant that the only breach in the principle of absolutism had come about by the wish and command of one of them, Alexander II, known as the Tsar Liberator. Succeeding his father, the stern martinet Nicholas I, towards the end of the humiliatingly unsuccessful Crimean War, he had perceived that many of Russia's ills were attributable to her archaic and repressive political and social system.

Accordingly reforms were instituted 'from above', which was the only method known or possible in Russia. As a first step in 1861 the serfs were freed. A year later the legal system was liberalised and units of local government were created in the Zemstva, bodies roughly akin to local councils. Secondary and university education was encouraged. The old forced levy by which a quota of serfs had been sentenced to the army for twenty-five years was replaced by a more equitable system of conscription. At the same time the coming of the railway age and some beginnings of an industrial and commercial revolution increased the general level of prosperity. Observers in the West began to predict that at last Russia was catching up with the rest of Europe.

Such a view was in any event over-optimistic. The freed serfs were now landless peasants, many poorer after their freedom than before. Industrialisation tended to create a new class of poor, the urban proletariat. There was still no real middle class in Russia and the possibility of participation in government did not exist save for the nobles and bureaucrats. Still, these were stages in development through which other European nations had passed; no doubt Russia, at a slower pace, would follow.

The hopes raised by Alexander's initial reforming zeal were disappointed as his own enthusiasm for modernisation seemed to wane. Perhaps he himself had expected too much by way of immediate results, certainly a nationalist revolt in Poland and repeated assassination attempts upon himself and his Ministers and governors helped induce him to turn away from domestic affairs towards a series of expansionist adventures in the

Balkans and Central Asia. Consequent upon this apparent change of Imperial heart and the frustrations it provoked there came a growth in the activities of the underground revolutionary societies in Russia. In 1879 the extreme terrorist group 'The People's Will' condemned the Tsar to death for his failure to carry his policies to their logical conclusion – some form of elected and representative Assembly. On March 31st, 1881, after a number of unsuccessful attempts, the sentence was carried out. Dismounting from his carriage to inspect the damage caused by a bomb which had missed him but landed among his Cossack escort, the Tsar became an easy target for a second assassin. A Polish student Grinevitsky rushed out of the gathering crowd and threw his bomb between himself and the Tsar. Grinevitsky died immediately, but Alexander, his legs nearly severed from his body and his stomach ripped open, had just enough strength to mutter, 'Take me to the Palace – to die there.'

His last wish was granted, in the presence of his son, the new Alexander III and his 13-year-old grandson, the future Nicholas II. Unknown to his subjects the dying Tsar's last official act had been that morning to consent to the establishment of a national representative council to advise on legislation. The project died with him.

Alexander's death and the manner of it was a climacteric in the history of Russia. The cause of moderate reform never really recovered from the blow. Russia had returned to what a Russian quoted by Count Munster had called twenty years before, 'absolutism moderated by assassination'.

The Tsar became again an omnipotent but distant being insulated from the people he ruled by bureaucrats, soldiers and policemen. For Alexander III this was not a difficult role. The shock of his father's death apart, he was temperamentally neither an innovator nor a reformer. A large, bald, bearded man, he seemed to epitomise 'the old Russia'. Queen Victoria said he was a 'sovereign whom she does not look upon as a gentleman'. If the observation had come to the notice of the Tsar of all the Russias he would have been unaffected. Obstinate, of limited intelligence, with a penchant for simple country pursuits, Alexander possessed the attributes of his own peasant subjects.

Englishmen, Germans and Jews he disliked equally, his French allies he bore as a necessary evil. Encouraged by his principal adviser, Konstantin Pobodonosteff, the Procurator of the Holy Synod, he adopted Nationalism, Absolutism and Orthodoxy as his watchwords and made them the bounds of his political opinions, judgments and ambitions.

In consequence, the national and religious minorities of the Empire suffered: the Poles and Finns, Lithuanians and Latvians were 'absorbed', and the freedom of the Jews was limited by the so-called Temporary Laws of 1882, which lasted for twenty years. During Alexander's reign, pregnant for the future, the first Marxist group was formed among the myriad other underground political movements in St. Petersburg. In London, Paris and Geneva émigré communities raised funds, pamphleteered and plotted. Their less fortunate comrades languished in the prison of St. Peter and St. Paul, or the fortress of Schlusselburg, or whiled away their exile in Siberia. Like many other autocrats before and since, when displeased by the face of domestic politics, Alexander took refuge in foreign affairs. At first the Dreikaiserbund, Bismarck's trades union of Emperors, attracted him. However the Bulgarian crisis of 1885–6 disabused his mind of the idea that Austria-Hungary and Germany might sacrifice any of their national ambitions to preserve the cause of unity among hereditary monarchs. From this realistic conviction (and for all his intellectual limits Alexander was a realist) grew the eventual Franco-Russian alliance secretly arrived at in 1894.

Although he had burnt his fingers in the Balkans there were other outlets for the Tsar's imperial ambitions. Russian foreign policy has always swung pendulum-wise east and west, so, thwarted in the west, Alexander looked east. In the 1880's and 1890's soldiers, sailors, administrators, merchants and adventurers with plans for expansion towards the Pacific found in their sovereign a sympathetic audience. Vladivostock, 'the Star of the East', became a base for an expanding navy and the Tsarevich Nicholas, on a tour of the Far East, pushed a wheelbarrow-load of soil along a plank and inaugurated the terminus of the Trans-Siberian Railway.

So Russia might be backward, with less than 20 per cent of her population able to read and write, and Russia might be poor with the lowest wages in Europe, even taking into account the lowest standard of living; Russia might also have the highest rate of infant mortality, the highest incidence of syphilis and drunkenness, of typhoid, cholera and death by famine, but she had her holy mission and would be a power to be reckoned with in the world.

Foreign visitors to Russia were struck by the contrast between the grinding poverty and appalling ignorance exhibited on all sides and the overweening sense of superiority of the Russians from prince to peasant. For the national arrogance was by no means a prerogative of the official or privileged classes. Million upon million of ignorant peasants, inured to pain and death, indifferent to hardship, illiterate and untravelled and super-stitiously wedded to an abuse-ridden Church, were loyal to a remote Tsar and accepted however imperfectly his vision of Russia's manifest destiny.

Somehow, for a few brief years the illusion lasted, sustained in part by the personality of the Tsar. But there was one limit on the power and actions of even a Russian Emperor – mortality. In October 1894 Alexander sailed on the Imperial yacht to Yalta, ostensibly to recuperate from dropsy, but in reality, as his doctors knew and his family guessed, to die there. A few weeks later the Imperial gun salutes were being fired in the Crimea for his successor, his 26-year-old son, Nicholas, now 'by the Grace of Almighty God, the Emperor and Autocrat of all the Russias, of Moscow, Kiev, Vladimir Novgorod, the Tsar of Kazan, Tsar of Astrakhan, the Tsar of Poland, Tsar of Siberia, of Tauride Chersonese, Tsar of Georgia, Sovereign of Pskov and Grand Duke of Smolensk, Lithuania, Volkyria, Podolia and Finland . . .'.

The recipient of these and many other honours was short and slight with a rather high-pitched voice and scarcely a drop of Russian blood in his veins. His handsome but blank face was given a little character by a neat beard and moustache, but his gait was self-conscious and his manner displayed the formality of shyness. His accomplishments were few: fluency in English, French and German, an interest in photography, a liking for tennis and swimming and a fondness for dogs. His serious reading was confined to one right-wing newspaper and his experience consisted of a brief formal spell as an officer of the Imperial Guard in St. Petersburg and a Grand Tour with special emphasis on the Far East.

His prejudices were as simple, and, because of his position, as important as those of his father. Unlike Alexander III, however, he did not dislike the Germans (he was to marry a German princess, and many of his principal officers and officials were of German origin), but held them in a sort of awe. Perhaps for that reason Nicholas was never able to rid himself of a kind of reluctant admiration for the bombastic Kaiser. Nor was he ever able to see through Wilhelm's transparently cunning overtures to friendship and co-operation which were certainly not intended to benefit Russia.

Like his father he had no particular love for the French but regarded them as a diplomatic necessity. His special hatred was reserved for Englishmen, Jews and Japanese. With regard to the first two races he put his contempt for both into one of his few recorded aphorisms, 'An Englishmen is a zhid (Jew).' His dislike of the Japanese, whom he normally referred to as 'monkeys', was no doubt reinforced by a nearly successful attempt on his life by an obscure fanatic during his only visit to Japan, in 1891, an event which brought the visit to an abrupt end, and left Nicholas with a considerable sword scar and severe headaches for the rest of his life.

Treated with a sort of affectionate contempt by his over-bearing father, the Tsarevich had been given virtually no tutelage nor preparation for the tasks ahead of him. Indeed on learning of his father's death and his own accession Nicholas II, as he now was, threw his arms round his sister Olga and confessed, 'I am not ready for it, I don't even know how to receive my Ministers.'

Ten days after Alexander III was buried in St. Petersburg, court mourning was suspended so that the new Tsar could marry the bride of his choice, Princess Alix of Hesse-Darmstadt. An acute observer of these disparate proceedings, which gave the new Tsaritsa the soubriquet among her subjects of 'the funeral bride', was Edward, Prince of Wales, representing Queen Victoria at both ceremonies. To her he wrote that Nicholas was naturally 'shy and timid', and to Lord Carrington, a member of his suite, he confided his worries at Nicholas' autocratic ideas and lack of worldly sense. Staying with the widowed Dowager Empress and the new Tsar and his bride in the Anitchikoff Palace, Edward (no mean judge, it might be thought, of matriarchs) was amazed at the control still exercised by the mother over her son, whom he decided was 'as weak as water'.

Very early in the new reign the Prince of Wales had put his finger on the contrast between Nicholas' personality and his position. Nicholas Alexandrovich Romanoff was pleasant, weak and indecisive, destined to move from domination by his parents to domination by his wife. He was a model husband and in time a doting father: a man who would have made a reasonable enough village squire, of the sort that the villagers would describe as 'not the man his father was'. Unfortunately, he was not a simple country gentleman, but autocrat of 133 million people over whom he was determined, as he declared, to maintain 'for the good of the whole nation the principle of absolute autocracy as firmly and strongly as did my late lamented father'.

The occasion for the delivery of this particular sentiment was the presentation of loyal addresses by the Zemstva to the new sovereign. The Zemstvo of Tver had asked hopefully for some move towards representative government. These were 'senseless dreams', said Nicholas, in a phrase which was to echo round Russia. Hopes that the new monarch might imitate his grandfather, the Tsar Liberator, were dashed to the ground. Liberal and progressive elements were forced to abandon the idea that once again reform might come from above. Both Kliuchevsky, the historian, and Lord Carrington independently predicted a revolution and the end of the dynasty. The Prince of Wales had expressed the hope that Nicholas would 'move with the times'. Plainly he would not. For the rest of his reign this weak, shallow man was to be a walking example of the dangers of the hereditary absolute monarchy, the principle of which he defended with religious intensity.

Eight years after his coronation in October 1902 Nicholas wrote to his mother, the Dowager Empress Maria Feodorovna,

In the sight of my Maker I have to carry the burden of a terrible responsibility and at all times, therefore, be ready to render an account to Him of my actions. I must always keep firmly to my convictions, and follow the dictates of my conscience.

Nicholas had not 'moved with the times' and from this highly personalised view of his duties and responsibilities he never wavered. Unfortunately, in this conviction Nicholas was confirmed by the adulation of his wife, who had translated herself from Protestant petty German princess, and a grand-daughter of Queen Victoria, to fervently Orthodox absolutist Tsaritsa. Never popular among the Russians, who called her 'the German woman', despite her mystical new patriotism, the Empress was nevertheless convinced that she and her beloved husband were the twentieth-century heirs of all those strong war-like Romanoffs of the past who, in her view, had ruled their simple loyal subjects for their own good and the glory of Holy Russia.

It is doubtful if any other princess culled from the pages of the Almanach de Gotha could have made Nicholas a much wiser or more reasonable monarch. As it was, the woman he did choose, and whom he loved passionately until the day of his death, was so inspired by an uncritical amalgam of love and near religious mania that she blindly confirmed his prejudices, excused his deceits and reinforced his worst judgments.

In most other European countries, even in the early twentieth century, many of these considerations – the psychological motivations of a monarch and his consort, their whims, fancies and illusions – would have been of little importance, but in Russia they were vital, since the whole governmental system was moulded round the omnipotence and implied omnicompetence of one man. Beneath the Tsar there did stretch a vast pyramid composed of tier upon tier of officials, Ministers, bureaucrats, generals and admirals, but all were ultimately without responsi-bility, their initiative as closely confined as their bodies within their dress uniforms. There was no Prime Minister and no Cabinet: Ministers had no collective voice or responsibility and could be ignored or dismissed at will. The official bodies such as the Council of State and the Senate, like individual Ministers, only tendered advice to the Sovereign and were in practice mere rubber stamps upon Imperial decrees.

A powerful Tsar, such as Alexander II, initiated policies both domestic and foreign himself. Under a weak Tsar, as Nicholas was despite his obstinacy, power rested with those who could influence or persuade him whether they themselves were Ministers, courtiers or mere favourites.

With no course of action is this more clearly illustrated than in Russia's approach to the war with Japan. At no stage did any one man, or group of men, positively advocate war. There was never a war party, as there was eventually to be in Japan. Even after the signing of the Anglo-Japanese alliance in 1902 apparently no group of statesmen or officials seemed to concern themselves overmuch with the question of where Russian policy in the Far East might lead. Certainly there was no committee formed of generals or admirals to examine properly the possibility of war and to prepare contingency plans should war break out. Russian policy makers seem simply never to have seen the warning in the fact that the Japanese had sought a Far Eastern understanding with Russia as an alternative to the English alliance.

Some part of the cause was the way in which Russia was governed, and some part the men who came to power under the system. Other nations in the nineteenth and twentieth centuries of course often pursued imperialist policies and thus 'drifted' into wars, Great Britain among them, in a surprisingly ill-thought-out manner. Nevertheless, the way in which Russia's policy developed provided a crushing indictment of her system of government. The most powerful statesman of the time was Sergius Witte. He was a man of undoubted force, drive and ability, and not untypically was of non-Russian (Dutch) origins. He had first made his mark as a railway administrator. 'Noticed' by the former Tsar Alexander III he became Minister of Communications and in 1892 Minister of Finance, but still kept within his control railway development as well as commerce, industry and labour relations.

His overall aim was the modernisation and industrialisation of Russia, and as part of this process he succeeded in returning Russia to the gold standard, and encouraging foreign, in particular French, investment. Neither by temperament nor interest was Witte excessively imperialist or expansionist in his outlook, but his concern with the development of the Trans-Siberian Railway brought him inevitably into the sphere of Far Eastern policies. Under Nicholas II it became his task to negotiate with Li Hung Chang, the Chinese Viceroy, on the subject of the Chinese Eastern Railway as an offshoot of the Trans-Siberian through northern Manchuria. Perhaps a little ingenuously, Witte argues in his memoirs, which were published after his death, that throughout his concern was purely with gradual commercial penetration. Nevertheless there can be no doubt that he recoiled from policies which were likely to lead to military confrontation with Japan, and it was no part of his intention to jeopardise newly-won economic advantages by participation in a costly war.

Curiously too, on the Russian General Staff where one might expect to find some eagerness for a warlike policy, there was little or none – at least directed against Japan. The Chief of the General Staff Obrusheff was not interested in that theatre at all, his concern being with the threat posed to Russia by Austro-Hungary and possibly her German ally as well. Perhaps it was an indication of his limitations as an all-round strategist, but to him the possibility of drawing off Russian forces to the East in the face of the obvious danger from the West was at least a nuisance, and at worst a disaster. Those who controlled the Imperial Navy, under General-Admiral the Grand Duke Alexei Alexandrovich, the Tsar's uncle, had a different view, though not a clearer one. Their long-standing obsession had been with the need for a warm-water port, since Vladivostock was only usable in the winter months with the aid of ice-breakers, and to them the newly acquired Port Arthur (plus nearby Dalny which could be developed as a civilian harbour) meant that Russia could now maintain a larger fleet in the Far East. But no one ever seemed to ask precisely what that fleet was meant to do. Port Arthur became the new prestige base and a great deal of money was spent on the fortifications and even more on the facilities at Dalny. However, Vladivostock was still maintained as a subsidiary and the 1,100 miles of sea between the two ports the Japanese could dominate from their home bases. Further, no one in the Russian Admiralty ever seemed to bother their heads much over the likely effect upon the Japanese of the establishment of a naval base and a civilian port on the Japanese doorstep, at the very time of the Russian overland penetration of Korea and Manchuria.

Part of the Russian blindness can no doubt be ascribed to the nature of the Imperial urge, common to other nations at the time, and the consequent competitiveness which afflicted all the Great Powers in matters of acquiring territory, naval bases and the like. Nevertheless there was also an element of the old Russian arrogance in the almost complete indifference shown to possible reactions by the Japanese. Muravieff, the Foreign Minister from 1896 to 1900, had put the sentiment in one sentence at one of the original conferences called to discuss the pros and cons of Port Arthur's occupation. Three of his colleagues, Witte, Vannovsky, the Minister of War, and Chiukhacheff, the Navy Minister, had all raised practical difficulties and stressed possible dangers; but Muravieff's view eventually found favour with the Tsar: 'One flag and one sentry, the prestige of Russia will do the rest.'

His successor as Foreign Minister, Count Lamsdorff, however, took the opposite point of view and regarded the whole Far East venture with apprehension. Such unfortunately was the Byzantine nature of the Russian governmental system that Lamsdorff's opinion didn't count. 'I can do nothing, I take no part in the negotiations', he confided to Witte. Lamsdorff, not a man of very forceful character in any event, came to be regarded by the Tsar as merely an official whose task was to execute the Imperial will, and during his tenure of office from 1900 to 1906 others either exercised more influence or put forward policies more attractive to Nicholas.

In November 1901 Witte wrote to Lamsdorff as follows:

An armed clash with Japan in the near future would be a great disaster for us. I do not doubt that Russia will emerge victorious from the struggle, but the victory will cost us too much and will badly injure the country economically – in the eyes of the Russian people a war with Japan for the possession of distant Korea will not be justified and the latent dissatisfaction may render more acute the alarming phenomena of our domestic life, which make themselves felt even in peacetime. Between the two evils, an armed conflict with Japan and the complete cession of Korea, I would unhesitatingly choose the second.

By this time Witte was undoubtedly beginning to have second thoughts about what he might well have seen originally as a successful piece of economic policy with no attendant dangers. Still, however sincere his conversion and however strong his objections, and no doubt he overstated both with the advantage of hindsight in his memoirs, he was too late. For by the new century there was a definite Far East lobby forming in the circles round Nicholas II.

Prominent among its members were two men, Alexander Bezobrazoff and Vladimir Vonliarliarsky, who were originally at least entirely outside the machinery of government. Both were former cavalry officers, but their interest in the Far East was not military but commercial. Way back in 1897 a Vladivostock merchant called Briner had acquired from the Korean Government a concession for the exploitation of the enormous forest areas in the north of Korea along the Tumen and Yalu rivers. Through the good offices of Vonliarliarsky and Bezobrazoff he managed to interest Count Vorontsoff-Dashkoff, the former Minister of the Court, in the project, and through him the Grand Duke Alexander Michailovich. One of Bezobrazoff's plans was that a railway could be built through the concession lands to link Port Arthur with the Trans-Siberian Railway. This idea, which in fact had some merit, failed to attract sufficient interest at the time, but Bezobrazoff's persistence did eventually persuade the Tsar to allow an investigation of the area by one of his Privy Counsellors, Neporozhneff, accompanied by two military staff officers. All three on their return were eloquent as to the area's strategic importance and commercial potential.

As a result of the report and more pushing of his contacts by Bezobrazoff the Briner concession was acquired under Imperial patronage in 1898, and on June 18th, 1900 the formation of the East Asian Development Company was approved by the Tsar, who had used a sizable amount of his private funds in assisting Bezobrazoff. In 1908 Witte, against considerable Court opposition, forced the dissolution of the Company. But nevertheless Bezobrazoff's course was set. By then he had succeeded in becoming a Far East expert. Along with his cronies Vonliarliarsky, Colonel Vogak and Rear-Admiral Abaza, the Russian military agent in China and Japan, he had acquired a position of considerable power and influence. In November 1902 Bezobrazoff was again in the Far East, on a two months' tour with two million roubles at his disposal from the Russo-Chinese Bank, the sanction for the loan having been given by Witte on orders from the Tsar. In May 1903 the ex-cavalry captain was appointed a Secretary of State, and Vogak was given an honorific post in the Imperial retinue.

Such advances had needless to say not gone unremarked by what might be called the Tsar's 'regular' advisers and Ministers. Adjustments of position were made to accommodate the new star in the firmament.

The Minister of War, Kuropatkin, had conferences with Bezobrazoff at Port Arthur, their visits to the Far East having happily coincided. Plehve, the Minister of the Interior since 1902, began to side with Bezobrazoff in an attempt to erode the influence of his rival for domestic influence, Witte.

On August 12th, 1903, to the surprise of both Kuropatkin and Witte, Admiral Alexieff, who compensated for his lack of sea-going experience by his position as protegé of the Grand Duke Alexei Alexandrovich and as rumoured illegitimate son of the Tsar Alexander II, was appointed Viceroy of the Far East with administrative and military control of the whole area plus the conduct of diplomatic relations with China, Japan and Korea. In his previous post as commander of the Pacific Squadron and the Kwantung garrison, the Admiral had been, to say the least, lukewarm about Bezobrazoff's dream of empire, he was now more enthusiastic.

On August 28th Witte, after ten years as Minister of Finance, was summoned by the Tsar and requested to bring his deputy, Pleske, with him. When they left the Peterhof Palace after a short audience, the ailing Pleske was Minister of Finance and Witte was President of the Committee of Ministers, an honorific post of no importance. In his diary Nicholas wrote, 'Now I rule.' In Darmstadt in the next month, visiting his cousins – one of whom was of course the Kaiser, always anxious to direct Russian interests away from the Balkans to the Far East – the Tsar took the opportunity of ratifying the statutes of the Far

East Committee. Among its members, along with the Ministers of War and Finance, were Bezobrazoff and Abaza.

Meanwhile the negotiations between Russia and Japan continued. Vainly, Baron Rosen, Russian Ambassador to Tokyo, tried to bring home to his masters in St. Petersburg the fact that there was a limit to Japanese patience, and that semi-official ventures such as those which surrounded the whole matter of the Yalu concession, while not being of any great economic value to Russia, did serve both to alarm the Japanese and provide them with a ready excuse for war. Rosen's military attaché continued even after his transfer to China to stress the strength and preparedness of the Japanese army to Kuropatkin, apparently to no effect.

The Imperial Viceroy telegraphed to the Tsar saying that from his point of view the diplomatic situation seemed hopeless, only to be informed that despite no slackening of the Russian negotiating position 'a war must not be permitted'.

About this time, according to Witte, Vyacheslav Konstantino-vich Plehve, the Minister of the Interior, observed to Alexei Nickolayevich Kuropatkin, the Minister of War:

What this country needs is a short victorious war to stem the tide of revolution.

Apparently Kuropatkin, now growing apprehensive and cautious, had rebuked Plehve for favouring a war policy. The War Minister's caution, however, like the Tsar's reluctance to countenance a war which he had in many ways encouraged, was ill-timed and ineffective. On February 4th, 1904 the Japanese Government approved the breaking off of diplomatic relations with Russia. On February 6th the Japanese Combined Fleet left Sasebo naval base and on February 8th attacked the Russian fleet at anchor at Port Arthur.

FOUR

'For Russia has been stricken'

THE DAILY TELEGRAPH

On the evening of February 8th a large part of the Russian Pacific Squadron lay at anchor in the roadstead of Port Arthur. The ships were ranged in three lines running east and west, the innermost consisting of five battleships, the flagship the *Petropavlovsk*, then *Sebastopol*, *Peresvyet*, *Pobieda* and *Poltava*. The middle line was headed by two more battleships, the *Tsarevich* and the *Retvisan*, followed by three cruisers, and the outer line of three more cruisers headed by the *Pallada*, which occupied the easternmost station. These were all the largest units of the fleet, destroyers and similar auxiliary vessels being within the harbour, except for two destroyers *Rastoropni* and *Bezstrashni*, which were on patrol 20 miles out to sea. During the day some of the capital ships had been engaged in coaling and in consequence large numbers of their ships' companies had been granted shore leave. The cafés of Port Arthur were full and a visiting circus was proving a great attraction. Earlier in the evening Madame Stark, the wife of Vice-Admiral Stark, the fleet commander, had entertained to a small party a number of senior officers, including Admiral Alexieff, the Viceroy and supreme commander, his Chief-of-Staff, Vice-Admiral Vitgeft and Stark's own second-in-command, Rear-Admiral Prince Ukhtomsky.

All these senior officers, of course, knew that events in the Far East were fast moving towards a climax and that war with Japan might be upon them at any time, but so far as their professional conduct was concerned they maintained the easy routine of peacetime. Admittedly Stark had raised the question of putting the fleet in a state of war preparedness, but he had been told by the Viceroy that such action would be 'premature'. Doubtless the Tsar's most recent instruction – that if war came it would be for the Japanese, not the Russians, to fire the first shot – weighed heavily with Alexieff. Whatever the reason, the 62-year-old Viceroy's lack of decision conveyed itself all the way down the line to his subordinates. Stark ordered the fleet to 'prepare to repel torpedo attacks', but as the order was unaccompanied by any further instructions most of his captains took the easy way out and did nothing. The two destroyers patrolled seawards with instructions to report any unusual activity to the flagship, and the *Pallada* as 'duty ship' had its searchlights manned; but for the rest of the Russian fleet the Japanese might not have existed. The great ships lay at anchor, full lights burning, guns unloaded; and those members of the crew on board turned in on their mess decks. On shore the fortress guns were still in their winter coating of heavy protective grease and the recoil cylinders of the most powerful land armament, the 10-inch guns on Electric Hill, were drained. The gun crews, like their naval comrades, were either at ease in their quarters or finding what amusements they could in the town. The night was clear and cold and a full moon shone on a calm sea. To the south-west the beams of Liaotishan lighthouse continued to shine a guide to the entrance of the harbour.

Meanwhile, off Round Island, about 60 miles east of Port Arthur, another fleet was making its disposition under the orders of a very different admiral between 6 p.m. and 7 p.m. For Vice-Admiral Togo, in command of the Combined Fleet which had left Sasebo two days before when negotiations had been broken off by the Japanese envoy at St. Petersburg, the war had already started.

Short and stocky, ten years Alexieff's junior, Togo had spent some of his naval career under the tutelage of the British in the training ship H.M.S. *Worcester*. Later, he had been the first Japanese officer to fire a shot in the Sino-Japanese War, and later still he commanded the naval operations which led to the capture of Port Arthur. Now, nine years later, Port Arthur was once again his chief objective, together with Chemulpo (the port of Seoul, the Korean capital) and Dalny, the Russian civil base. According to his intelligence reports Russian ships were to be found at all three points and it was Togo's intention to destroy as many of his enemy's war vessels as possible in three simultaneous actions.

Accordingly, the fleet divided. To Port Arthur sailed the destroyers (still called torpedo boat destroyers) of the 1st, 2nd and 3rd Flotillas, totalling eleven ships, while the 4th and 5th Flotillas of eight ships made full speed towards Dalny. These were both purely naval attacks, but the force destined for Chemulpo, under the command of Rear-Admiral Uriu, had a different composition and purpose. The war vessels under his flag were cruisers and torpedo boats, and together they provided the escort for three troop transports carrying 2,500 troops, a temporary wharf, sampans, launches and other landing equipment.

Rarely have two adversaries presented a bigger contrast at the beginning of a war. The Russians, confident of their strength, had scarcely moved a company of troops or a ship on to a war footing. Static, almost inert, both navy and army, despite recently arrived military reinforcements, merely waited for an attack which no doubt many senior officers thought the Japanese would not dare to make. The Japanese, in order to start the war at all, had to put troops into Korea and to do that they had first to neutralise Russian sea power. It was an earnest of their determination and vigour that it was decided that both operations should be attempted at once.

Just before 11 p.m. the *Shirakumo*, the leading Japanese destroyer, came within sight of the two patrolling Russian destroyers. These, to the surprise of the Japanese, turned about and returned to Port Arthur so that their captains might report to Admiral Stark. Guided now by the searchlights of the *Pallada*, Captain Asai in command of the 1st Flotilla led his ships into the roadstead and along the line of Russian battleships, each destroyer in succession discharging its torpedoes and then turning away at full speed. In the Russian fleet all was confusion. The destroyers *Rastoropni* and *Beztrashni* arrived to make their report at the same time as the noise of explosions made it unnecessary. The *Pallada* was the first ship to be struck, being hit amidships, and one of her coal bunkers caught fire.

Almost immediately afterwards the *Retvizan* shuddered as a 200-square-foot hole was blown in her port side. The *Tsarevich* was torpedoed in the stern, her bulkheads shattered and the steering compartment flooded. All three ships got under way as soon as possible in an attempt to reach shallow water, but the *Pallada* grounded near to the lighthouse on the west side of the harbour entrance, while the *Retvizan* and *Tsarevich* both came to grief in the narrow gullet of the harbour, almost blocking it for the passage of other vessels.

On the other Russian ships searchlights blazed and guns and even small arms were fired out to sea. Officers shouted orders and ships' crews scurried hither and thither, but their assailants had long since departed.

Meanwhile at Dalny the Japanese had drawn a blank, for there were no Russian warships there at all. In fact there was only one ship of any description in the harbour and that was a British merchantman which had embarked Japanese subjects from Port Arthur and Dalny under charter to the Japanese consul. She only narrowly escaped being torpedoed nevertheless, and the disappointed captains of the 4th and 5th Flotillas, realising their mistake, returned to the fleet rendezvous at Round Island.

At 8 a.m. on February 8th, that is 16 hours before the launching of the attack on Port Arthur, Rear-Admiral Uriu (another officer who like his superior Togo had profited from British naval training) was receiving from the captain of the destroyer *Cheyoda* a report on the state of affairs at Chemulpo, the third objective of the Japanese fleet.

When the *Cheyoda* had left at midnight on the 7th there had been two Russian warships in the port, the cruiser *Varyag* and the gunboat *Koreetz*. To Uriu, with five cruisers and four torpedo boats, this was no opposition at all. The admiral's main concern was the presence of British, American, French and Italian warships recently arrived 'to protect national interests'.

If a battle had to be fought in order to land the troops under his command, the presence of foreign neutrals presented an alarming prospect of possible diplomatic incidents. Nevertheless Uriu had his orders, the synchronisation of the three attacks upon Port Arthur, Dalny and Chemulpo was vital, and he continued on his course. As it turned out, events played into his hands diplomatically as well as militarily. Just as the Japanese arrived off the port, at about 2.30 p.m., the *Koreetz* was seen to be leaving – in fact as it transpired later she was heading for the 'safety' of Port Arthur. Although war had not been declared it was obvious to the Russian captain that the Japanese intended hostile action. In the confusion which followed the *Koreetz* fired two rounds from one of her light guns and then turned tail back into the harbour. Those two small calibre shells fired from the gunboat were thus the first fired in the war, and this fact the Japanese later seized upon for propaganda purposes.

Undeterred by either the *Koreetz* or the *Varyag*, Uriu's transports anchored and began to disembark troops. By 3 a.m. of the next morning all were ashore and soon on their way by rail to Seoul, still a neutral capital, just as Chemulpo was a neutral port. Seemingly indifferent to such niceties, the Japanese admiral 3 hours later assembled all his ships, transports as well as cruisers and torpedo boats, off the mouth of the harbour and sent a message to the neutral warships politely requesting them to leave, and one to Captain Rudneff of the *Varyag* informing him that unless the Russian warships left the harbour he would be forced to attack them where they lay at anchor.

The neutrals protested to no avail, and Rudneff gallantly accepted the challenge on the morning of February 9th. Sailing past the neutral ships at 11 a.m. with the band on deck playing the Russian national anthem 'God preserve the Tsar', the *Varyag* followed by the *Koreetz* headed for the open sea and the waiting Japanese. The action lasted little more than an hour and the result was a foregone conclusion, for the Russians were both outnumbered and outgunned. The *Koreetz* fired a few ineffective shots and then accompanied the heavily damaged cruiser back into harbour. There the crews were disembarked, and the wounded put under medical care. Then the *Varyag* was scuttled and the *Koreetz* blown up along with a Russian merchant ship, the *Sungari*, which had arrived some hours previously.

Admiral Uriu's squadron watched over the approaches to Chemulpo for some time and then on the morning of February

10th anchored in Asan Bay. That day the Japanese Emperor formally declared war on Russia.

By that time, however, at Port Arthur Vice-Admiral Togo and Rear-Admiral Dewa, commanding the cruiser squadron, had already followed up the destroyer attack. Three Russian ships were now disabled and the Japanese took advantage of the fact on the morning of February 9th: sailing to within 9,000 yards, their battleships and cruisers opened fire on the rest of the Russian fleet. This time the shore batteries replied, inflicting some minor damage on the attackers, but the fleet itself seemed to be in much the same inert state as the night before. Indeed Alexieff, the Viceroy, had given orders that the fleet was not to engage the enemy, but in effect to rely for protection on the shore batteries.

At 1 p.m. Togo, perhaps over-prudently, withdrew his squadrons to rejoin Uriu's ships in Asan Bay, where he learned for the first time of the successful action at Chemulpo. By now the news of the first armed clash was being telegraphed round the world. 'First blood to Japan' was a much-overworked headline in English and American newspapers.

Alexieff in Port Arthur began 'devotedly to inform' his Imperial master in St. Petersburg of the triple reverse inflicted by the hitherto despised enemy.

In fact the damage inflicted by the Japanese upon the Russian fleet in these first hours of the war was not formidable. A cruiser and a gunboat destroyed, two battleships grounded and a cruiser temporarily put out of action, plus some superficial damage to four more cruisers in the second attack on Port Arthur, were something of a disappointment to Togo, who, like most sailors of his time, placed too much store on the accuracy and destructive power of torpedoes. Nevertheless the comparatively minor losses were no real indication of what the Japanese had achieved. In one bound Togo had vindicated his country's claim to be recognised as a first-class sea power, with a navy equal in skill and striking power to that of many a European nation. At the same time he had demonstrated that in the Far East at least Russia had to recognise his fleet's superiority: the Russians had suffered damage, and been forced on to the defensive. Togo had seized command of the sea, causing

Japanese hopes to soar, and Russian confidence to plummet. Perhaps most important of all, by crippling some units of the Russian navy and demoralising many of its senior officers, he had ensured that there would now be a land battle for Korea and perhaps Manchuria as well.

Nor had Japanese initiatives been by any means exhausted by these first blows. Togo was at one and the same time disappointed by the scale of damage inflicted by the torpedo attacks and encouraged by the obvious lack of preparedness on the part of the Russians. Plainly, more had to be done, and could be done.

The grounded *Tsarevich* and *Retvizan*, nearly blocking the harbour entrance, suggested another way of neutralising the Russian fleet without at the same time risking the Japanese battleships and cruisers under the shore batteries. Accordingly, Togo ordered that five old merchant ships be loaded with coal dust and fitted with explosive charges and asked for volunteers to man these ships, take them into Port Arthur and sink them in the narrow harbour entrance. The admiral was overwhelmed by volunteers for this dangerous task. Finally seventy-six officers and men were chosen and on the night of February 23rd, accompanied by an escort of torpedo boats, they sailed their slow, ancient vessels into Port Arthur, expecting success and accepting their deaths as a likely consequence. The Russians, however, were becoming alive, if not in attack, at least in defence. The merchant ships were met by blazing searchlights and roaring shore batteries. On the slow-moving merchant ships the Japanese 'suicide squads' did their best, but in a rough sea, their eyes blinded by the searchlights and their ships damaged and hard to manoeuvre, the captains failed to place their vessels according to plan.

Two ships were halted and virtually destroyed by Russian gunfire, and the remaining three were sunk by their crews too far out to sea to block the harbour. Surprisingly, the attendant torpedo boats managed to rescue all but one of the seventy-six seamen, many of whom were convinced that the operation had been totally successful.

The following night the Japanese 4th Destroyer Flotilla

launched another torpedo attack, as a result of which it was
discovered that Russian cruisers could move in and out of the
harbour quite freely. The Russians had in fact moved all their
ships inside the harbour with the exception of the grounded
Retvizan, which now did duty as a guard ship, sweeping the
harbour approaches with her heavy guns. None of the torpedoes
fired in the attack at the *Retvizan* reached her, the Japanese
probably overestimating the range so that the torpedoes ran out
and sank.

On the morning of February 25th Togo tried yet another
approach, through indirect bombardment of the harbour and
its installations in the hope of either damaging ships or frustrat-
ing the repairs being carried out on those already damaged.
The bombardment was attempted at a range of about 9,000
yards by Togo's battleships, observations being kept by his
cruisers. Within the harbour the Russian cruisers *Askold*,
Bayan and *Novik* suffered damage, twenty-two Russian
sailors were killed, and twice that number wounded. After
about an hour however the fortress guns were beginning to make
life on the Japanese ships extremely hazardous and the squadron
was withdrawn.

Thus in this rather indecisive way ended the first phase of
operations at Port Arthur.

At first sight it looked as if everything had gone in favour of
the Japanese. Certainly all the initiatives had been on their side.
In the next months there were to be two further attempts, on
March 26th and May 3rd, to block the harbour with old
merchant ships, but neither were to meet with complete success.
For the basic fact was that so long as the Russian fleet remained
in harbour under the protection of the shore batteries, it was
nearly impossible for the Japanese to destroy it, or to seal off the
harbour without unacceptable risk to their own warships.

Nevertheless, as a fighting navy the Port Arthur fleet for the
moment ceased to function. The Russian theory of the fleet 'in
being', which by its mere presence could deter the Japanese,
had been disproved. The bluff had been called. Only at Vladivostock could the Russian navy be seen to be carrying out
anything like the true purpose of an active fighting force. At
first with the aid of ice-breakers (as the harbour was frozen

until March), Rear-Admiral Jessen led out his cruiser squadron consisting of the *Rossiya*, *Gromoboi*, *Rurik* and *Bogatyr*, to destroy and harry Japanese shipping and troop transports, successfully avoiding the counter-force under Rear-Admiral Kamimura which had been detached from the main Japanese fleet. Unfortunately, though, for the Russians, the squadron at Vladivostock could always be outnumbered by Kamimura's combination of cruisers, light cruisers and destroyers, so that the scope of its operations was naturally limited. In addition, Admiral Alexieff ordered that Jessen's sorties must be confined to a day's sailing from Vladivostock.

So the powerful Russian fleet being in effect neutralised, Japanese troops continued to land in Korea. First at Chemulpo, and then at Chinampo when that port was ice-free, the divisions of General Kuroki's 1st Army poured ashore and advanced towards Pinyang (Pyongyang), the most important town in North Korea, 150 miles north of Seoul. The eventual objective was obviously the river Yalu, which marked the frontier between Korea and Manchuria, but before that line was to be reached the Russians at last bestirred themselves. On February 20th General Kuropatkin, the former Minister of War, was appointed to command the land forces in Manchuria. On March 12th he left St. Petersburg and by March 27th he had reached Harbin. On March 8th there arrived at Port Arthur Admiral Makaroff. Formerly Port Admiral at Kronstadt, he was regarded as Russia's most energetic admiral, and was the obvious replacement for the incompetent and uninspiring Stark.

Both Kuropatkin and Makaroff were men whose professional reputations had extended beyond the borders of their own country, but the situation they found on taking up their new commands must have given them considerable cause for concern. Neither of their services were reacting quickly enough to the Japanese danger. The Russian armies were being mobilised and concentrated all too slowly, while the navy at Port Arthur was indulging in indiscriminate mine-laying, an essentially defensive operation. Overall both commanders found themselves still under the direction of the Viceroy, Admiral Alexieff, who was an uninspiring sailor and seemed unlikely to prove himself much of a soldier. Weighed down by his responsibilities as the Viceroy of the 'Imperial Lieutenancy of the Far East', he could not make the transition from civil governor of vast territories to military commander of the forces fighting the Japanese. The fortress of Port Arthur, the Pacific Squadron, the port of Dalny, Korea, Manchuria, all these and a considerable part of the Russian army were his, contributing both to his self-importance and his worries, for he was directly responsible to the Tsar; yet he could not seem to realise that unless he galvanised both navy and army into action he was likely to lose them all to the Japanese.

Luckily Makaroff was made of sterner stuff. He realised that the Pacific Squadron was there to be used. The threat of action had patently failed to deter the Japanese, and now the only course was action. Within days of his arrival the squadron was being put through its paces. On March 12th four battleships and a cruiser steamed out of Port Arthur to gain much-needed practice in fleet manoeuvres. Ten days later the same force repelled Japanese cruisers on course for Port Arthur. As a result, alerted to the increased effectiveness of the Russians, Togo tried again during the night of March 26th–27th to seal the entrance to Port Arthur. Once again however shore batteries and searchlights prevented the suicidally gallant Japanese from placing their ships correctly, although the reports rendered to Togo once again gave him hope that the operation had been successful. It came as a new disappointment to find that Russian ships spurred on by their energetic commander, could still make their way to the open sea with apparent ease. In fact, although late in the day, the Russian fleet was becoming a force with which to be reckoned, instead of a collection of floating batteries moored in the harbour of Port Arthur. As Makaroff, not without reprimands to incompetent officers and a quota of near accidents, forced the Pacific Squadron into fighting shape, Togo decided that time was not on his side. Therefore a fleet action had to be provoked if possible while the advantages of skill and training still lay with his own men.

The device was a simple one. A cruiser squadron was to act as bait to lure Makaroff out towards the main Japanese battleship fleet which was to be in waiting and in communication by wireless telegraph. At the same time it was hoped that perhaps some of Makaroff's fleet might come to disaster in the minefields which the Japanese had been laying in increased density round the approaches to the port.

The ruse worked better than perhaps Togo might have expected. On the night of April 12th Makaroff, on board the cruiser *Diana* which was acting as guard ship, actually saw some destroyers apparently engaged in laying mines outside the harbour. When these had been identified as Japanese, he had bearings taken and ordered that the area should be swept the next day. Unfortunately, the orders were never carried out, both Makaroff and his officers presumably being over-absorbed in the events of the next morning.

Just after daylight the Japanese 2nd Destroyer Flotilla arrived and was engaged by Russian destroyers. The *Strashni* was set on fire and sunk, and the Russian cruiser *Bayan*, coming to the rescue, was in turn drawn towards the Japanese 3rd Cruiser Division. At 8 a.m. the battleships *Petropavlovsk*, with Makaroff on board, and *Poltava* joined the three cruisers, *Diana, Novik* and *Askold*, and gave chase to the Japanese cruisers. These continued to fire at long range, while retreating eastwards in accordance with instructions. Forty minutes later Makaroff realised what was happening when six Japanese battleships appeared out of the mist to his front. Makaroff was a brave man and a daring commander but he realised he was near the jaws of a well-laid trap. The Russians promptly turned about and headed at full speed for the protection of Port Arthur. By 9.30 Togo realised that he had failed, perhaps because the trap had been sprung prematurely. Disappointed, he turned away while the Russians, led by the flagship, prepared to return to harbour. Ten minutes later there were two enormous explosions, heard by sailors in both fleets and spectators on shore. The first was a mine and the second the magazine of the *Petropavlovsk*. A third explosion released a cloud of smoke and steam as the boilers burst and the flagship disappeared with nearly all her complement of some 700 men. Seven officers and 73 men were picked up, including the Grand Duke Cyril, blown from the bridge, but not the commander of the Pacific Squadron, Vice-Admiral Makaroff, nor his guest the distinguished war artist Vassili Verestchagin, on board the flagship specifically to observe a sea battle.

Rear-Admiral Prince Ukhtomsky recovered as quickly as any, and on board the *Peresvyet* took control. With the *Pobieda* he began to patrol the harbour mouth as the rest of the fleet came in. At 10.15 there was another loud explosion, and the *Pobieda* suddenly heeled over with an enormous hole blown in her bows. The second disaster within minutes cast the Russians into panic. Apparently thinking they were being attacked by submarines, gun crews loosed off in all directions. Again Ukhtomsky asserted himself and led the way into harbour signalling the rest of the squadron to follow. This it did in some sort of order, the *Pobieda* herself limping slowly in, though in no danger of sinking.

At 11 a.m. Togo withdrew his battleships, leaving the 3rd Division cruisers to observe until it was certain beyond all doubt that no Russian ships would venture out of harbour again that day.

The news of the disaster reached St. Petersburg during the Easter holiday, and when the official report was published it cast a pall of gloom over the traditional festivities. A day later the correspondent of the *Daily Telegraph*, describing the requiem service held in the Admiralty Church on the bank of the Neva attended by Madame Makaroff, the Minister of Marine and the Diplomatic Corps and countless naval officers, ended his report with the words:

For Russia has been stricken, and as yet the bulk of the nation has not realised how terribly.

Even in Japan there was a torch-carrying ceremony at Nagoya for the souls of those drowned in the *Petropavlovsk*, but Togo took the opportunity on April 14th and 15th of bringing his battleships and cruisers close inshore to shell both the forts and gun emplacements at Port Arthur and to try the effects of high-angle fire in the inner harbour.

'Thus ended,' wrote the correspondent of *The Times*, 'the three days' engagement which, in the opinion of most, destroyed any faint hope which may have existed that the Russians might be able to equalise again the balance of naval power in these seas.'

FIVE

'They will not dare, they are unprepared'
GENERAL KUROPATKIN

The death in action of one admiral, however popular or distinguished, should not in the normal way plunge a whole navy into a state of melancholic inertia. However, such was the effect of the death of Makaroff and the sinking of his flagship. Admittedly the admiral had gained a considerable professional reputation from his works on naval tactics and his practical concern with naval construction, particularly in the sphere of ice-breaking vessels. He was also extremely popular with the lower deck as well as with his fellow-officers, something of a rarity in Tsarist Russia. But his last taste of action had been as a young officer in the Turkish war, nearly thirty years ago, and for all his qualities he was no Nelson. The fact that he was regarded as irreplaceable was more a reflection on the state of the Russian navy than an endorsement of his own reputation.

That service had not distinguished itself in what had been scarcely two months of warfare. The battleship *Petropavlovsk* sunk, the *Tsarevich*, *Pobieda* and *Retvizan* damaged; the *Varyag* and *Koreetz* sunk at Chemulpo; the destroyers *Boyarin*, *Stereguchi* and *Vnushitelny* and *Bezstrashni* damaged and the mine-layer *Yenesei* totally destroyed; the *Strashni* sunk: it was a dismal record. Yet even this did not give a complete picture of the state of the Pacific Squadron, for there were no compensatory achievements and little evidence of improvement.

On two occasions when the squadron had been on exercises under Makaroff's command there had been collisions between battleships, the second resulting in the suspension from duty of the captain of the *Sebastopol*. This was bad enough, but the sinking of the *Yenesei* provided a classic example of professional incompetence. Not only was the mine-layer blown to bits with scarcely a survivor by one of her own mines; but it was only realised after her sinking that there was no independent record being kept of where exactly she was laying her mines. Thus it was quite possible that Admiral Makaroff and his flagship were victims not of cunningly laid Japanese mines but of badly laid Russian ones.

Later on during the war the Japanese were themselves to suffer a series of misfortunes from collisions and groundings and the like, often during night operations, and so perhaps, in fairness to the Russians it should be remembered that in many ways this was an experimental war. In both the two most recent naval conflicts, the Sino-Japanese War and the Spanish American War of 1898, one adversary had so clearly outclassed the other that few lessons of general application could be drawn. In the following four years all aspects of naval technology – engines, guns, torpedoes, armour, mines and wireless telegraphy – had advanced by leaps and bounds as each maritime nation had endeavoured to outclass the other in the arms race. With every generation of warships laid down each naval power hoped to gain some advantage over its rivals. Yet since few of the ships were tried in action, the superiority achieved was purely statistical. It fell to both Russians and Japanese to learn the quality of their own and the enemy's ships the hard way.

Because of this background of an international navy race with each nation eyeing narrowly the building programme of the other, something of a myth had grown up about the relative strengths and quality of the warships in the Russian and Japanese navies. For so long had Navy Ministries and admirals been considering another inch of armour, a knot or two of extra speed or some increase in gun calibre as denoting automatic superiority, that when the Japanese won their first successes it was assumed that these must be solely and inevitably due to technical superiority. As an amplification of the theory it was argued that the British, the acknowledged masters, had built the Japanese navy for their allies, whilst the Russians had to make do with the outdated and inefficient products of their own ship-building industry.

Unfortunately the facts do not easily fit the theory. First, so far as foreign-built ships were concerned, both the Russians and Japanese bought ships from foreign yards, and the Russians, even more than the Japanese, tended to buy a foreign prototype or design as with the prototype of the 'Tsarevich' class, modelled on a French design, and follow it up with ships of their own construction (in this case the *Suvoroff, Imperator Alexander III, Borodino* and *Orel* and one other ship still uncompleted during the war). Both adversaries also acquired foreign patented engines, guns and armour, the Russians most often patronising their French allies, but also buying from the U.S.A. and Germany, while the Japanese tended to buy from Britain, although not exclusively. In fact there was little if any sentiment in these deals. Both nations were bent on buying the best available ships for their own needs and both the Russians and Japanese entered the war with considerable numbers of destroyers and torpedo boats built at the Yarrow, Laird and Thornycroft yards in Britain.

So far as their own shipyards were concerned, the Russians had at first sight a considerable advantage over the Japanese. Theirs was a well-established industry with among others the Baltic Engineering Works, the Nevsky Works, the Putiloff armaments concern and the Kolpino Steel Works, all dating back to the eighties of the previous century. The Japanese ship building industry on the other hand was still in its infancy when war began. Thus throughout the course of the war – an incredible situation for a naval power – the Japanese were only really capable of maintaining and repairing their existing warships, not of building new ones. Certainly they had no facilities, even if they had had the time, to replace any of their capital ships or first-class cruisers lost in action.

However the outright purchasing of foreign vessels did have some advantages to balance against the obvious risks, and these did weigh against the Russians. For Russian ships took considerably longer to build than their English, French, German or American equivalents. Perhaps the biggest disadvantage native shipbuilders suffered under was simply climate, which adversely affected both construction and launching; but in addition Russian working organisations and all the shipyards and armament works were government-controlled and bureaucracy-ridden, and functioned no more efficiently than the government machine itself. In consequence the naval organisation presided over by the Grand Duke Alexei Alexandrovich (who was said to like 'slow ships and fast women') tended to spend too much time and money on producing warships which took five or six years in construction, and which when they finally did join the fleet were already out of date.

Finally, one of the most pernicious of Russian naval habits, that of 'improvements', should be mentioned. Whether because of the long-drawn-out building programme of most vessels, or because of the over-close relations between Imperial Navy and State-owned shipyards, there was a tendency for senior officers to impose their own requirements upon the shipbuilders during construction, often to the detriment of the ship itself. The 'improvements' most frequently took the form of extra armament or armour or provision for carrying more ammunition or coal, all of course with the object of giving the vessel more fighting power or endurance. Unfortunately, such impositions often slowed the ship down or made it less manoeuvrable and in some cases dangerously reduced the vessel's stability by increasing the weight carried above the water-line.

The Japanese had by contrast six modern battleships (*Fuji, Yashima, Hatsuse, Shikishima, Asaki* and *Mikasa*) as its main striking force, all British-built, all less than six years old, and supported by excellent armoured cruisers. Their fleet was thus more uniform than the Russian's and more compact, and it had fewer ships which fell behind the latest developments in gunnery, armour or engines. Nevertheless, the Russians had a considerable numerical advantage overall, and consequently possessed what the Japanese did not, a reserve of warships in case of loss in battle. Finally, it should be said that to assume automatically that a battleship built in 1896 was in every way superior to another built in 1894 would be to subscribe to the 'arms race' by paper comparison type of thinking, forgetting that the ultimate test of a warship's quality is trial in battle. And in this respect, more important than the ships themselves were the officers and ratings who manned them and the navy to which they belonged.

Here the Japanese possessed undoubted advantages. For the Russian navy with its complement of 65,000 men in 1902 (the Royal Navy had 122,600, the French 53,250 and the Japanese 31,000) was in a number of ways unlike any other. It was a navy geographically divided between the Baltic, the Far East and the Black Sea, and of the three fleets the Black Sea Squadron could not by international agreement move freely through the Bosphorus and was therefore bound by the confines of an inland sea. Indeed ships for the Black Sea Squadron had to be built at Nikolaeff and often spent their whole life on the sea in which they were launched. Consequently, in calculating naval strengths, whether of ships or personnel, a considerable element of the Russian navy had simply to be written off in relation to the war with Japan, as it was unable to play any part in the conflict.

Another peculiarity was imposed by the conditions of the Russian climate. Until Port Arthur was acquired there had been no ice-free port in winter, therefore no active sea-going training could take place for roughly six months of every year, ships' companies spending the winter months in barracks on shore. So officers and men of the Imperial Navy had considerably less sea experience than their opposite numbers in the other principal navies of the world. They were in effect less professional, and there was something of a tendency in official circles to regard a sailor as a form of soldier who by chance had to spend some part of his life at sea.

Further, the Russian navy was a conscript service, about 10,000 fit men over twenty-one years of age being chosen by lot each year to serve for seven years on the active list and three on the reserve. Now lower deck life in any navy in the early twentieth century was hardly a bed of roses, but for a Russian unlucky in the annual ballot it meant seven years in which he received poor food, poor pay, was forbidden to marry, and had hardly any chance of promotion. With only six months' sea service a year in an age of increasing naval technological complexity this was hardly a system likely to transform an ill-educated Russian peasant into the very model of a happy, efficient seaman.

The officers, save for one or two junior grades, were all

volunteers, and though not the aristocratic incompetents of some legends they were drawn largely from the minor gentry and professional classes. Many were of the Baltic squirearchy, of German origin, which supplied much of the public service of the Tsar. Plainly as in all services, some were good, some bad and some indifferent; but in general the navy in Russia was not regarded as either a smart or a prestigious service, and indeed was not even particularly popular, so the standard of officer recruit was not high. Further, the Imperial Navy under its Grand Ducal master was beset by all the vices of favouritism, conscription and bureaucracy inseparable from an absolutist and incompetent state system.

Perhaps one or more of these faults would in isolation not have been too serious – they were present in other navies, including the British, recognised as the 'mistress of the seas' – but the combination of them all put the Russians at a considerable disadvantage in relation to the Japanese.

They too had basically a conscript navy, but with as well a considerable number of volunteer recruits to the lower deck, generally with sea-going experience before service. And their officers were imbued with such enthusiasm, compounded of patriotism and professionalism, that British naval officers who met them complained that they had virtually no interest outside service life, and were consequently very dull off-duty company.

Overall, perhaps the most important factor in the comparative development and quality of the two rival navies was that for Japan, an island power, a navy was both a natural growth and a necessity; whereas for Russia, where a naval and maritime tradition hardly existed, the build-up of a large fleet dated only from 1880 and was really an adjunct of the imperial policy in the Far East. Russia however, unlike Britain, had not needed a navy to acquire an empire, and the 'new' navy was still regarded as something of a luxury (like the Baltic Fleet, which had essentially protective tasks in time of European war), fulfilling a passive rather than an active role. In many official circles it was thought enough for such a fleet to be 'in being' to deter an enemy.

In any event, it was a sorry comment on the Imperial Russian Navy that Makaroff's successor as commander of the Pacific

Squadron, Vice-Admiral Skrydloff, could not even reach his ships at Port Arthur – he could get only as far as Vladivostock by train – for they were now completely confined by the patrolling Japanese, and seemingly quite incapable of regaining control of the sea from the enemy.

Nevertheless Togo, and behind him the Great General Staff under Yamamoto, and the Japanese Cabinet, could have no grounds for complacency. The land battle stretched ahead and there were already rumours that the Russians were planning to send out their Baltic Fleet, comprising some of their most modern battleships, very similar in armament and speed to the Fuji class, to redress the balance in the Far East. Further, while the Japanese had no naval reserves, Russia had a number of ships being built and refitted at Kronstadt. What state of readiness such ships and their crews were in was not known accurately but the Japanese had prudently to assume that any or all of them might be used in the future against them. Even at Port Arthur, where the Viceroy Alexieff had temporarily returned to his old profession, and hoisted his flag in the *Sebastopol* and appointed his chief-of-staff, Vitgeft, as second in command, there were still three undamaged capital ships, and repairs were being rapidly carried out on the *Tsarevich*, *Retvizan* and *Pobieda*. The cruiser *Pallada* was also under repair, but the *Bayan, Askold, Diana, Novik* and *Boyarin* were all serviceable, as were over twenty destroyers and ten first-class torpedo boats. Under any control but the dead hand of Alexieff this was a force which could have inflicted considerable damage upon the Japanese. And although it continued to skulk in harbour protected from direct attack by the shore batteries and suffering occasional indirect bombardment by the Japanese, Togo could not assume that it would fail for ever to retaliate. He and his captains could now cruise the Yellow Sea almost as they pleased, but he would have been foolhardy to bank on that state of affairs continuing. C. S. Forrester has pointed out in his *Age of Sail* that naval commanders, far from underestimating their enemy, often make the mistake of forming exaggerated views as to his power and resources. For Togo, this was an almost unavoidable error: with the information available to him at the time, he would have needed almost superhuman

prescience to gauge the depths of apathy and inertia to which
the Russian naval commanders at Port Arthur had sunk. He was
right for the moment at least to act as he did, i.e. to risk no
direct attack upon Port Arthur, but to patrol, observe and cover,
whilst ensuring at the same time that the landings of Japanese
troops in Korea continued undisturbed by the Russian
fleet.

The dramatic death of Makaroff had captured world headlines
and tended to draw attention away from the necessarily more
slow-moving developments on land. But on March 27th, as has
been seen, Kuropatkin had arrived at his headquarters and the
time could not be far off when the two opposing armies would
be joined in battle.

There was of course a certain irony about the appointment
of the former Minister of War as commander-in-chief of the
Russian armies in the field, though no doubt not an irony that
that particular individual now took much pleasure in savouring.
Like almost all Russians in senior naval and military posts
before war broke out he had seriously underestimated Japanese
resolution. Even when war seemed imminent he was heard by
Count Kokovtsoff to say, 'they will not dare, they are un-
prepared, they are only putting on airs, thinking that we shall
be frightened and will believe them'. Some time previously
he had also likened the occupation of Manchuria to the easy
conquest and colonisation of Bokhara. No doubt there were
similarities so far as the native population was concerned, but
to take that view, confidently and in simplicity, was to discount entirely any possibility of action by the Japanese.

Looking back with the advantage of hindsight in his memoirs
Kuropatkin was to suggest that he, and perhaps he alone, had
seen all along the inherent dangers of Russia's penetration into
the Far East. If so, he was remarkably silent on the subject at
the time. He may have criticised details of the policy in practice,
such as the vast expenditure on the creation of a civil port and
harbour at Dalny while neither Port Arthur nor Vladivostock
had been completely fortified or re-equipped; but as far as the
general project was concerned there is no record of any opposition. Even a recent visit to Japan, where he had undoubtedly
been impressed by the efficiency of her army, had failed to

provoke the then Minister into a realisation of the dangers of war.

Witte paints a picture in his memoirs of Kuropatkin as a place-seeking sycophant fawning upon the Tsar and loading the Tsaritsa with flattery. But Witte's view of Kuropatkin's character and abilities was no more flattering than Kuropatkin's own estimate of the worth and achievements of Witte, and an explanation for the Minister's blindness is probably to be sought at a less personal level. Kuropatkin, in common with most senior Russian army officers, saw the main threat to his country on her western frontier, from Germany and Austria-Hungary, separately or together. Any policy which drew Russian forces away from the west was therefore inadvisable at best and at the worst positively dangerous. But this view was not entirely accepted by the Tsar who certainly at the beginning of the century placed great store upon his friendship with the German Kaiser, and though Kuropatkin would perhaps have preferred Russia not to take on the burdens of a Far Eastern empire, the decision once having been taken within the Tsar's circle of intimates he had to accept it, or resign. Witte's evidence may suggest that the General was not the resigning type; but this is hardly strong criticism, for there were few men of principle around Nicholas II, and his servants went on serving whatever was the current policy until sacked.

In any case, Kuropatkin as a soldier would no doubt have preferred, once a decision had been made, to see it put into practice wholeheartedly. In the military sphere, of course, this simply had not happened. The events of the first few weeks of the war had shown that diplomatically and strategically the situation had been grossly misjudged by those who wielded influence in Russia. Contrary to the advice tendered to St. Petersburg by Alexieff, who had in turn received it from his naval and military staffs, the Japanese obviously could defeat or at least neutralise the Russian fleet, and land troops in Korea and Manchuria.

Before the opening of hostilities one of Kuropatkin's generals had said of the Japanese, 'we will only have to throw our caps at them and they will run away'. A number of cartoons had appeared in the Russian press, depicting the Japanese as comic monkeys, vicious and irritating no doubt, but always fleeing from clean-limbed Russian soldiers and sailors or being contemptuously crushed by the Russian bear. 'Monkey' was a favourite term of abuse used by the Tsar himself for any Japanese – he normally described Japanese diplomats he received in those terms in his private diary. Now these contemptible Orientals, previously seen with typical Russian arrogance as scarcely human or comically quaint, were proving themselves to be a serious and frightening enemy. Whatever his past views may have been, and they may well have been mixed for a number of reasons, it was now Kuropatkin's duty to defeat this enemy. The navy, perhaps due to its indecisive handling by Alexieff, for whom he had little regard, had obviously failed, so it was now up to the army.

The choice of land against sea operations was immediately a happier one for any Russian. Despite attempts by various rulers from Peter the Great to Alexander III to make Russia a sea power, her strength and prestige still lay in her massive army of 1,100,000. These sturdy peasants, loyal and disciplined, prepared to give their lives if necessary for Tsar and Holy Russia, were not only the nation's pride but in many ways the very backbone of the regime. Behind the first million men there were in reserve nearly 2½ million more who had all passed through the system whereby every able-bodied man between the ages of twenty-one and forty-three served, unless lawfully excused, for four years with the colours and for thirteen more in various categories of the reserve. Even then the resources of the Empire were not exhausted for there were in addition 345,000 Cossacks, 12,000 Caucasian native troops and a national militia of nearly 700,000. No wonder that over the years German, Austrian and British generals had lived in apprehension of being forced to take on a nation with virtually unlimited resources of manpower.

Indeed what a later generation was to call the 'Russian steamroller' created a myth of its own, not only of unlimited power, but of virtually limitless ambitions as well. As an example, in 1904 Archibald Wavell, one day to be a Field-Marshal and the penultimate Viceroy of India, had just joined his regiment, the Black Watch, stationed in central India. Within days of his arrival, however, there was the news of the

Japanese attack on Port Arthur, whereupon his battalion, with a number of others, was immediately despatched for the North-West frontier to be ready to withstand any attempt by the Russians to invade India via Afghanistan.

Yet the overwhelming statistics were something of an illusion. True, Russia could not be defeated in Russia. The combination of manpower, acreage and climate ensured that; as Napoleon had discovered and Hitler was to discover. Yet when Russian troops had been deployed outside Russia or on the periphery as in the Crimea in 1854, or in the Turkish War in 1877, they had not demonstrated many of the military skills. Courage, doggedness, even a sort of fatalism they displayed, but these were luxuries easily indulged with inexhaustible numbers of men. But the hardy ingenuity of the British, the *élan* of the French and the sheer professionalism of the Germans were seemingly beyond the range of Russian military thinking or practice.

At the outbreak of war there were in Russia and the Caucasus 25 army corps consisting basically of 2 infantry and 1 cavalry division each, a total of about 31,000 men per corps. In Turkestan there were 2 similar army corps and in Eastern Siberia another 2. In the war area itself, exclusive of garrison and technical troops, Russia had 100 battalions of infantry, 35 squadrons of cavalry, 25 artillery batteries and 13 companies of field engineers, making a round total of 84,000 men. Obviously with the advent of hostilities this force could, and would, be reinforced from Europe. There are considerations other than sheer numbers which affect the effectiveness of armies, however, notably disposition and quality. And here Russia had disadvantages to contend with. Less than any country in Europe could she denude her home bases of troops, for the Russian soldier at home performed the dual role of fighting man and policeman. Finland, Poland, Turkestan and many districts of Russia proper simply could not be left without considerable garrisons for fear of local uprisings. Of course other empires had similar problems – the Habsburgs were not likely to take all their non-Hungarian troops from Hungary, nor the British to remove all their regiments from Ireland – but these involved minor commitments compared with the vast numbers of troops

necessary within Russia to preserve law and order. Perhaps
the situation can best be indicated by the fact that a Russian
general's only experience of active service throughout his whole
career could be in the suppression of civil disturbances,
and indeed a number at the time of the Russo-Japanese
War had successfully founded their reputations on just that
one activity.

Another limitation on the sending of troops to the Far East
was simply distance. During the whole course of the war a total
of 5 regular army corps, 2 reserve army corps, and 1 extra
division totalling 210,000 men were actually sent to the East.
All of them, plus horses, artillery, ammunition, equipment and
warlike stores had to travel by the only route, the Trans-
Siberian Railway and its extension from Harbin, by the Chinese-
Eastern and Manchurian railways.

The total length of the railway from Moscow to the Liaotung
Peninsula and Port Arthur was nearly 5,500 miles, almost
certainly the longest line of communication in any war. Along
this line, often single-track and in fact not completed in one section round the southern edge of Lake Baikal until well on into
the war, had to travel every addition, whether of men or
material, that the Russians made to their armies facing the
Japanese. Thus although the Japanese army, with less than
250,000 field troops at the beginning of the war and 400,000
trained and semi-trained men in reserve, was considerably
outnumbered by the Russian overall, so far as men who could
actually be deployed on the battlefields of Manchuria were
concerned, the Japanese could maintain the advantage as
long as they could land enough of their army in Korea and
Manchuria before Russian reinforcements could make up the
balance.

Russia's superior numbers also did not give her an automatic
advantage in the quality of her fighting troops. In this context
there must be considered the different approach to the war by
the two combatants, dictated by strategic considerations as
much as any other, which make what is always a difficult
comparison even more so. Japan from the start determined to
deploy in the theatre of war almost the whole of her army
including the crack Imperial Guard Division – indeed she was

bound to do so for hers was a fight to the death almost on home territory. Russia on the other hand was compelled to use those formations nearest to hand, that is her 'Siberian' divisions, which were not up to the standard of training and organisation of her best European divisions. Further, the Russians showed very little disposition to move their best divisions to the battle front. Perhaps it would be an exaggeration to suggest that because, for instance, the Imperial Guard cavalry and infantry stayed firmly in St. Petersburg and few of its officers volunteered for detachment on active service, the Russians simply did not bother to put their best force in the field. Nevertheless there had always been a feeling, especially in the officer corps, that service in the Far East was slightly 'second class', perhaps even not to be taken too seriously. Such attitudes are not uncommon in armies or were not in peacetime. Lord Cardigan, it will be recalled, in command of his militarily and socially smart 11th Hussars, despised officers who had served in India. Still, even that supreme military snob did not refuse action in war in the Crimea. Fifty years later, however, the Russian military 'establishment' appeared to be quite content to preserve such outworn attitudes in a time of national emergency.

Nevertheless, though the troops in the Far East were not the best that Russia possessed, they formed a good cross-section of her army save in one respect: the cavalry arm. At first sight this may seem paradoxical, because by far the largest proportion of the horse soldiers employed were Cossacks. Certainly, they had superb romantic titles: Siberian Cossacks, Ussurian Cossacks and the Trans-Baikal Regiment of Cossacks. And they had also a worldwide reputation for daring and horsemanship, plus a dashing uniform of fur hat and kaftan festooned with cartridge belts and ornamental daggers. They were nevertheless not particularly good soldiers. Their organisation was tribal, and their discipline and training were very much their own affair. They also provided their own horses and most of their own equipment, which fact set them apart from the rest of the army. Almost mercenaries in outlook, they may well have been excellent at harrying the Turkoman tribesmen, or putting down civilian unrest, when their 'separateness' was an advantage, but the sophisticated disciplines required of cavalry in twentieth-century warfare were foreign to their mental make-up and indeed their military purpose.

Luckily however for the Japanese, the cavalry arm was also the weakest in the Japanese army, although for a very different reason. As one British officer put it 'the Japanese are not natural horsemen'. This was true, but only time would tell whether in what was just about the last decade of cavalry's utility in war it really mattered if either army was not particularly well provided for in lancers, hussars or dragoons, in the new age of machine-guns, barbed wire, magazine rifles and hand-grenades.

Finally, what of training, discipline, morale and all the other imponderables, which made up the good or bad fighting soldier? The Russian officers presented a wide diversity of military and educational attainments and, curiously in a despotism, lacked that homogeneity of professionalism present in other comparable armies. Similar criticism could be made of the men they commanded. They too, though subservient to authority, seemed to lack that spark of military enthusiasm which galvanised, say, the German or French conscript. Some part of the reason was no doubt educational, for the average Russian was woefully ignorant and unskilled, but the sheer size of the organisation also militated against a high professional standard. With so obvious a numerical superiority, why bother with professional standards? Marksmanship, map reading and individual field training, even literacy, were no doubt important in other smaller armies, but the Russians had the Tsar, the Orthodox Church and more bodies than almost any other three armies put together. It was not without significance that alone among European armies Russian soldiers carried their rifles with bayonets fixed even on the rifle range. When the order to active service came, the bayonet scabbard was discarded, for ultimately the answer to the problems of battle was to be not musketry, but numbers and cold steel.

If courage and endurance were the virtues that the Russians relied on, what of the Japanese? French and then German trained, these almost unknown Orientals were facing their first conflict with Europeans. The Russians certainly still held them in contempt, but perhaps a more balanced view could be obtained from a nation which had trained them. In May 1904 Albert Hopman, a naval captain, was sending his report to the Admiralty in Berlin from his post as observer at Port Arthur. It was naturally a naval report, but the implied comment on the yet untried Japanese army would have offered no comfort for Kuropatkin:

Having seen these examples of a fanatical spirit of attack and endeavour, and comparing it with the apathy and indifference of the Russians, I can see only a black future. One can hardly imagine that the Japanese army has a different spirit. It has the same blood, the same nerves, as the navy.

By the time that Kuropatkin actually arrived at his head-quarters on March 27th a number of moves had of course already been made by the Japanese. Enough of their 1st Army had been put ashore in Korea and moved north via Pinyang towards the Manchurian frontier on the Yalu river to justify the landing of the commander himself, Major-General Baron Kuroki. In the opening stages Kuroki had directed the operations from Ujina, just over 3 miles from Hiroshima, which remained the main Japanese base throughout the war, but now the larger part of his army was established in Korea, and his staff moved to Chinampo on March 17th.

The army itself was moving north steadily and methodically, its progress hampered by the thaw which had turned the rudimentary roads, which in summer were dust tracks, into rivers of mud. The employment of 10,000 Korean coolies in addition to the soldiers normally assigned to transport and baggage train duties was some indication of the difficulties of the terrain. Nevertheless the Japanese succeeded in keeping transport, even if of the most primitive kind, moving and the flow of food and ammunition to the forward units was maintained. In addition, as they advanced, signals sections set up telegraph poles and wire along their route and sappers carried out what they could in the way of road repairs for the benefit of their comrades who would need to follow them.

On the Russian side Alexieff had mobilised the troops in the territories under his jurisdiction, soon after the first Japanese troops had landed at Chemulpo near Seoul. In fact the mobilisation worked reasonably well, an infantry battalion taking about two weeks to gather in its men while cavalry and artillery tended to take a little longer. However, a number of units were found when mobilised to be still under their war strength. The first formation which was actually put to active use was Major-General Mischenko's Cossack Cavalry Brigade which had already been in an advanced state of readiness. As the Japanese advanced north Mischenko and his 2,000 men moved south to carry out patrols on the Korean side of the Yalu.

Russians and Japanese first clapped eyes on each other on March 23rd, but the Russians confined themselves to observation and hardly bothered to return the fire of the Japanese infantry before galloping off to report. It was soon quite obvious to the Japanese that the Russians intended to offer no resistance in Korea. Accordingly the Japanese had shifted their point of disembarkation from Chemulpo, which was used from February 8th to March 1st, northwards over 100 miles to Chinampo. Whether the Russian decision not to fight in Korea was taken for strategic reasons or diplomatic ones, it is difficult to say; certainly the Tsar's original instruction that the Japanese must appear the aggressors had weighed heavily with Alexieff, and this, combined with the Viceroy's natural sloth and tardiness, no doubt made the decision not to fight in a technically neutral state doubly attractive. As both the Viceroy's predictions made before war broke out (i.e. that the Russian fleet would deter the Japanese and that because of this the Japanese could not land in Korea) had been proved false, it is tempting to regard him as already a spent force. But this would be wrong, for Alexieff still exercised considerable influence over both naval and military decisions. Further, his judgment was not always at fault on subsequent occasions.

So far as the coming battle was concerned, it was at least clear that it would be impossible for the Russians to engage the Japanese 1st Army with the troops available in February and March. Even by the beginning of April Kuropatkin had at his disposal only 23 squadrons of cavalry and 8 battalions of infantry ready for action, in addition to Mischenko's cavalry brigade. A few weeks later, however, as mobilised units came on to a war footing Lieutenant-General Zasulich was able to take command of 15,000 infantry, 5,000 cavalry and over 60 guns, and Alexieff made it known that he now favoured a strong resistance to be made along the Yalu. Unfortunately this was not the view of Kuropatkin, who wanted to fight a mere rear-guard action. Though he was, at least technically, subordinate to Alexieff, he sent orders to Zasulich instructing him to stand on the Yalu but 'not for a decisive action with the enemy in superior numbers'. On April 25th Kuropatkin's instructions to Zasulich were still that he should fight a delaying action only.

The next few days the Japanese spent preparing for their attack on the Russian positions. The Yalu was at this time of year a wide muddy river swiftly flowing with water from the recent thaw. Under cover of heavy and accurate artillery fire they prepared a number of crossing positions with the intention of keeping the Russians guessing as to which they would use. Throughout, the Japanese movements were methodical and superbly organised. Each artillery battery, for example, was carefully sited and then hidden, foliage and whole trees being used as camouflage. Though camouflage was common practice in later wars, in 1904 it was something of an innovation, and was certainly not a precaution observed by the Russians, who in the days before the battle behaved with a complete lack of caution and allowed Japanese officers on the opposite bank equipped with field glasses and telescopes to plot a large number of positions with considerable accuracy.

In the event, Japanese preparations paid off, for in the artillery duel preliminary to the main battle a considerable number of Russian guns were knocked out by accurate counter-battery fire while not a single Japanese gun firing from a prepared position was hit.

The infantry preparation of the two sides clearly indicated their different approaches to the coming action. General Sir Ian Hamilton, the senior British observer with the Japanese, with his experience in the Boer War fresh in his mind, noted with approval the way in which the Japanese used every available bit of concealment and the speed with which they used their entrenching tools to dig themselves in. On the other bank of the river, however, Russians could be seen exposing head and shoulders to view or shot quite happily. Sir Ian also watched the Japanese capture without much difficulty three of the islands, Chukodai, Kinteito and Kyurito, opposite Wiju, and then speedily erect pontoons and bridges. At the same time Japanese torpedo boats carried out a series of feints near the mouth of the river 15 miles away, to keep the Russians guessing as to the eventual point of attack. As a result, in the last few days of April the Russians were still strung out upon a 20-mile-long front while the Japanese were concentrating, apparently unknown to their enemy, for the final push.

When the time came for the eventual infantry attack the Japanese found that they had succeeded in confusing the enemy almost beyond their own expectations. On the other side of the river, although individual soldiers and regiments fought with great bravery, the command situation was in confusion. General Zasulich had two conflicting series of orders from Alexieff and Kuropatkin, and worse still, at a crucial stage in the battle he virtually lost touch with General Kashtalinski, his second-in-command. Colonel Gromoff, whose responsibility it was to keep the two generals informed and thus co-ordinate the actions of the two wings of the army, failed so badly in his task that he was afterwards court-martialled, and, although acquitted, committed suicide. These mistakes in command, perhaps not vital in the face of any enemy less efficient than the Japanese, in the event proved disastrous. At the end of the final action on May 1st the Japanese had crossed the Yalu successfully and the Russians were in retreat, with at least 1,400 dead, a total of 3,000 casualties and 600 men taken prisoner. Japanese total casualties were approximately 1,000 men, a third of those suffered by their opponents.

In reasonably good conditions, with modern weapons which favoured defence rather than attack, an Oriental army had beaten a European one for the first time for centuries. The occupation of Korea was now put beyond doubt. Two days later another attempt was made to block Port Arthur, which, though not entirely successful, demonstrated yet again the Japanese superiority at sea. On May 5th the Japanese 2nd Army began to disembark at Pitzuwo.

On the same day Admiral Alexieff left Port Arthur by train for Harbin, taking the view that that fortress was now in danger, not only from the sea but from land as well.

SIX

'What are hosts whose hearts are cold?'

JAPANESE MARCHING SONG.

In departing from Port Arthur at 11 a.m. on May 5th, as he announced 'by command of the Tsar', Admiral Alexieff showed a fine appreciation of both strategy and self-preservation. Unfortunately the strategy was not his own, nor that of his subordinate naval and military commanders, but that of the enemy.

As early as April 24th Admiral Togo and General Oku, the commander of the Japanese 2nd Army, had met on board the battleship *Mikasa* to settle the details of disembarkation. The force, consisting of three divisions and an artillery brigade, had already been shipped to Chinampo on board seventy transports with cruiser protection and was now awaiting orders. This operation, be it noted, had been completed before the battle of the Yalu had been fought and won. When the news of Kuroki's victory was known, on May 3rd the first transports sailed for Houtushih on the coast of the Liaotung Peninsula opposite to the Elliott Islands. The landing place had a double significance. Historically, it was very near to Pitzuwo where the Japanese troops had landed in 1894 to fight the Chinese; strategically it provided an excellent cutting-off point for an army which had as its object, as had its predecessor ten years before, the isolation of Port Arthur.

Strangely, although the Russians were perfectly well aware of the details of the Japanese campaign of 1894 and although the landing place was within 60 miles of their own fleet, the landings were completely unopposed. Rather to their surprise the Japanese encountered no mines, no destroyers, nor any opposing troops, only a detachment of Cossacks which trotted off at their approach. Nevertheless, Togo kept a force of destroyers and torpedo boats on watch and the fairway of 8 miles between the Elliott Islands and the mainland was blocked by anti-torpedo nets and booms to keep the anchorage secure.

General Oku landed with his H.Q. on May 10th, the whole army being on shore three days later. As a final refinement a cableship then completed the connection with Korea, and thence to the Imperial H.Q. in Tokyo. While the Japanese completed their disembarkation, in Port Arthur the Russians talked.

On May 5th the Viceroy had left, but not without some advice for those he left behind. At a meeting of the destroyer captains he suggested that they might take some action against the Japanese transports, now known to be disembarking troops. Immediately they raised a number of difficulties, principally the presence of the Japanese escorting vessels. 'Well,' said Alexieff according to Captain Bubnoff who was present, 'talk it over with Admiral Vitgeft', and left for his train.

That particular officer, however, who as the senior Rear-Admiral was now in command of the fleet, was even less decisive. Again according to Bubnoff, 'he was a very hard worker, but in no way a fighting admiral, for he would not take any responsibility on his shoulders'. As a result there were a number of meetings of flag officers and captains who behaved more like delegates at a trades union congress than officers of a disciplined fighting service. A memorandum was drawn up and signed by all present and sent to Alexieff in answer to his second suggestion telegraphed from Harbin, that some action should be taken. The key sentence in this extraordinary document was that if action were taken it 'might mean annihilation, in which case the Fleet (i.e. the Baltic Fleet) when it arrived from Kronstadt, would meet with no support from Port Arthur'. Vitgeft then handed over his responsibilities to Rear-Admiral Reitzenstein, who was told to work out a plan of attack. He in turn held a number of discussion groups as a result of which nothing at all happened, and the Japanese were allowed to land undisturbed as if engaged in peace time manoeuvres.

It is difficult to credit that three Russian senior naval officers,

Alexieff, Vitgeft and Reitzenstein, should all behave in this manner. None of them were admittedly in the first flush of youth – the photographs which survive show them all as elderly, heavily-built and bemedalled figures – but age alone cannot account for their inactivity in face of obvious danger. Perhaps some explanation can be found in the rapidly developing pattern of reaction between the two enemy forces on land and on sea. Plainly the Japanese navy was superior to the Russian fleet in eastern waters, there could seemingly be no thought of a Russian naval victory until reinforcements arrived from Europe. On land, Japanese soldiers and, perhaps more important, Japanese generals, had shown themselves at least the equals of the Russians. Already it was obvious that the next battles would occur north-west from the Yalu river, further into Manchuria, towards Mukden and the line of the railway (the source of all reinforcements for Kuropatkin), and in the Kwantung Peninsula around Port Arthur. The rest of the Liaotung Peninsula, of which the Kwantung Peninsula formed the tip, was becoming almost neutral ground, over which Japanese armies were beginning to march merely to get to the battlefields. A Russian preponderance of force existed in the Mukden area and this was likely to increase as more reinforcements arrived, and from Kuropatkin's point of view prudence suggested that he should wait in this position of advantage for the Japanese to attack him. There was also the consideration as to how far the Japanese would want to advance into Manchuria, and how far they could advance. Even with his own incredibly long lines of communication, fifteen days' travel from Mukden to Warsaw, the most westerly Russian military district, Kuropatkin could still calculate on the problem set to the Japanese by their own lengthening supply line. However, all this ignored the problem of Port Arthur, and it was on the subject of that fortress that the Russians were, understandably, most indecisive.

Port Arthur was a prestige possession, the one warm-water port, and a fortress which had signalled Russian domination of the area. Now that the bluff of the 'fleet in being' had been called, it was still a powerful land fortress, with a naval potential, if only as a base for the new fleet which it was rumoured would soon sail from Europe. For the Japanese, too, Port Arthur possessed importance beyond its strategic significance, fought for and won as it had been by their troops in the Chinese War and then wrested from them by the Europeans. It was now a matter of prestige to retake it. On the more practical plane it would be impossible for the Japanese to win in Manchuria and Korea, yet leave Port Arthur in possession of the enemy. Despite the poor performance so far of the fleet within its protection, those ships were still a potential danger to any future operations.

In the first weeks of May, as Japanese troops continued to land in the Kwantung Peninsula, the 'problem' of Port Arthur was the main consideration for every Russian with responsibility in the war, whether he was in St. Petersburg, Harbin or Port Arthur itself. The question was, should it be evacuated, fought for to the last man or given up? Admittedly the question was not put in those stark terms, but that was the essence of it. In St. Petersburg the idea of surrender was almost unthinkable, but the nearer the scene of action it became much more of a possibility. For Kuropatkin, there were many attractions in the idea. The troops in Port Arthur, numbering over 40,000, could still perhaps join his forces, giving him a valuable reinforcement, and he would then no longer have to consider two theatres of operations but be able to consolidate one front against the Japanese. Naval officers, on the other hand, despite their misuse of the fortress, jibbed at the idea of evacuation, which would give the Japanese a base, even if all the Russian warships in it were destroyed. Again, to give up Port Arthur would mean an end to the war at sea, for then there would be no point in sending out another Russian fleet from Europe. It would also mean that the Japanese too could concentrate their land forces, and advance freely upon Kuropatkin.

So the arguments went to and fro, while Japanese naval shells landed in Port Arthur and the military and civil population awaited their fate. After the event, no less an authority than Admiral T. Mahan, of the U.S. Navy, the author of the best-selling *The Influence of Sea Power upon History*, took the view that the Russians should have disposed of their fortress, now revealed as but an encumbrance, at least in their indecisive hands. No doubt Kuropatkin would have agreed with him, from the military point of view. But no such decision was taken, and the Russians waited upon the initiative of the Japanese. Perhaps they had one final justification, since if there was to be a siege of Port Arthur, and that was not yet certain, no one, Russian or Japanese, could predict its outcome. For by 1904 sieges were rather out of fashion, the very word smacked of the formalised warfare of the days of Vauban and Turenne. Though there had been sieges in the last fifty years or so – the British had laid siege to Delhi, occupied by mutineers, and a year before to Sebastopol, fortified by the redoubtable Todleben – there had been no recent experience by which to judge a siege with modern weapons, more powerful artillery, machine-guns, mines and the magazine rifle. There were two possible exceptions which could not fail to influence the minds of Russians and Japanese respectively: in 1877 in the Russo-Turkish War the cream of the Russian army on its way to the Straits through the Balkans had been held at bay for an incredible time and suffered enormous losses at Plevna, which had not even been a true fortress but a fortified encampment based on a small Bulgarian town, while the Japanese on the other hand had captured Port Arthur itself from the Chinese within the memory of all, and within the experience of many Japanese officers. Thus although both examples presented obvious disparities with the present situation of Port Arthur it is easy to see why Russians thought that the modern port could be impregnable, whilst the Japanese were over-confident in their belief that having taken the fortress once they could take it again.

So far, in considering the events in the early weeks of May, it has appeared that the initiatives were largely in the hands of the Japanese, and so after the battle of the Yalu they were, certainly in the military sphere. From the Yalu Kuroki's 1st Army followed the retreating Russians to occupy Fenghuang-cheng, nearly 100 miles beyond their river crossing, by May 6th. While the 2nd Army under Oku continued its consolidation after its landing at Pitzuwo, the 4th Army commanded by General Nozu began on May 19th to disembark, again against no resistance, at Takushan almost midway between Pitzuwo and the mouth of the Yalu river. This army proceeded to advance on a course parallel to that of the 1st to the north, thus cutting straight across the Liaotung Peninsula in a north-westerly direction.

Yet, between the occupation of Fenghuangcheng and the landing at Takushan the Japanese suffered one of their most severe setbacks of the whole war.

Whilst the Japanese armies cautiously but steadily felt their way inland and Russian senior commanders disputed tactics (Kuropatkin and Alexieff, for instance, now both together in Liaoyang, were arguing as to whether their headquarters should be evacuated in favour of Harbin), Admiral Togo was again active at sea.

On May 12th mine-sweeping operations began in and around the bays in the vicinity of Port Arthur, with a view to a time when troops might have to be put ashore with naval support as part of a direct attack upon the naval base. It was unspectacular but trying work, and there was danger from two sources, the guns of the fortress and the mines themselves, which the Russians had laid apparently haphazardly, but in considerable numbers. By May 16th a torpedo boat had been blown up and sunk with most of its crew, the destroyer *Miyako* had struck a mine and sunk in a little over 25 minutes, and two gunboats had collided in a fog at night. It was not however the old minefield which inflicted the greatest damage on the Japanese. Captain Ivanoff of the Russian mine-layer *Amur* had watched the movements of the Japanese closely, especially those of the more powerful vessels, battleships and cruisers, which patrolled off Port Arthur, protecting the operations of the mine-sweeping force. These large ships tended to follow a definite pattern each day, and Ivanoff, who showed much more initiative than most of his superior officers, determined to use this dangerous habit to their disadvantage.

On the morning of May 14th, aided by a low-lying fog, he took the *Amur* out as unobtrusively as possible, and although at times he could see the masts of the Japanese ships above the fog, succeeded in laying a number of mines in the likely path of the Japanese squadron, about 10 miles from the shore. The next day the Japanese appeared and followed their customary routine. About 10 a.m. a dull far-off explosion was heard on shore, and the Japanese seemed to be in some confusion. Soon two more explosions, the second much louder than the previous two. From the shore it was not possible to discern accurately what had taken place, but the Japanese ships had in fact suffered a fate almost parallel to that of the *Petropavlovsk* and the *Pobieda*. The first explosion had been the battleship *Hatsuse*, flying the flag of Rear-Admiral Nashiba, striking a mine which disabled her steering gear. The battleship *Yashima* almost immediately struck another mine or possibly two. While the *Yashima* was listing heavily the third explosion occurred, striking the *Hatsuse* amidships. An enormous cloud of smoke and steam rose up, and within a matter of minutes the *Hatsuse* disappeared below the surface. The Japanese admiral, however, did not suffer the fate of Makaroff. With about 200 of his crew, many of whom were badly injured, he was picked up by the other ships in the flotilla. Soon after, the *Yashima* was taken in tow, but it proved impossible to keep her afloat, and a few hours later she had to be abandoned and sank off Encounter Rock. Earlier on in the morning of the same day, the Japanese had also suffered loss among Rear-Admiral Dewa's cruiser squadron. In turning in a fog to the south of the Liaotung Peninsula, the *Kasuga* rammed the *Yoshino* amidships, which sank rapidly, drowning a large part of her crew, who were unable to find friendly ships in the dense fog.

The last of the Japanese misfortunes was suffered on May 17th when the destroyer *Akatsuki* struck a mine and sank immediately, and the tragedy of the loss of the flagship came to an almost farcical conclusion. Admiral Nashiba, after being fished out of the water, had transferred his flag to the dispatch vessel *Tatsuta*, but that small ship that same evening ran into another fog and ran aground on the westernmost of the Elliott Islands. The Admiral was rescued but the *Tatsuta* remained aground for a month.

Thus, in a short space of time, the Japanese had lost two battleships, one cruiser, a destroyer, a gunboat and a considerable number of experienced sailors. Luckily for them, Admiral Vitgeft had none of the qualities of his subordinate Ivanoff, for though the loss of the *Hatsuse* and the damage to the *Yashima* were visible from Port Arthur, Russian battleships were not allowed out for fear of mines and there was no effort to pursue the advantage except that destroyers were sent out 'to worry the damaged battleship but not to attack'. Needless to say, with such orders, the destroyer captains scurried back to the protection of Port Arthur shore batteries as soon as the Japanese battleships and cruisers turned their attention upon them.

Still the Japanese suffered a grievous loss, and Togo's naval operations had now to be continued with even greater regard to the safety of his remaining battleships. Further, the *Hatsuse* incident showed that there was nothing of the inevitable in the eclipse of the Russian navy: the Vladivostock squadron was still active, within its limits, and a considerable nuisance to the enemy, and it was only at Port Arthur that the naval authorities were seemingly incapable of action.

Although the sinking of the *Hatsuse* could not be concealed from the outside world, and especially the enemy, the Japanese admitted publicly to none of their losses, and did manage to keep secret the loss of the *Yashima*. This secrecy was not as a matter of pride or of concealing bad news from their own people, but merely a part of their inflexible rules of security. Japanese censorship of news was a considerable irritant to the swarm of military observers and correspondents now present in Korea and Manchuria. General Sir Ian Hamilton, the senior military observer with the Japanese army in the field, was himself somewhat taken aback to find that there was no 'most favoured nation' policy in favour of allies as far as news was concerned. Even the British were not taken into Japanese confidence about present operations or future plans.

Perhaps with Sir Ian his Japanese hosts were a little too rigid, but in general their policy was a wise one. The Russians, on the other hand, seemed to care little about security or intelligence – forgetting perhaps that it was a former Tsar, Nicholas I, who when asked how he was so well informed about British dispositions in the Crimea had said, 'I read it in *The Times*.' The Russians were never able to obtain accurate information about Japanese troops in Manchuria, and often made the most serious underestimates. Their intelligence throughout the war was poor, especially in the face of a dawning solidarity of Oriental races throughout the Far East. By contrast, the Japanese, while giving away no secrets themselves, employed a considerable number of spies, some Japanese, but many Chinese, who were more willing to work for Japanese than Russian masters, and also possessed the facility of language and appearance which enabled them to mingle undetected with the local inhabitants.

On the Russian side there was also always the possibility of leaks of information from their own nationals, either through carelessness, or objection to the Tsarist regime. Aware of this, Japanese intelligence agents made approaches to members of the subject nationalities within the Russian Empire, the Poles being an obvious choice. Pilsudski, a future President of an independent Poland, was one of the young men so approached. But at this stage there was little those inside Russia could do, for the war was still to be won or lost in the Far East.

Nevertheless, in April, three weeks before the battle of the Yalu, the Russians sustained, at least in their view, a most important diplomatic defeat, for on the eighth of that month the Anglo-French *entente* was signed. This formal recognition that Britain and France were prepared to find some measure of agreement and patch up old quarrels was the culmination of a lengthy period of talks and negotiations. A year before Edward VII had paid his famous official visit to Paris. On the first day of his stay there had been shouts from the crowd as his open landau passed of 'Vivent les Boers' and 'Vive Marchand' (the French officer ousted by Fashoda by Kitchener) and even 'Vive Jeanne d'Arc'. The same evening the King's reception at the theatre had been cold to the point of rudeness. However, a few gracious words in the interval to Jeanne Granier, an actress whom the King had seen perform in London, thawed the atmosphere a little. From then on, by the exercise of his considerable charm, Edward went from strength to strength, so that on his departure from the capital there were large crowds shouting, 'Vive Edouard.' The British Ambassador wrote to Lord Lansdowne, the Foreign Secretary, saying that the visit had been 'a success more complete than the most sanguine optimist could have foreseen'.

Edward's VII's triumph in Paris very successfully put the seal of royal diplomacy on the work of politicians on both sides of the Channel. So, on April 8th, 1904, it was possible for the *entente* to be signed with hardly a word of criticism by parliaments, press or public, either French or English. The agreement itself was basically concerned with the burying of colonial disputes as far afield as Madagascar, Siam, the New Hebrides and West Africa and even including the question of French fishing rights off Newfoundland, a problem which dated back to the Treaty of Utrecht.

Most important, the British had henceforth a free hand in Egypt, in return for which the French had the same facility in Morocco. Each country had graciously given to the other something which belonged to neither of them. Still, spheres of influence were the stuff of early twentieth-century rivalries, as the Russo-Japanese War itself demonstrated, and a colonial compromise between two of the principal rivals in the race was significant enough, not least for the other contenders.

The Kaiser was cruising in the Mediterranean when he heard the news of the Treaty, and commented, 'The Treaty makes me think in a number of respects.' For the Kaiser to think about any international development in which Germany had played no part was generally the precursor to the conviction that he and the German Empire should have played a part, and not a small one, and that this failure should be remedied as quickly as possible. In a speech a few weeks later it was not surprising that he warned his subjects to 'clear their eyes' and 'toughen their resolution in case it becomes necessary to intervene in international affairs'. Officially at least, Germany welcomed the Anglo-French understanding, but in private von Bülow, the Chancellor, wondered about secret compacts between France and Britain and Holstein and in his tortuous way concluded that while the British would be quite content to see France at war with Germany, it was doubtful whether in that eventuality they would help their new ally.

Such thoughts, though dangerous, were all in the realm of speculation. In reality the *entente* had no direct effect upon present German policy. Far different was the case with Russia. The Tsar was now presented with the unwelcome fact that his principal, indeed his only, ally was now pledged to friendship with a nation he particularly disliked, which was in turn committed to a military alliance with the enemy with whom even now he was at war. Forgetting that the British had before the war warned him confidentially, through the French, of Japanese intentions, he could now only see the *entente cordiale* as a development highly disadvantageous to Russia's conduct of the war. From the outset Britain had 'held the ring' for Japan, now she had seduced away the French to the extent at least that any future co-operation with Russia was bound to be tinged by consideration for British susceptibilities and interests.

Meanwhile, there were none but discouraging reports from the actual theatre of operations. The stocky blue-clad Japanese infantrymen continued to force their way steadily inland with a crystal-clear object in mind, the encirclement of Port Arthur.

To the north of the Liaotung Peninsula the armies of Generals Kuroki and Nozu continued to drive towards Kuropatkin's main force. There the object was for the Japanese to meet and if possible defeat the Russian army, wherever it might be encountered. A number of battalion-level skirmishes occurred, but at this stage no full-scale pitched battle. For the good reason that the Russians, since the Yalu, had been steadily withdrawing. Indeed, considering their vastly superior numbers and the feeble opposition they faced, the Japanese made comparatively slow progress. As there were no real roads, only tracks, General Sir Ian Hamilton was perhaps a trifle unfair when he suggested that this was because of their Germanic habits of thoroughness which in the Japanese almost became a military vice. This characteristic he had first observed on the banks of the Yalu: they would not move, he said, 'until they had completed their most minute preparations,' and he predicted that in consequence they might well run into difficulties if they met a 'first-class general'. However, they did not, as the Russians did not apparently possess even a senior officer with dash and initiative enough to harry the steady Japanese advance.

One gets an impression that perhaps Sir Ian, fresh from the campaigns on the South African veldt, became somewhat impatient with this slow, steady warfare along the tracks and in the man-high millet fields of Korea. However, he used his enforced leisure to good account to record his impressions of the Japanese soldier. The man in the ranks reminded him forcibly of the Gurkha though 'better educated, more civilised, on the other hand not so powerful or hardy'. As Sir Ian, although a Gordon Highlander, had in his time commanded Gurkhas, no higher praise could be decently contemplated. The officers, on the other hand, obviously disconcerted him. Courteous rather than friendly, they managed at a staff officers' reception to organise a military band to play the Gordon's regimental march in his honour, but they kept him outside their confidence in spite of his obviously pro-Japanese enthusiasms. The Japanese suspicion of all foreigners and their tremendous security-consciousness might account for their coolness, but perhaps also this tall gangling British general, apparently rather effete and something of a chatterbox, in his turn disconcerted them.

Their own generals were inclined to be silent men, but when they did talk, it was to some purpose, revealing that they had painstakingly analysed the deficiencies not only of the Russian army, but of the British and the British-Indian armies as well. Sir Ian confided to his scrapbook his hopes that the British would remain friends with their new allies, and at the same time he worried about the fate of a degenerating Europe, faced in the future with the challenges of less civilised, tough, militaristic 'barbarians' from without – a sentiment that would have been echoed by the Kaiser, who had sent to the Tsar his specially commissioned allegorical representation of Europeans resisting the 'Yellow Peril'.

Hamilton's consolation, however, lay in the poor performance of the Russians. 'The Russian soldier is the worst shot existing in any great army in Europe', he wrote, and as a former Commandant of the British Army's School of Musketry at Hythe he was no mean judge of such matters. The Russian infantryman was still trained to 'volley firing': each soldier took aim and when the whole formation had its butts nicely into the shoulder and the muzzles pointing, presumably, at the enemy, the officer gave the order to fire. The catch lay in the 'presumably', for no officer could tell if any or all of his men were firing high or low, or whether or not they had an enemy in their sights when he gave the order. Volley firing had been appropriate, and effective, in the Peninsular and Waterloo days when muskets were inaccurate at 100 yards, but with the modern magazine rifle whose range was at least ten times that distance, it was a ponderous and slow anachronism. No wonder Sir Ian found his mind wandering back to the Boer riflemen of three years ago who had carried out such accurate and economic slaughter of the flower of the British infantry.

Certainly, the Japanese with their close Germanic formations presented excellent targets even when they changed from conspicuous blue uniforms to khaki drab. But the Russians in formation were even closer and when they bothered to dig trenches dug nothing much below chest depth. So the senior British observer could console himself, as he watched the Japanese outclass the Russians, with the thought that the Japanese was 'not as good as the best of British infantry but', and it was a significant 'but', 'only the best'.

Thinking ahead in terms of future world conflict, as did almost all the correspondents and observers in Korea, civilian as well as military, Sir Ian found himself with two sets of conclusions and comparisons. Plainly, the Japanese had up to the moment shown themselves superior to the Russians. But were the Russians putting forward their best generals and their best troops? Was it fair to regard this as a balanced conflict of East and West? The Japanese were obviously the best that any independent Asiatic or Oriental nation could produce, patriotic, fearless and the masters of modern military technology. But where did the Russians stand? Were they themselves of the East or the West? Hamilton came to the view that they were betwixt and between, suffering from the disadvantages of both cultures. However, he was still left with the difficulty that he was a soldier from a democracy trying to identify the causes of competence and incompetence in armies that were both the products of autocratic, militaristic states.

Meanwhile, the Japanese private soldier, indifferent to such fine distinctions, trudged steadily on, never tiring of his marching song, which was translated by Mr Maxwell of the London *Evening Standard*, and rendered into verse by the senior British military observer. It contained more truth and fewer inaccuracies than most soldiers' songs, and was more high-flown in sentiment and considerably more printable than anything likely to be uttered by Sir Ian's own beloved Jocks or Gurkhas:

> Vaunt not Russia's vast dominions,
> Boast not of her legions bold,
> What is vastness in a desert?
> What are hosts whose hearts are cold?
>
> Thousands starving, traitors lurking,
> Coffers empty, lack of grain,
> How shall Russia stand against us,
> Stand the long and weary strain?
>
> March then with our sunlight banner
> Waving proudly in the van,
> March beneath that glorious emblem,
> Down with Russia! On Japan!

To the south of the Liaotung Peninsula, less remarked by foreign observers, the army of General Oku operated with a much more precise objective than their comrades in the north. The Kwantung Peninsula with Port Arthur at its tip is joined to the Liaotung Peninsula by a narrow neck of land with Chinchou Bay to its north-west and Hand Bay to its south-west. At its narrowest point the neck is little more than 2 miles wide. The area is a hilly one, the hills being steep, rugged and bare, and the principal height is Nanshan Hill, which commands almost the whole area, giving excellent observation and fields of fire. Held by the Russians, Nanshan was the key to the Kwantung Peninsula, but if it once fell to Japanese hands the peninsula would be cut off from the north, and from besieged Port Arthur.

So the task of isolating the Kwantung Peninsula was assigned to Oku's 2nd Army, consisting of the 1st (Tokyo), 3rd (Osaka) and 4th (Nagoya) Divisions, assisted by the navy which was deployed in Chinchou Bay.

Perhaps because of fear of mines or Russian land batteries, and the dangers for capital ships in shoal waters, Togo, ever mindful of his duty to preserve his battleships and cruisers, told off for the naval operations what could hardly be described as a fleet of first-class ships. He selected two 600-ton gunboats, with the *Tsukushi* of 1,370 tons, by no means in its first youth, plus an old Chinese vessel captured in the Sino-Japanese War.

All told these four ships could bring into action only twenty guns of medium calibre, the heaviest armament being the two 10-inch guns of the *Tsukushi*. Nevertheless, the naval support was thought sufficient as this was to be an infantryman's battle, and Nanshan would have to be taken by direct assault in conditions which would allow little room for manoeuvre or dispersal.

On the Russian side the command was with Major-General Fock. General Stoessel, however, in command of the Port Arthur area, also exercised an overall control over Fock's dispositions, and he ensured that for once the Russian forces were not without naval support: two destroyers and a gunboat left Port Arthur and stationed themselves in Talien Bay to give support to the eastern flank. The Russians in and around Nanshan had constructed earthworks and dug defensive positions, and although these were not constructed with any great skill, they presented a formidable obstacle to the enemy, being reinforced by mines and barbed wire. Strategically, the only advantage possessed by the Japanese was that of Mount Sampson, which from 4 miles to the north-east commanded the heights of Nanshan. So far as numbers were concerned the Russians were well supplied, being able to deploy over 10,000 men, artillery and infantry, in a position which from coast to coast extended scarcely 3 miles. This time there could really be no excuse for the Russians. They were not faced by overwhelming numbers, surprise, or even superior generalship. As Repington, now *The Times* correspondent, put it,

If a Russian Division of 8,000 to 12,000 men, backed up by 50 or more siege guns and 16 quick-firing field guns, cannot hold 3,000 yards of front, strongly entrenched and secure on the flanks, against the rush of infantry in the open restricted to a frontal assault, it is hard to say what position it can expect to defend with success.

Actually, the numbers were not quite correct, as Colonel Repington could not estimate how many of his reserve battalions General Fock would use; and the Russians had more field guns than he thought. But the point he made was a valid one. If the Russians couldn't repulse the Japanese here in front of Port Arthur, what hopes were there of holding that fortress when its time came, as it would if the Nanshan position fell?

Oku's main attack began in the early morning of May 26th with an artillery barrage which lasted for 3 hours. The Russians replied with vigour and in kind, and when the 3 hours had elapsed the defensive positions seemed to have been very little affected, although foreign observers judged that this was the most intensive artillery duel they had so far witnessed during the war. However, the 3 hours elapsed, Oku gave his order for his infantry to advance. In the centre was the Tokyo Division, Osaka on the right and Nagoya on the left. There was next to nothing in the way of cover, and the troops were in densely packed formations. Suffering considerable casualties, the Japanese pressed on until they were within 400–500 yards of the Russian trenches. There they paused to use their entrenching tools, and await the supporting movement of the artillery and their infantry reserves to replace those already killed and wounded. By mid-day both sides were running short of field artillery ammunition, each Russian gun, for instance, having by 11 a.m. exhausted its allowance of 150 rounds. Although Major-General Fock had not used his reserves for 7 hours the Russians had held back three Japanese divisions. At Port Arthur there was a feeling that from reports received the Japanese were likely to retire or at the least accept stalemate.

It was not however in Oku's nature to accept defeat. From mid-day until 3.30 p.m. forlorn groups of Japanese continued to rise from their shallow trenches and attempt to advance into withering rifle and machine-gun fire. Whole companies and even regiments were scythed down. Knowing that the Russians had laid mines in front of their positions, suicide squads volunteered to explode them by discovering them in the only way possible. In the event, these fanatical bodies of men found that heavy rain had exposed many mines so that their sacrifice was not called for, but many were killed just the same by small arms fire at short range from the Russian trenches.

At 3.30 General Oku, where others might have given up, changed his tactics slightly. For 30 minutes his artillery plastered the Russian positions, and then the infantry went in again, led as usual by their officers, sword in hand, shouting 'Banzais' to the Emperor and Japan, but this time with engineers also in the van equipped to cut or bridge barbed-wire entanglements.

At last the Russian left flank, assaulted time and time again by these 'scientific fanatics' (the phrase was Sir Ian Hamilton's), began to show signs of crumbling. Immediately, the Japanese artillery was shifted to this sector in the hope of neutralising the Russian machine-guns. Major-General Fock failed to react to the new situation and summon up his considerable reserves, although asked to do so by his subordinate commander, General Nadyein.

The Osaka Division on the Japanese right, and therefore on the Russian left, began to make headway against the 5th East Siberian Rifle Regiment which was simply overwhelmed by numbers. The Osaka men, regarded semi-humorously in Japanese as being somewhat careful of their own skins, utterly disregarded casualties and swept into the Russian trenches; while at the same time their comrades in the other two divisions began at last to make their way over the obstacles and defence works to their own fronts. Fock reported to Stoessel that his position was becoming critical, and was ordered to retire. The Russians blew up their arsenal at Tajangshen and a general retreat in the direction of Port Arthur began.

At 7.20 p.m. exhausted but victorious Japanese infantrymen hoisted the Rising Sun flag on the top of Nanshan Hill. By 8 p.m. the three divisions bivouacked down in a continuous line of positions from Chinchou Bay across the promontory to Hand Bay. On a final note, almost of farce, about this time a flotilla of Russian destroyers left Port Arthur to attack the Japanese gunboats in Chinchou Bay, but the *Vnimatelni* struck a submerged rock on the way and was abandoned, and so the rest of the flotilla returned to port without apparently finding the Japanese ships.

When the next day the casualty lists were calculated, the Russians had over 700 men buried on the field, without taking into account losses in the retreat. The Japanese had 4,855 killed and wounded. Much of the disparity was of course accounted for by the fact that the Japanese were attacking, often quite recklessly, in the open, while the Russians were defending from behind earthworks. Nevertheless another factor, and one which was little credit to Fock's generalship, was the large proportion of the Russian force which, though present on the battlefield, was never actually committed to action. The Japanese estimate was that of 18,000 men present only about 3,500 were ever brought to the firing line. They themselves brought about 29,500 infantry to battle of whom a large proportion were killed and wounded in the first hours of the engagement.

Officially in St. Petersburg the battle was described as a strategic withdrawal. In Manchuria on the ground the Japanese now consolidated their line across the peninsula and in the process occupied Dalny without a shot being fired. This civilian port, with its wharves, graving docks and workshop facilities, once the pride of the Russian Far East colonisers, was now at the disposal of the Japanese navy and ready, almost unharmed as there had been no demolitions, to receive the Japanese 3rd Army.

On the day of the battle Admiral Togo formally announced to the world that the Liaotung Peninsula was under blockade, that is, it was banned to neutral ships. In a sense the announcement was superfluous, for the Kwantung Peninsula was isolated, General Stoessel's command was cut off from Kuropatkin to the north, and the world could now await the news of the siege of Port Arthur.

SEVEN

'The Japanese are naturally a military race'
THE RUSSIAN HIGH COMMAND

For the rest of the world following the campaign through its daily newspapers the Siege of Port Arthur was now 'on'. Armchair strategists and the general public could sit back and prepare themselves for each episode to unfold like an exciting serial story. Until now the movements of various Japanese armies commanded by generals with outlandish names, each one of which, in his photograph, looked like any other, had been somewhat confusing. Inevitably the naval battles had appeared more clear-cut and comprehensible. A number of newspapers battled hard to make the land campaign more understandable by producing maps, but unfortunately the place names were even more outlandish than those of the generals, with the added complication that almost every town had in effect three names: first the Chinese Manchurian name, then the Japanese or Russian version, and finally the rendering of either into something reasonably pronounceable by an Englishman, Frenchman or German.

The national attitudes to the combatants were of course also reflected in the newspapers. The British papers, irrespective of their political complexions, regarded the Japanese victories almost as their own. However there was beginning to appear in the reports both of the military correspondents and foreign reporters a sort of envy to mix with their admiration of the Japanese, and a certain uneasiness perhaps as to what the future might hold. This tendency was made more explicit by those who later expanded their despatches into book form. Britain's was an Empire, where, apart from Canada, Australia and New Zealand, white men held dominion over coloured whether black, brown or yellow: and the victories now being recorded in the Far East were those of a newly arisen Asiatic nation, defeating a nation which for all its defects had been considered hitherto the most powerful in Europe. It was a disturbing phenomenon indeed. No correspondent specifically warned his readers of any danger in a Japanese resurgence, but many felt obliged to point at the Russian complacency and unpreparedness before hostilities and to hope that their own country would never be caught out in similar circumstances.

Neither the German nor the French press seemed particularly worried by any threat from Japan, and both concentrated upon likely effects of the war in Europe. German correspondents revealed themselves as unimpressed by Russian military organisation and methods, while the French press, well served by correspondents in St. Petersburg, was adept in producing gossipy pieces on the decision-making and personality conflicts in the inner circles of the Tsar – there was however little sign of sympathy for their ally's predicament.

In Russia itself the press had no alternative but to reflect the overwhelming national sense of disappointment as official bulletin succeeded official bulletin and there was no news of a Russian victory on land or sea. In the early days of the war there had been patriotic fervour and confidence even among those sections of the community not normally noticeable for their enthusiasm for the regime. The merchant communities of Moscow had started fund raising for comforts for the troops, and there had been patriotic demonstrations by students, those of St. Petersburg University marching to the Winter Palace to cheer the Tsar. This was the time when Nicholas II could write to the German Kaiser and say that the prospect of war had 'stirred the generally sleepy nature' of his people. Now those days were far behind. Enthusiasm for the patriotic funds had petered out amidst allegations of corruption, there were stories of conscripts and reservists failing to report for duty, and the students had returned to their normal state of unrest. Even Leo Tolstoy, who although a pacifist but in his youth a soldier in the Crimea, had felt a sort of reluctant enthusiasm for the Russian cause in the early days, had now relapsed into pessimism as defeat followed defeat. The only sections of society which seemed to see any benefit from the war were those groups dedicated to revolution who hoped that from Russia's present misfortunes might spring their own opportunities.

Meanwhile officially inspired journals still attempted to minimise Russian defeats and exaggerate Japanese losses; and the Tsar and the Tsaritsa continued to do their duty at railway stations giving their formal blessings to troops leaving for the front.

The news that Port Arthur was now surrounded and about to be put to the test was greeted almost with relief. Here at last was a clear-cut issue, no question of surprise or cunning strategem, but simply Japanese against Russians in circumstances that seemed to offer no unfair advantage to either side.

Yet before the siege proper began there was another battle to be fought, and this arose out of the conflicts and indecisions of the Russian High Command. The site of the battle was the overgrown village of Telissu (which as an illustration of current difficulties over nomenclature was variously rendered as Telissu Te-li-ssu, Tokuriji by the Japanese, and as Wa-jang-kou by many military commentators). In a sense the outcome hardly mattered, for though the battle was fought near the junction of the Port Arthur and Liaoyang stretch of railway and the Fuchou river, it was not a conflict for a particular position so much as a clash for prestige, with an eye to an advantage in future initiatives.

Ornithologists will tell one that the cock birds of many species fight for territory, as well as for future superiority with regard to mates and food, yet the actual decisive battle may occur almost anywhere. So it was with Telissu.

In the first part of June there had been considerable movement of both Russian and Japanese subsidiary formations accompanied by a number of essentially unimportant skirmishes. Nevertheless it was possible to distinguish even at this point quite different objectives. On the part of the Japanese, the first objective was to capture Port Arthur as soon as possible, the second to drive the Russians out of Manchuria, and the third to destroy the Russian fleet present in the Far East without risking the Japanese fleet too much in the process. The third

objective of course depended upon the first, and it might seem
at first sight that the Japanese High Command was pursuing
disparate objects in a rather dangerous manner. Nevertheless,
in Japanese eyes, the overall necessity was speed of attainment
before Russian reinforcements by land and sea could give them
numerical superiority. Japanese confidence too was increasing
with every triumph. And perhaps temperament was an important factor, for despite their habit of careful reconnaissance and
preparation before all their military operations, Japanese commanders were beginning now to reveal a degree of reckless
desperation in many of their decisions. Hitherto it was the
Russians who had been feared for their almost complete indifference to losses; now the Japanese were showing an even more
frightening combination of meticulousness in planning and
fanaticism in execution.

On the Russian side the objectives were almost the converse
of the Japanese: first, to relieve Port Arthur; second to out-
number the Japanese warships by sending out the Baltic Fleet;
and third to delay the advance of the Japanese northwards until
Russian reinforcements could arrive by way of the Trans-
Siberian Railway.

Comparing the two sets of objectives, Japanese aims can be
seen to depend on a level of attainment which, despite the risks,
they were confident they could achieve. Russian aims, however,
were less well defined: what for instance if Port Arthur could
not be relieved? Whereas each Japanese aim was self-sufficient,
and a considerable advantage could be achieved at each stage,
each Russian objective, even if attained, still left a question
mark hanging over the next move.

A bird's-eye view in early June of the Liaotung Peninsula
would have revealed a large number of seemingly disparate
troop movements: columns of Japanese, now wearing, instead
of their earlier blue, a drab khaki uniform less conspicuous and
of a light material more suitable for summer campaigning, filled
the valleys and tracks and paths moving steadily northwards.
Reinforcements were still being landed from the sea, at an
increased pace now that the captured port of Dalny was cleared
of mines. These were largely infantry movements, although
each infantry division had its cavalry element, riding stiffly on

sturdy ponies, and its much larger artillery contingent. In the south of the peninsula the divisions nearest to Port Arthur were being augmented and regrouped so that by June 6th, when General Nogi took over command from Prince Fushimi, the new force could properly be called the 3rd Army. While it remained static, looking to the south and Port Arthur, the 1st, 2nd and 4th Armies moved on, with Liaoyang in the north as their general objective.

Russian troop movements were less purposeful. Their soldiers too had changed their uniforms, the officers' white tunics and soldiers' white blouses having given way to grey. Their cavalry, better mounted and appearing more at home in the saddle than the enemy's, were much in evidence observing and occasionally harrying the Japanese columns. Nevertheless at this early stage it would have been difficult to distinguish any significant pattern of deployment and the Russians seemed unaware of the steady build-up of Japanese forces.

In fact, to move from the bird's-eye view to the close-up, there was considerable dissent raging in the higher reaches of the Russian command. Once again it was resolving itself into a conflict between Kuropatkin and Alexieff.

Basically, the General was opposed to any forward movement until he had enough reinforcements to give him numerical superiority, the Viceroy on the other hand was insistent that some move must be made to relieve Port Arthur. The disagreement was ultimately resolved by a Council of War at Tsarkoe Seloe at which the views of General Sakharoff, the Minister for War, Admiral Avellan, the Minister of Marine, and Plehve, the Minister of the Interior, were taken. The decision, backed by the authority of the Tsar, was that Kuropatkin must try to relieve Port Arthur. By May 27th he had indicated to Alexieff that if ordered to do so his only course would be to try to break through General Oku's 2nd Army. A few days later he was ordered by telegraph from St. Petersburg to make the attempt. It is impossible to tell with what determination Kuropatkin embarked on the task. Under his own command at Liaoyang he had 36,000 infantry and 6,000 cavalry; opposing the Japanese 1st Army under Kuroki was a force under Lieutenant-General Count Keller and Major-General Rennenkampf of 23,000 infantry and 4,000 cavalry, and standing against Kuroki was Lieutenant-General Stackelberg's force. This was ordered to advance, but it was given little extra assistance by way of reinforcements save that of General Samsonoff who commanded an independent but small cavalry brigade of little over 1,600 men.

The temptation to believe that Kuropatkin was not putting his whole heart into the operation is difficult to resist. Otherwise, he was incredibly misinformed about the strength of the Japanese forces with which Stackelberg would have to contend. Admittedly, the Japanese had, in contrast to their enemy, managed to preserve an absolute security clamp-down on all their troop movements; but what in that case were the Russian cavalry doing whose duty it was to report on enemy strengths and movements to the Commander-in-Chief? Kuropatkin's orders to Stackelberg were in reality a mass of contradictions and ambiguities.

Your Excellency's Army Corps is detailed with the object of drawing upon itself the greatest number of the enemy's forces and thereby weakening his army operating in the Kwantung Peninsula.

Your advance, therefore, against the enemy's covering troops must be rapid and energetic, in the hope of crushing his advanced detachments should they prove to be weak in numbers.

In the event of your encountering superior strength decisive action will be avoided, and in no case will you allow the whole of your reserves to become engaged until the conditions are entirely clear.

The object of our southerly movement is the capture of the Nanshan position and thereafter an advance on Port Arthur.

It is difficult to conceive of a worse set of orders and one wonders if they were drafted more for the benefit of the War Council in St. Petersburg than for the unfortunate General Stackelberg.

Incredibly too, no instructions were sent to General Stoessel in Port Arthur to attempt anything in the way of assistance or diversion from the south at the time that Stackelberg would be battling to reach him from the north.

By the first week in June it was obvious to the Japanese and to General Oku in particular that the Russians planned some move to attempt a relief of Port Arthur. It was to be expected in any case, but now it was public knowledge, and a common subject for comment even in French and German newspapers which had picked up reports from the Russian press. On June 13th, therefore, on the principle of never allowing the Russians to gain the initiative, the Japanese 2nd Army moved north to the attack. On the 15th the real battle began, the Japanese having in their advance virtually swept aside the Russian cavalry screens. The details of the battle are perhaps not important. Sufficient it is to say that it was fought in difficult terrain, hilly if not actually mountainous, which gave no positive advantage to either side, but that the Japanese took their opportunities while the Russians did not. Consequently, the Japanese managed to outflank the Russians and virtually surround them, Stackelberg having contributed to this situation by over-concentrating his own men. Once again there was little coordination between Russian commanders, in this case Stackelberg and his subordinate general, Gerngross. When Stackelberg found his position untenable, he ordered a withdrawal which, since it had to follow three mountain passes with the Japanese commanding the heights with artillery, rapidly became a rout. Gerngross towards the end of the day was severely wounded. The Japanese did not pursue with cavalry but merely shelled their retreating opponents.

Both sides had fought with great gallantry for the best part of three days, but in the end the Russians had not only been repulsed but had lost in the process vast quantities of ammunition and stores and sixteen artillery pieces. More significantly, although the Japanese in their recklessness had lost just over a thousand men killed and wounded and missing, Russian losses were well over three times that number, the Japanese alone burying some 2,000 Russian dead on the immediate field of battle. Further, the Japanese captured about 500 Russian prisoners, while the Russians took none.

The forces engaged had been roughly equal in number, about 30,000 on each side, so the attempt to relieve Port Arthur had been a signal failure, and had proved, so far as such things can be proved, that man for man and general for general the Japanese were the superiors of their enemy in a straight fight. Henceforth, if they were to think of victory, the Russians must first seek material and numerical advantages of a high order.

As well as teaching these melancholy lessons the battle of
Telissu was also noteworthy in that it revealed to the world
for the first time in a not particularly favourable light those
Generals Samsonoff and Rennenkampf who were to figure
within ten years as the army commanders in an even more
disastrous action, when 370,000 Russians were to be defeated
in East Prussia at a battle which the victorious Germans called
Tannenburg.

At this point the question might be asked, what did those in
power in Russia think of the chances of success? Certainly
Alexieff, who had once worried lest the Tsar should wish to
terminate hostilities too soon and give the Japanese an easy
peace, must have changed his view considerably. In many ways he
was now only of nuisance value, not knowing which way to turn
though still exercising some influence at St. Petersburg. When
he insisted that Port Arthur must not be given up, however,
he was merely reinforcing the conclusion of the Tsar and his
advisers that for the Russians at this stage to surrender the
fortress, however strong the strategic arguments, would be
politically impossible. Indeed, as will be seen when the Japanese
viewpoint is considered, they were perhaps wiser than they knew.

Kuropatkin was the key man, and perhaps the most reliable
way of establishing his opinions is to consider the instructions
and advice he gave his troops. The relevant documents were
later captured by the Japanese, and subsequently found their
way into the hands of Major C. M. Crawford and Captain J. B.
Jardine, two of the British military observers attached to the
Japanese army. These documents, along with many others on
the organisation, arms and even uniforms of the Japanese had
been distributed among the Russians certainly down to battalion, and possibly company, level.

On tactics the High Command had this to say:

The attack of the Japanese is a continuous succession of waves,
and they never relax their efforts by day or by night. If the enemy's
front is narrow, they seek to outflank it, if extended, to pierce it.

Then there followed an analysis of the way in which the
Japanese always sought to confuse the enemy by simultaneously
making a feint attack and a real one; and of the skilful manner

in which Japanese soldiers used the terrain to their own advantage. The document also pointed out that the Japanese were more inclined to make night attacks than the Russians, and that their infantry fire, though often wild, was certainly more rapid than the Russian. Throughout, the mobility of both infantry and artillery is much commented upon. Finally, the document concludes, 'It is impossible not to admire the bravery and activity of the Japanese, due chiefly to their light equipment and to their natural fondness for the offensive.'

In another document the inferiority of the Japanese cavalry, particularly so far as horse management was concerned, was stressed, but one has the feeling that perhaps this was the only real point of criticism the Russians could find. Elsewhere is to be found the observation that: 'Lightness of heart, ingeniousness, perseverance, unselfishness are the chief qualities of the Japanese soldier'; and another that 'The Japanese are naturally a military race and take easily to a soldier's life, adapting themselves readily to military disciplines, while the non-commissioned officers and men observe even the minutest details of army discipline.'

To which praise another British observer, Lieutenant-Colonel A. L. Haldane, could only add his own comments: 'It would seem that the Japanese never forget that, after a long fire fight, when their own condition seems least hopeful, that of the enemy is no better and often worse. Inspired by such a belief, and determined to lose their lives rather than yield an inch of ground, once gained, it is not to be wondered at that unbroken success has shone upon their arms. . . .'

Such in essence could not have been far from the opinion of the Russian commander-in-chief, and the prospect could not have been anything but alarming. Inevitably both Russian soldiers and foreign observers gave much thought to what pushed the Japanese on to his feats of bravery and endurance. Both Sir Ian Hamilton and the correspondent of the *Evening Standard*, while attending Japanese military funerals, reflected upon the problem. Previously Orientals had been regarded as fatalistic to the point of inertia. Yet here were private soldiers imbued with Shintoism, some sort of offshoot of Buddhism, a religion which seemed to possess no moral code save stoicism in misfortune, promised little in the hereafter and merely enjoined implicit obedience to the Imperial will, inspired to acts of courage almost beyond the comprehension of Europeans.

The Russians, on the other hand, once thought of as unnaturally ready to fight and die for the Tsar and Holy Russia, now seemed to be afflicted with the very vices of fatalism and inaction formerly attributed to the East. Even more surprising, those qualities of mechanical proficiency and organisation and preparation, thought of as the prerogative of the European, seemed totally absent from Russian practice but implicit in every Japanese action from platoon march to divisional deployment.

In these circumstances it is difficult to think that Kuropatkin could even at this stage have contemplated an all-out Russian victory. Still, he was now committed to a holding action in the north of the Liaotung Peninsula from his position at Liaoyang, and a siege operation at the tip of the Kwantung Peninsula. The summer season with its heavy rains was approaching and perhaps with August out he would then have sufficient reinforcements to fight the decisive battle.

If such were his views, the Japanese could not have been more content for it meant that their strategy had succeeded. Soon General Oyama would be leaving Japan to take over immediate control of the four Japanese armies. The old Marshal Yamagata Aritomo, Chief of the Great General Staff, final authority on all military matters, dominant among the Genro or senior counsellors and perhaps the most powerful voice in Prime Minister Katsura's Cabinet, was prepared at the age of 66 to give up active control in the war theatre to his Chief-of-Staff. Accordingly, Oyama with his Chief-of-Staff Kodama left for the front with the blessing of his former chief gracefully expressed in the traditional poetic form:

> One who always
> Went first to war
> now, because of the passing years,
> sends others off to war.

However, from Japan, Yamagata continued to exhort his protégés. On July 16th he wrote to General Nogi, 'The speedy fall of Port Arthur is the most important element in the victory or defeat of our whole army.'

Much concerned about the danger from Russia's Baltic Fleet the old Marshal continued to stress the importance of taking Port Arthur at all costs, but in a sense his encouragement and advice was hardly necessary. Oyama and his subordinate generals had been in little doubt of their overall strategy from the beginning. What was true of a battalion attack was true also of bigger operations, a real attack and a feint. Kuroki and the Yalu river advance had been the feint, designed to keep Kuropatkin occupied in the north while the real attack on the very symbol of Russian dominance in the Pacific, her warm-water port and naval base, was mounted in the south.

However, because of Russian passivity, the Japanese were enabled to carry on two separate but related operations simultaneously. Under Oyama, who had besieged Port Arthur when it was held by the Chinese, Nogi and the 3rd Army encircled Port Arthur; while the 1st, 2nd and 4th Armies, under Kuroki, Oku and Nozu respectively, moved steadily northwards, at the same time holding the ring for Nogi and drawing ever closer to Kuropatkin at Liaoyang.

In the circumstances and with his now confirmed reservations about meeting anything like an equal force of Japanese, Kuropatkin was in effect deprived of all immediate initiatives.

Thus the Kaiser's letter to the Tsar dated June 6th, 1904, contained a good deal of not untypical advice and comment,

I only hope to goodness the General (Kuropatkin) won't jeopardise the final sucess of your Forces by rashly exposing them to an 'échec' before the whole of his reserves have joined him, which are, as I believe, still partly on the way. The old proverb of Napoleon I still holds good, 'la victoire est avec les gros Bataillons', one can never be too strong for the battle, especially respecting the artillery. An absolute superiority must undoubtedly be established to ensure victory.

Such advice must have been just as welcome and helpful as the famous cryptic exhortation from the same source to the shy and incoherent Nicholas on another occasion, 'My advice to you is more parades and more speeches.'

However, in the remainder of the letter Wilhelm showed the other side to his nature, his deceit as well as his brashness.

First he related how the French Military Attaché in Berlin was alleged to have said that his country had not sent their fleet to help to keep Port Arthur open pending the arrival of the Baltic Fleet only because of 'other Powers'.

'After many hints and allusions,' wrote the Kaiser, 'I found out – what I always feared – that the Anglo-French agreement had one main effect, viz, to stop the French from helping you!'

'Il va sans dire,' he went on, 'that if France had been under the obligation of helping you with her Fleet or Army I would of course not have budged a finger to harm her, for that would have been most illogical on the part of the Author of the Picture, "Yellow Peril!"'

It is an unfortunate comment on the abilities of 'Dearest Nicky' that he was perhaps taken in by this farrago of half-truths and nonsense from his 'affectionate cousin Willy'.

Nevertheless, even such an 'insignificant person' (the phrase was the Kaiser's) might have noticed that while on the one hand his Imperial cousin was currying favour by saying that he intended to dissuade 'Uncle Bertie' (Edward VII) from any attempts to mediate between the combatants, Bülow, his Chancellor, was at the same time taking every advantage of Russia's predicament to extract the most favourable terms for Germany in the negotiations for the commercial treaty between the two countries signed on July 28th. In fact at this moment the British were not concerned to mediate, the French had no intention of interfering, and Germany could not close her eyes to the advantages she gained in Europe while Russia was occupied in the Far East, to say nothing of further advantages which might accrue in the future were Russia to be defeated either on land or sea. The Kaiser had of course by way of common politeness congratulated the Tsar on the bravery of his soldiers and sailors, but had said nothing, rather significantly, of the abilities of the higher command. In this at least Wilhelm showed some uncharacteristic self-control.

While the two rival armies engaged in their marching and manoeuvring the time was coming when the Russian navy at Port Arthur was to be forced into some form of activity. Alexieff, after the failure to relieve the port, was anxious that something should be done, though he was careful never to define exactly what it should be, and Admiral Vitgeft, who had confessed to his captains, 'I am no leader of a fleet', was therefore reluctantly pushed towards action. In early June a number of rather abortive naval councils had been held at which no positive decision had been reached. Meanwhile both mine-laying and mine-sweeping by both sides continued and the presence of Japanese mines provided an excellent excuse for Vitgeft's inaction. However, on June 15th Alexieff's order was read out to the senior officers, the fleet was to put to sea and engage the enemy, choosing the most favourable opportunity and taking every precaution. It was a typical Alexieff order, in that it insured against failure, but it was an order which had to be obeyed. In the next few days the *Tsarevich*, *Retvizan* and *Pobieda* (now repaired), together with the *Sebastopol* and *Poltava*, five cruisers and sixteen destroyers, were prepared and provisioned for sea. Many ships' guns had been landed ashore to help in the defences, and this secondary armament was now largely returned to its rightful place on board.

On June 20th Vitgeft issued his orders:

By order of Admiral Alexieff the squadron, having completed the repairs to the ships which were damaged by the enemy before war was declared, will now put to sea so as to afford assistance to our comrades on land in defence of Port Arthur. With the help of God and St. Nicholas, the wonder worker, who is the protector of mariners, we will endeavour to fulfil our duty loyally and conscientiously and to defeat the enemy, who have already lost some ships by striking some mines. The little gunboat *Bobr* has shown us what can be done in very difficult circumstances. May God be with us.

The plan was if possible to attack the Japanese base on the Elliott Islands, but Vitgeft's overpowering mood of pessimism and gloom did little to encourage his officers and men. In reality the Russian situation had improved somewhat in the last few weeks. On June 13th the Vladivostock squadron had again been active sinking a Japanese transport carrying the eighteen 11-inch howitzers intended to provide the heavy armament for the siege of Port Arthur. In addition, repairs to the three damaged battleships had been successfully completed and their presence in the Russian line of battle was bound to surprise the Japanese. Nevertheless Vitgeft, a fat man of melancholy visage at the best of times, boarded his flagship as if on the way to a funeral. At 5.40 a.m. on June 23rd the fleet left harbour, and by any standards it was a formidable array. Preceded by dredgers towing minesweepers and eight destroyers, there followed in line ahead the six battleships and four cruisers followed by four more escorting destroyers.

Certainly the appearance of this strong and well-balanced force was a considerable shock to the Japanese. Two days before, *The Times* correspondent in Tokyo had dismissed the Port Arthur squadron from his calculations: the harbour was so well mined, he said, that the Russians either could not or would not take to sea. Stoessel was apparently prepared to use his guns on land to blow up the ships if necessary. Now here was this derided fleet sailing out to do battle.

Immediately the destroyer *Shirakumo* watching the harbour entrance steamed off at full speed to report to Admiral Dewa off Encounter Rock. He wirelessed the signal to Togo more than 30 miles away at his base in the Elliott Islands, 'enemy fleet is leaving harbour'. Though Togo had with him only four battleships, eight cruisers and six destroyers he immediately gave orders to raise steam and at 9.50 a.m. the Japanese weighed anchor and headed for the enemy. Meanwhile wireless messages were summoning any other available vessel in the vicinity. By 2.50 p.m. the hills round Port Arthur were visible from the *Mikasa*, Togo's flagship. With him were the *Asahi*, *Fuji* and *Shikishima* and twelve cruisers. On the port side of his main battle fleet steamed all the available destroyers and torpedo boats, totalling over thirty, which had hastened to the Admiral's alarm signals. By 6 p.m. the Russians were 20 miles from Port Arthur, the Japanese were about 10 miles to their south, and at last the two fleets could see each other. Both fleets changed their bearings so that soon they were steering a parallel course about 8 miles apart. Togo determined to join battle and the *Mikasa* began to close to the Russians even though only about half an hour of daylight remained.

The dead Makaroff might have weighed the chances of destroying the main part of the Japanese Fleet against losses on his side. Vitgeft however, incredibly, would not accept the challenge and turned his fleet away and towards Port Arthur. The appearance of a Japanese fleet in such numbers and at such speed had totally disconcerted him. The prospect of a night action with Togo's torpedo boats moving in among his ironclads so completely unmanned him in fact that he preferred the perils of the 23 miles return to safety to an action which might have turned the balance of the war.

As soon as the Russians were seen to be avoiding battle Togo sent in his destroyers to harry the rear section of battleships. With great courage, almost desperation, the Japanese destroyer captains attacked at full speed again and again, discharging scores of torpedoes at close, nearly suicidal range, well below 1,000 yards.

Almost incredibly, not one hit was made, and only when the Russian Fleet was moving into the roadstead did the *Sebastopol* suddenly rock to the force of an explosion. Once again, though, the damage was inflicted by a mine, not a torpedo, but the *Sebastopol* limped on with a heavy list to port in the company of her consorts.

Eight more attacks were made by the Japanese, but with no more result than that the next day the Russians were able to collect a considerable number of torpedoes run ashore, still unexploded. They in their turn had inflicted very little damage on their adversaries, one Japanese destroyer and four torpedo boats having been hit, three sailors killed and four wounded. On shore the Russian garrison, which had watched the fleet's return, was sunk in despondency and another rift was created between soldiers and sailors. The Japanese destroyer crews were consumed by a different more honourable emotion, sheer fury at the complete failure of their many attacks. At home in Russia sentiments were well expressed by the St. Petersburg correspondent of the *Echo de Paris*:

Public opinion has not been very deeply affected by the reverses on land as it counts upon the large forces under General Kuropatkin to restore the fortune of Russian arms. It is however exasperated by the naval defeat of June 23rd, which was not even the result of a battle.

The only consolations apparent to the Russians were the continued harrying operations of the Vladivostock Squadron under Skrydloff. These consisted of raids on the Japanese coastline, the sinking of transports carrying men and armaments, nothing heroic or spectacular, perhaps, but they did ensure the permanent diversion of Kamimura's cruisers from the Port Arthur area. Skrydloff could not always count on such achievements as the destruction of the Japanese siege guns, but his activities were at least not underrated in Japan, where Tokyo crowds demonstrated outside the house of their own admiral, breaking windows and shouting that he should either come to grips with Skrydloff or commit hari-kari.

Officially, however, the Japanese oligarchy was well satisfied with its senior commanders. The promotion of Oyama on his imminent departure for the theatre of war was the opportunity to make up the successful divisional generals to the rank of full general, along with Kodama, Oyama's Chief-of-Staff. Togo and Yamamoto, the Minister of Marine, both became 'Kaigun Taisho', the highest rank in their service, roughly equivalent to Admiral of the Fleet. Rear-Admirals Uriu and Dewa were raised to Vice-Admiral. At Liaoyang at about the same time Kuropatkin distributed 250 St. George Crosses for bravery, but no Russian general, and perhaps understandably no admiral, was promoted.

On June 29th a fast Russian destroyer broke the blockade at Port Arthur to make Niewchuang and returned a few days later with more orders from the Viceroy. This time the fleet was ordered 'to put to sea in good time and make for Vladivostock, if possible avoiding an action'. This order, after the customary officers' meeting, was refused by Vitgeft on the grounds that action could not be avoided.

By July 28th, however, the necessarily complicated and time-consuming system of communications between Alexieff and Vitgeft and St. Petersburg had produced a more precise instruction. Vitgeft was now to 'take the squadron out of Port Arthur'. The order came not before time, because by then Japanese howitzers were lobbing shells into the town and the naval basin, aided at times by observation from a captive balloon. The *Tsarevich* was hit, the *Retvizan* damaged, and Admiral Vitgeft himself slightly wounded by a shell splinter.

On the same day as Vitgeft received his final set of instructions it must have been obvious to all that the 'small victorious war' so ardently desired by Plehve was not in any way living up to its expectations.

However, the Minister of the Interior was not to live to see the result of either his domestic or his foreign policies. On his way to the Baltic Station, whence he was to go to Peterhof for an audience with the Tsar, Plehve was literally blown to pieces, despite his armour-plated coach and the policemen lining the streets, by a bomb tossed into his lap by Yegor Sazonoff.

It was not insignificant that no one, not even in official circles, or among the investigating police, seemed to regret the Minister's death. Even more indicative of the crazy rottenness and incompetence of the whole Russian internal system was the fact that though Sazonoff, a Jew, had no doubt good reason to kill the organiser of the Kishinev pogrom, the assassination operation was made possible only with the active connivance of Evro Azeff, a state-employed agent provocateur.

EIGHT

'We shall meet in another world'

ADMIRAL VITGEFT

On July 27th General Nogi's 3rd Army, supported from the sea by Togo's battleships and cruisers, captured the so-called 'position of the passes', thus effectively sealing off the small Kwantung Peninsula from what might be called the 'mainland', the Liaotung Peninsula. Meanwhile to the north the Motienling pass had been taken and the 2nd Army had occupied Niewchuang, both moves bringing the Japanese nearer to Kuropatkin's headquarters at Liaoyang.

By July 30th the Russian forces in the Kwantung Peninsula had retired into the lines of Port Arthur. Up till now there had been a certain amount of movement in the war, even though it had consisted chiefly of the steady advance of Japanese armies and the complementary withdrawal of Russian ones. Although Russian generals had shown themselves almost universally inept and appallingly bad at co-operating with each other, they had possessed room and opportunity to manoeuvre. Now the two main areas of conflict were 'settling down', almost at the two extreme points of the theatre of war, Liaoyang and Port Arthur. Individual Russian regiments and commanders – and generals for that matter – had throughout shown no lack of physical courage, but there had seemed to be an almost complete lack of military planning and preparation, and an equally fatal failure to ensure any properly organised command structure. Now there was little room left for that sort of planning, the wider concepts of strategy could be forgotten, and there was little room left even for tactical manoeuvre. Especially at Port

Arthur soldiers, from general to private, could prepare themselves for a slogging match.

With this change in the mode of warfare it was noticeable that Russian performance improved. There were no victories in July for Kuropatkin to report to St. Petersburg, but resistance to the Japanese improved, vigorous counter-attacks were mounted and every position gained by the Japanese was paid for with considerable casualties. One British observer had noted that even in nearby open country Russian troops had a 'fortress mentality' about fighting, particularly apparent no doubt to the British with their experience in South Africa fresh in their minds. Now at Port Arthur the Russians need not concern themselves with the niceties of outflanking movements and the like, they could dig themselves in to fight or die.

It is not too fanciful to discern at this stage a change in the whole war which cast shadows forward to the world conflict which was to open ten years later. Certainly the foreign military observers, British, French, German, Italian and Austrian, watched each step in the present conflict with future wars in mind. However, it is unlikely that with all their expertise they could appreciate that with the next phase they were being allowed a peep into the future. From now on, many of the old concepts of soldiering could be abandoned. The cavalry, for instance, with their swords and lances, and the horse-artillery, equipped with light guns designed to be mobile enough to co-operate closely with the mounted arm, could really all be packed away like toy soldiers. It was no longer important or significant that in this area the Russians were superior, for a good seat on a well cared for horse was no longer a very significant military factor. Both sides had now cast off their smart colourful uniforms in favour of something that could provide some camouflage for its wearer. And the regimental bands too had disappeared – in the first phase of the war both Japanese and Russian battalions had charged the enemy with bands playing and colours flying. From now on even the officers' swords, the very symbol of military panache and pride, were less important than hand-grenades. Machine-guns, barbed wire, booby traps, grenades and mines were now the weapons. Round Port Arthur the Russians began to experiment with live electric currents, mines detonated by touch or electric charge and even a primitive flame-thrower. Only two weapons of the next war were absent: submarines and aeroplanes, although the Russians at home were experimenting with underwater craft and the Japanese did use a balloon for artillery spotting. Certainly there were many lessons to be learnt both from the material point of view and from the conduct of the two combatants.

The position at Port Arthur into which the Russians now withdrew was by no means a simple port and town, nor was it in the conventional sense a 'fortress'. East to west, from Shuangtan and Pigeon Bay to the outer western trenches, the distance was nearly 12 miles. North to south from the northern-most (Amtsushan) forts to the mouth of the outer harbour was some 5 miles. The southern centre of the position was the east and west harbours, shading off to the west into mud flats exposed at low tide to an area over 3 square miles. Almost the whole of the usable harbour was protected from the sea by the promontory ending in the Tiger's Tail, save for the half-mile wide gullet leading into the outer harbour mouth. North of the harbour was the New Town in which the railway terminal was sited, to the east lay the Old Town, with the main road from there leading to the north. Dotted around the whole of the town and harbour complex were the fortresses and battery sites. These were placed almost entirely on the hills and features of high ground which ringed the harbour in an almost regular formation except for the Erlungshan (Dragon's Nest) Mountains to the east which formed a continuous line of hills nearly 3 miles long.

It was on this, the eastern side of the position, that the Russians had dug and constructed trenches. Elsewhere they relied on individual fortresses and batteries. All in all the defensive system for Port Arthur fitted into no coherent pattern for reasons which went back to the time when the Russians had first taken over from the dispossessed Japanese in 1898. Originally the military engineers had planned to build six permanent fortifications for protection from attack by land, but these plans had to be modified when it was realised, rather late in the day, that on such hilly ground one fort was liable to be masked from the other by dead ground. Consequently, a number of minor 'fortifications' or 'intermediate works' were built to fill the gaps. The numbering and the manning of these two series of works was never co-ordinated. In addition, behind the fortresses a ditch 20 feet deep and 20 feet wide was excavated, and the spoil thrown up as a parapet. Despite the labour and time involved in this particular work the Russians in fact made little use of it.

Since the original planning stage in 1898 all the fortification construction had made very slow progress, partly because a large part of the available money was diverted to the construction of the civilian port at Dalny. Still, the military engineers seemed to have little sense of urgency and even at the time of the outbreak of war in February 1904, five years after their commencement, few of the fortifications were absolutely completed. With the outbreak of war, efforts were made, particularly with the siting of batteries, but some of the old Chinese works had in the end to be repaired and refurbished and pressed back into service. In addition a number of new trenches were dug round the perimeter and connected with the outlying batteries. Barbed-wire entanglements were erected wherever possible. Unfortunately, though, even with this relatively unsophisticated form of defence the Russian lack of foresight was again revealed – barbed wire was not available in sufficient quantities, so the Russians were forced to improvise and put up a series of lines of telegraph wire taken from the railway stores. The supporting posts were wooden and not iron, and therefore more difficult to embed in the rocky ground but easier for attackers to demolish. In one other respect the defences were not as strong as their face value might have indicated, again through a lack of the proper up-to-date materials, in this case iron or steel plating. The fortresses were constructed without proper reinforcement such as was by then being used in Europe to cover batteries and emplacements. The concrete used was from 3 to $4\frac{1}{2}$ feet thick, and on the coastal batteries even thicker, proof against medium artillery, certainly, but inadequate against concentrated shelling by heavy howitzers should the Japanese be able to bring them to bear.

In a sense, of course, no position is impregnable against determined and repeated attacks by a well-equipped enemy and it would be wrong therefore to think that Port Arthur, because it had certain deficiencies, was anything but a very formidable proposition indeed for the Japanese now assembling for its assault.

One other aspect of the defence of the port should however be mentioned and it provides a clearer insight into Russian military defects than any examination of shortages of materials or other lack of preparations. It was the question of the actual command of this, the most important Russian position in the war. Before the investment of Port Arthur became a certainty the Viceroy, Admiral Alexieff, had drawn up a general command structure which was adequate if not over-precise. However, with the closing in of General Nogi's 3rd Army as the Russians retreated, the situation became more complicated. The Russian field army in the Kwantung Peninsula abandoned any likely future possibility of active operations and concentrated itself within the confines of the Port Arthur position. At this time Lieutenant-General Smirnoff was the commandant of the fortress, and Lieutenant-General Stoessel the commander of the fortified zone. Technically, though, Stoessel was senior in his rank to Smirnoff and his real command was the 3rd Siberian Corps. This force was composed of the 4th East Siberian Rifle Division under Major-General Fock and the 7th East Siberian Rifle Division commanded by Major-General Kondratenko, and it was independent of the fortress troops. Within the fortress itself the artillery was the responsibility of Major-General Byeli.

When the siege of Port Arthur became imminent Kuropatkin, presumably with the concurrence of Alexieff, though possibly on his own initiative, telegraphed Stoessel on July 3rd ordering him to leave on one of the destroyers which could still manage to avoid the Japanese blockade. If he had done so the command would have rested, or rather remained, with Smirnoff. This was obviously Kuropatkin's intention as it was clear that the presence of two lieutenant-generals with ill-defined powers might easily lead to disagreement and friction. Incredibly, however, and for what reasons of his own it is difficult to surmise, Stoessel suppressed the telegram and stayed on in Port Arthur tacitly assuming the command over the head of Smirnoff.

Almost equally incredibly Kuropatkin took no further action and allowed Stoessel to remain in charge with Smirnoff as his notional subordinate.

Lower down the scale the command set-up was by no means uncomplicated, although for less curious reasons. Major-General Nikitin commanded the artillery of the 3rd Siberian Corps; but once his guns were inside Port Arthur he and all his men came under the orders of Major-General Byeli. Under Stoessel and Smirnoff Kondratenko was placed in command of all the land forces; but Byeli was not responsible to him nor apparently to Stoessel, but to Smirnoff as commander of the fortress. This division of artillery and infantry repeated itself all the way down to battery and battalion level, and there was further division on a geographical basis between eastern, northern and western sectors of the defence. Still, ammunition and food seemed plentiful, Kondratenko at least was a brave and deservedly popular commander, Stoessel had distinguished himself during the Boxer Rebellion, and the 42,000 Russians were in many ways in better heart about the coming struggle than they had been in any of the last three months of defeats, humiliations and withdrawals.

For the moment, though, the next move was not with the soldiers but the sailors, but not, let it be said, on the initiative of their immediate commander Admiral Vitgeft. Throughout late July and early August, as Japanese troops had closed in on Port Arthur and as shells (under the direction of Major-General Teshima, newly appointed 'in charge of siege artillery') had started falling in the town, the correspondence between Alexieff and Vitgeft had become more and more acrimonious. What was to be done with the fleet? Alexieff favoured a sortie so that the Port Arthur ships could link up with those at Vladivostock, and thus form a considerable force with which to harry the Japanese. No doubt he would also have liked to see an augmented fleet under the command of the active Skrydloff rather than the almost unbelievably useless Vitgeft. Certainly, he toyed with the idea of replacing Vitgeft with one of his junior flag officers. In any event the active course, any active course, was preferable to the fleet being simply bottled up and bombarded at anchor without doing anything to engage the Japanese navy at sea.

Nevertheless, just staying at anchor and contributing some of his armament to the land battle was exactly what Vitgeft did propose, backed up by his council of flag officers and captains. In their view the risks of a sortie were too great to be contemplated.

Alexieff, faced with what amounted to almost direct disobedience to his orders, appealed to St. Petersburg and the authority of the Tsar. Nicholas telegraphed to the Viceroy as follows, 'I fully share your opinion concerning the importance of the squadron making a speedy sortie from Port Arthur, and breaking through to Vladivostock.'

Meanwhile, another message had arrived at Mukden from Port Arthur, beginning, 'The squadron cannot go out', and ending, 'I have begun indirect fire on the Japanese troops.' Alexieff, reinforced by the Imperial will, would have no more of Vitgeft's attempts to avoid battle and telegraphed on 7th August as follows:

I again reiterate my inflexible determination that you are to take the squadron out of Port Arthur. I must recall to you and all serious officers the exploit of the *Varyag*. The failure of the squadron to proceed to sea regardless of the Imperial will, and of my command, and its extinction in the harbour in the event of the fall of the fortress will, in addition to the heavy legal responsibility, leave an indelible spot on the flag of St. Andrew and on the honour of the fleet. You are to make known this telegram to all admirals and commanding officers and are to report its receipt.

Faced with an order couched in these terms even Vitgeft could hesitate no longer and accordingly preparations were immediately made to take the fleet to sea on August 10th. Landed guns were replaced, stores and ammunition replenished, and steam raised. There was still however time for Vitgeft to send one last valedictory message by destroyer to Chefoo and thence to his ultimate superior:

In compliance with the commands of Your Majesty, transmitted to me by the Viceroy in a telegram, I am steaming out with the squadron in order to break through to Vladivostock. I, personally, and a conference of Flag Officers and Captains, after taking into consideration all the local conditions, were adverse to this sortie, which, in our opinion, cannot meet with success, and will hasten the capitulation of Port Arthur, which I have reported time after time to the Viceroy.

It is not difficult in military and naval history to find examples of fine words and protestations of determination being used to cover up or supplement a lack of physical force. But on August 10th, 1904 exactly the reverse situation applied, for behind the mine-sweeping flotilla at 9 a.m. on a fine but misty morning there steamed six capital ships, *Tsarevich* (flag of Rear-Admiral Vitgeft), *Retvizan*, *Pobieda*, *Peresvyet* (flag of Rear-Admiral Prince Ukhtomsky), *Sebastopol* and *Poltava*. Following these giants were three armoured cruisers, *Askold* (flag of Rear-Admiral Reitzenstein), *Pallada* and *Diana*. It was a considerable force by any standards, protected as it was by the light cruiser *Novik* and eight destroyers, adequate not only to fight its way to Vladivostock, but to do battle with any comparable Japanese Fleet.

In fact the ships which Admiral Togo was able to deploy at short notice were a match, but no more, for the Russians. Warned by his destroyer watch on Port Arthur of the appearance of the Russian Fleet, it was not until Vitgeft's command had steamed about 25 miles on its course for Vladivostock that Togo had it in sight, if not yet in range. Immediately under command the Japanese admiral had four battleships, the *Mikasa*, the *Asaki*, *Fuji* and *Shikishima*, three armoured cruisers and eight protected cruisers, with which to meet the Russian squadron of six battleships and three armoured cruisers. Later in the day other Japanese ships were to join the Admiral in answer to his signals, but for the first part of the action the fleets were approximately equal. In one respect, however, Togo seemed to have an advantage in that seventeen destroyers and twenty-nine torpedo boats were able, because of their high speed, to join him almost immediately. However, these smaller craft, although obviously outnumbering the eight Russian destroyers, were of scarcely any value while the Russian fleet was undamaged, and while daylight lasted. Only at night, or against damaged ships, dare Togo risk destroyers or torpedo boats against battleships or cruisers. Thus in main armament (12-inch guns) and secondary (6-inch) there was little to choose between the fire power of the Russians and the Japanese. The detailed breakdown was as follows: the Russians deployed 15 × 12-inch guns, 8 × 10-inch, 88 × 6-inch, and 6 × 4·7-inch; the Japanese deployed in their main fleet 20 × 12-inch, 2 × 10-inch, 14 × 8-inch, and 110 × 6-inch. In these circumstances there was only the experience of the Japanese commanders and crews to be weighed against the lack of battle experience of the Russians, plus the disadvantage suffered by ships which have been a long time idle in harbour and subject to bombardment, as had been for instance the *Retvizan*, which still shipped a considerable quantity of water owing to shell damage, and the *Tsarevich*, which had both engine and steering problems.

By about 11.30 a.m., the two fleets were some 12 miles apart, but it was not until past noon when the gap had been reduced to about 13,000 yards that the first ranging shots were fired by both sides. There followed a period of manoeuvres during which Togo tried unsuccessfully to steam his line of ships across the line of advance of the Russians. The aim was to 'cross the T', in then current naval parlance, so as to be able to concentrate the broadside of a whole fleet upon the leading ships of another. In this object Togo failed, and indeed found himself virtually unable to head Vitgeft off from the southeasterly course necessary to get him eventually to Vladivostock via the Straits of Korea.

On neither side could this have been regarded as the likely outcome after nearly two hours of engagement. No one could argue that Vitgeft was the superior Admiral, nor that the Russians' slowly executed unpractised manoeuvres were the equal of the rapid Japanese changes of course. Nevertheless, time and time again, Togo found that Vitgeft's ships were able to circle round the Japanese rear and to pursue their chosen course. On the occasions when the two fleets found themselves in the classical position of sailing on parallel opposite courses, it also became obvious that the Japanese possessed no clear superiority in long-distance gunnery, the *Mikasa* herself taking a considerable number of hits from the 12-inch guns of the *Tsarevich* and the *Retvizan*.

By 2 p.m. the dilemma for Admiral Togo was acute. The Russian fleet was now steaming at 12 to 13 knots to the southeastwards and although the Japanese battleships were capable of 14 knots the distance between the fleets was still over 10,000 yards; and while the maximum range of a 12-inch gun was 15,000 yards, nothing like accuracy could be expected beyond about half that range. It looked therefore as if there was a very good chance that the Russians would make Vladivostock. Togo could still close and fight out a duel to the death at point-blank range, bringing his cruisers into action as well as his battleships, but the cost to his own fleet was bound to be considerable, and what would then be left of the Japanese navy to face the Baltic Fleet when it arrived in Far Eastern waters?

He therefore decided upon a combination of speed, manoeuvre and long-distance gunnery. Not so decisive, not so final, but his objective was to force the Russians back into Port Arthur. For if Vitgeft escaped he had won; and again if he lost literally every ship in close action and in the process Togo lost even on a one for two basis, the Russians in the long term would still have won.

It was at this stage, therefore, that the cruisers under Rear-Admiral Dewa were put into separate play and ordered to engage their Russian counterparts. Unfortunately for them the old adage about 'ships fit to stand in the line of battle' was once again proved. The Russian battleships immediately concentrated on the enemy cruisers, especially Dewa's flagship the *Yakumo*, inflicting considerable damage. Prudently Dewa fell astern of the Russian fleet, out of range.

So the chase resumed as the sun sank lower in the sky, and only gradually did the Japanese gain on the Russians. Not until 4.30 p.m. was there any considerable change discernible in the Russian line, when the *Poltava* was seen to be lagging behind her consorts, and they slackened pace to keep company with her. The range was consequently reduced to less than 9,000 yards and every gun that could be brought to bear in each fleet was concentrated on the other. The *Poltava* was surrounded in founts of spray, but the *Mikasa* was hit again, one turret being put completely out of action. In the *Shikishima* one 12-inch gun burst and another was temporarily disabled. On board the *Asaki* two guns burst due to overheating. Again, the *Mikasa* was hit, a gaping hole blown in her starboard side only a few feet above the water-line.

Then suddenly at 6.40 p.m. there occurred what can only be described as a stroke of luck for the Japanese and of disaster for the Russians. On leaving Port Arthur Vitgeft had bade his close friends farewell, saying, 'We shall meet in another world.' Now his prophecy was fulfilled. Two 12-inch shells struck the *Tsarevich*. The first near the foot of the mainmast killed Vitgeft and his staff navigation officer and seriously wounded his Chief of Staff, Rear-Admiral Matusevich, and the Flag Captain. The second burst on the roof of the conning tower and killed or wounded every man at that vital post, including the navigator and the helmsman whose dead body jammed the wheel hard to starboard. Entirely out of control, belching smoke, the flagship lurched round in a wide full circle, nearly colliding with both the *Poltava* and the *Sebastopol*. The *Retvizan*, her captain not realising what had happened, followed the *Tsarevich* at first, and then taking in her plight steamed rapidly towards the Japanese in a gallant attempt to draw fire and allow the flagship to recover. The *Peresvyet* followed the *Retvizan*, for the same reason as the *Retvizan* had followed the *Tsarevich*, putting the Russian line in complete confusion. Of a line of six battleships two now remained on their original course, three steered to starboard and the enemy, while the flagship having turned full circle came to a halt.

Once again the task of restoring order after the death of a Commander-in-Chief fell on the shoulders of Prince Ukhtomsky, who could read the signal 'Admiral transfers the command', hoisted by the now stationary *Tsarevich*. Once again he signalled 'Follow me', to the rest of the fleet. Unfortunately, however, both topmasts of the *Peresvyet* were shot away so Ukhtomsky's flags could only be displayed on the bridge rails where they were hardly discernible. In any event, no admiral's flag was now on show on the *Peresvyet* so that some captains thought that Ukhtomsky, not Vitgeft, was killed. During this chaos the Japanese closed to a range of 4,000 yards and steaming on a parallel course fired every available gun, concentrating especially on the *Retvizan* and the *Peresvyet*, the two nearest ships. The captain of the *Retvizan* in desperation tried hard to ram the *Mikasa* and might well have succeeded had he not in his turn been struck by shell splinters. In agony he was just able to order his ship to return and conform with the rest of the squadron before he collapsed.

However, his gallant gesture had not been wasted: the *Tsarevich* was again under way, and Togo was once again reminded of the dangers of loss to his own battle fleet. The Russians were now retreating north-west back to Port Arthur, but still firing their guns. In some measure the Japanese had succeeded in their object, there would now be no breakaway to Vladivostock. The light was failing, perhaps destruction could safely be left to his overwhelming force of destroyers and torpedo boats. So all through the night these small fast ships made attack upon attack upon the limping Russian force, which now consisted of the five battleships, *Retvizan, Peresvyet, Pobieda, Sebastopol* and *Poltava*, the cruiser *Pallada* and three destroyers. To the surprise and chagrin of the Japanese not a single hit was scored and by the next morning a much relieved Russian squadron was passing safely into the inner harbour of Port Arthur.

The fate of the other Russian ships was dreary and humiliating. The *Tsarevich* was unable to keep up with her sister ships. Commander Shunoff, her senior uninjured officer, thought first of a renewed attempt at Vladivostock as she was now unmolested by the enemy. Unfortunately, however, it was soon found that her shell-torn funnels and other damage had so increased her fuel consumption that this would be impossible. Therefore with the *Novik* and three destroyers she made for the German port of Kiaochow where she and the destroyers were interned. Meanwhile the *Askold* and another destroyer made for Shanghai where they too were interned, and the *Diana* accepted the same fate at French Saigon. Most of the ships were in fact too badly damaged to do much else, as in all cases necessary repairs would have taken longer than the 24 hours allowed in a neutral port. Nevertheless, it was a humiliating end to a naval action. Only the *Novik*, after coaling at Kiaochow was capable of showing any more fight. After numerous adventures she reached the island of Sakhalin, but was cornered by the Japanese cruiser *Tshushima* while coaling at Korsakovsk. In the action which followed the 6-inch guns of the Japanese almost destroyed the Russian ship armed only with 4·7s. Finally, the

Novik was scuttled in harbour, but the captain and the crew could find some consolation in the state of their opponent which limped away holed on the water-line and with a considerable list.

So ended the last sortie of the Port Arthur Squadron. The casualties were not disproportionate, the Russians lost 74 dead and 394 wounded, the Japanese 69 killed and 131 wounded, nearly half of these being on the flagship *Mikasa*. In fact, the battle was decisive. Prince Ukhtomsky decided on his return, after a council of war, that no more attempts would be made to reach Vladivostock. This however was not known to Admiral Togo who could never quite ignore the battleships present in the fortress harbour.

Perhaps the most curious feature of the Battle of the Yellow Sea, as it came to be called, was that despite the tremendous battering inflicted on the ships engaged (15 heavy hits on the *Tsarevich*, 22 on the *Mikasa*) no battleship was sunk, nor seemingly came within any danger of sinking. Indeed, although the Russians had had one battleship, two cruisers, a light cruiser and five destroyers put out of the war by scuttling, internment and grounding, not one single ship had been destroyed by direct enemy action. Nor had the Japanese lost a vessel.

Almost equally remarkable was the failure of a large force of fast Japanese destroyers to strike with as much as a single torpedo a squadron of slow-moving, poorly handled and damaged ships on the return journey to Port Arthur.

Finally it should be noted that although the Kaiser in his usual cousinly way sympathised with the Tsar on the subject of the 'incompetence of the Port Arthur admirals', the Russian fleet had acquitted itself, once at sea and until the disastrous strike on the *Tsarevich*, much better than might have been expected.

Vitgeft's last performance had in short been nothing like as bad as his own gloomy forebodings suggested. On both sides this fact was noted and may well have affected the future conduct of the war and prolonged its duration. The Japanese remained cautious, preserving their precious battle fleet, while the Russians began to think hopefully of the possible performance of another battle fleet under an admiral more skilled and belligerent than the unfortunate Vitgeft.

NINE

'There will be nothing for me to do in the Far East by September'

ADMIRAL ROZHESTVENSKY

The primary object of Admiral Vitgeft's sortie from Port Arthur had been a link-up, with or without an action fought on the way, with the cruiser force at Vladivostock. This, of course, had not been attained, but, perhaps surprisingly considering the state of the highest councils of the Russian navy, plans had been made for the Vladivostock cruisers to 'receive' the battleships and cruisers making their way northwards from Port Arthur. In the event the failure of the Port Arthur squadron was to have unfortunate repercussions for the Vladivostock force as well. But meanwhile on August 12th there was cause for rejoicing, but not for a naval or military victory, in St. Petersburg. At Peterhof, at the fortress of St. Peter and St. Paul, at the naval base at Kronstadt and eventually all over Russia, guns boomed out a salute of 300 rounds. In his diary a delighted Nicholas wrote:

A great never-to-be-forgotten day when the mercy of God has visited us so clearly. Alix gave birth to a son at one o'clock. The child has been called Alexis.

In due form Russian soldiers and sailors fighting in the Far East were informed by special order of the day from their Commander-in-Chief of the birth of His Imperial Highness Alexis Nicolaievich, Sovereign Heir Tsarevich, Grand Duke of Russia. A month or so later Nicholas' diary was to record the baby's first haemorrhages which caused his doting parents to suspect and then have confirmed that he was a haemophiliac and therefore unlikely, even if he lived, to succeed his father.

That this domestic tragedy, a closely kept secret from the Russian people, sorely affected the dynasty-conscious Nicholas and his wife there can be no doubt. It is arguable that many later events, particularly those springing from the Tsaritsa's adulation of Rasputin, who seemed able to induce temporary 'cures' of the Tsarevich's condition, might not have occurred if Alexis had been an ordinary healthy boy.

However, the uxorious Autocrat of all the Russias had been already besotted with the trivia of domestic life before his son was born, and to suggest as some have done that the whole fate of the Romanoff dynasty and the Empire it ruled might have been different if its heir's blood had clotted in the normal way is merely to indulge in romantic fantasy. With or without a healthy successor Nicholas II was a singularly inept and shallow-minded ruler whose very qualities attracted the worst of advisers. With a healthy son he would have been no less inept and shallow-minded and his advisers no wiser.

As far back as June 20th Nicholas had presided at a meeting of one such set of advisers, the Higher Naval Board. It consisted of General-Admiral the Grand Duke Alexei Alexandrovich, Admiral Avellan, the Minister of Marine, and Admirals Niloff, Wirenius, Dubassoff and Birileff. Also present was the comparatively junior 55-year-old Rear-Admiral Zinovy Petrovich Rozhestvensky.

It was the first appearance on the stage of the Russo–Japanese War of a man whose name for a variety of reasons was later to resound round the world. At the meeting the decision was taken to send the Baltic Fleet to the Far East to relieve Port Arthur, and with the combined fleet so formed to destroy Togo and the Japanese navy.

Confidence in the success of such a project was high, at least to judge by the utterances of the chosen instrument of the Higher Naval Board. In an interview a few days later with the St. Petersburg correspondent of *Petit Parisien* Rozhestvensky didn't actually state categorically that he had orders for the Far East, but he made it clear that even if he had, 'there will be nothing for me to do in the Far East by September. The Japanese will have capitulated long before then.'

By August the Japanese showed no signs of capitulation, but

the plans for the Baltic Fleet, or as it was now called, the Second Pacific Squadron (the 1st or what remained of it being at Port Arthur), still proceeded, despite the fact that the Port Arthur squadron had been ordered to leave Port Arthur. The news of Vitgeft's failure to escape to Vladivostock, followed by the information that the fleet now returned to the beleaguered fortress was sorely diminished, struck no small blow. The next information concerned the fate of the Vladivostock cruisers.

Unfortunately, the plan by which these were to organise their movements so as to coincide with, and assist, the Russian main fleet remained general only, and no serious attempts had been made at co-ordination. Consequently, it was only on August 11th that the news reached Vladivostock by way of the destroyer *Ryeshitelni* that Vitgeft had left Port Arthur. As quickly as possible the three cruisers *Gromoboi*, *Rossiya* and *Rurik* made ready and put to sea on August 12th under the command of Rear-Admiral Jessen. But by yet another unfortunate turn of fate the news of Vitgeft's death and the return of the Russian fleet to Port Arthur arrived at Vladivostock a little after he had left. A torpedo boat despatched with the information which made his expedition pointless from the start failed to catch up with him. Maintaining a reasonably high speed the three cruisers were off the Korean coast on the parallel of Fusan by the dawn of August 14th. Jessen decided to await Vitgeft there and began to steam along the parallel.

No Russian ships of course appeared to greet their comrades, but in the afternoon four Japanese armoured cruisers were sighted. These were the *Idyamo*, *Adyuma*, *Tokiawa* and *Iwate*: about half of Kamimura's force for watching the straits, the Japanese admiral having moved to this latitude on hearing of the Russian fleet's departure from Port Arthur 24 hours before it was known at Vladivostock. What the Japanese admiral did not know was the fate of that fleet, a fact which may have influenced his subsequent course of action. Not knowing therefore if a superior Russian fleet might not appear at any minute, Kamimura behaved with considerable caution. Although superior to the Russians in both numbers and gun strengths, the total Japanese broadside being 12 × 8-inch and 27 × 6-inch as opposed to the enemy's 6 × 8-inch and 21 × 6-inch,

Kamimura elected to fight the action as far as possible at long range, often as great as 9,000 yards, at which distance Japanese superiority in marksmanship, apart from their greater number of guns, began to tell.

Admiral Jessen's squadron manoeuvred at speed and with great skill but as well as their numerical disadvantage they had to cope with the fact that the light favoured the Japanese gun-layers who had the sun behind them, making the task of spotting the fall of shell for them easy, and for the Russians correspondingly more difficult. After nearly an hour of this action the *Rurik* became the principal victim and from then on drew more and more of the fire of the Japanese cruisers. Her steering gear was disabled so that she could only be steered by use of her engines, then the engine compartment itself began to fill with water from a hit below the water-line. Both the *Rossiya* and *Gromoboi* tried most gallantly to draw fire from their sister ship, but to little avail. At the end of several such attempts the *Rossiya* had a fire aboard and both she and the *Gromoboi* had a number of guns disabled. A little after 8 a.m. the appearance of two more Japanese cruisers, the *Nanina* and the *Tabachiko*, decided Admiral Jessen's course for him: the *Rurik* must be abandoned to her fate. Accordingly the two other Russian ships set course for Vladivostock, and so continued a running fight for upwards of an hour until, rather inexplicably, Kamimura abandoned the chase. On the Japanese admiral's return to the *Nanina* and the *Tabachiko* it was to find these two cruisers still picking up survivors from the *Rurik* which had sunk at 10.20 a.m. with 170 of her crew. At 9.45 her last gun had ceased to fire, then Lieutenant Ivanoff, her senior unwounded officer, ordered the last torpedo to be fired, the Kingston valves to be opened and the ship scuttled. Of the total of her crew 625 officers and men were rescued by the Japanese, of whom 230 were wounded. Happily among these survivors was the gallant Ivanoff whose conduct was later recognised by an official notification that for the rest of his service he was to be known as 'Ivanoff trinadtzate' (13th), he being the thirteenth officer of that name in the Imperial Navy list. For the rest of the Russian navy the battle of Ulsan (so called after the Korean port near the central action) was the melancholy end to what had been regarded by all as a welcome contrast to the performance of the squadron at Port Arthur. The Vladivostock cruisers had harried the Japanese coastline and transports, and in the end succumbed gallantly to superior force. For months after the action the *Rossiya* and *Gromoboi* were too damaged to take to sea, and when they did the latter ran upon a rock and was again severely damaged. The *Bogatyr* was also damaged, and for many months only the *Rossiya* was fit to put to sea. From August 14th there was no effective Russian naval force at Vladivostock, while at Port Arthur the guns were being dismantled from the warships to assist in the land defence. If Japanese naval power were to be broken in the Far East then that task must fall upon the shoulders of Rear-Admiral Rozhestvensky, at present at St. Petersburg over 18,000 miles away, who had assumed command of the Baltic Fleet on August 12th.

At about this point in the August of 1904 it was possible to distinguish a change in the tempo and indeed the whole pattern of the war. It happened in many ways. The areas of conflict became much more closely defined. The objectives of the combatants also became clarified and at the same time individual commanders, both Russian and Japanese, became 'characters' whose decisions and personalities assumed importance.

Some part of the process was of course due simply to the mere effluxion of time. The 'style' of Kuropatkin or Kuroki for instance was now becoming familiar to the watching world. Nevertheless, the men and the measures which emerged in the late summer of 1904 were, with a few exceptions, to last for the rest of the war.

On land the two theatres of operations were around Port Arthur and Liaoyang, but with the important difference that Port Arthur had an intrinsic importance whereas Liaoyang was just where the main body of the Russian army happened to be. It was there that Kuropatkin had decided to concentrate, collecting together his steadily arriving reinforcements and abandoning altogether any projects for the relief of Port Arthur. In this decision one can discern the eclipse of the influence of Admiral Alexieff, the Viceroy. From henceforth, decisions in the military sphere were made by the General, not the Admiral, although it was too early yet to banish Alexieff entirely from the councils of the Russians in the Far East. Nor would it be right to think that Kuropatkin, relatively free from Alexieff's selfish indecision, was now about to embark upon an offensive policy. On the contrary, he had shown himself an extremely cautious general. If a parallel could be found in Russian military history it was not with Skoboleff, his former chief, the dashing victor over the Eastern tribesmen, but Kutuzoff, who retreated beyond Moscow in 1812 saying 'so long as we keep a force capable of resisting the enemy we can hope to end the war satisfactorily'. For all his confident words before the war, Kuropatkin now thought in terms of withdrawal along his line of communications as far back as Mukden or Harbin, far beyond his present position at Liaoyang. Like Kutusoff he was prepared to fight a war by ordering a retreat.

This meant inevitably the death knell to any hopes which might still have been entertained in Port Arthur that that garrison would be relieved by the Russian army to the north. Kuropatkin was only prepared to stand and do battle against the armies of Generals Oku, Nozu and Kuroki if he had a considerable advantage numerically, and even with reinforcements he was not prepared to take further risks by trying to break through to the south.

To many, no doubt, Kuropatkin's caution, to call it no worse, was a surprise and a disappointment. Even by the fairly undemanding standards of Russian generalship better might have been expected from one who until the outbreak of war had occupied the key post of Minister of War. Kuropatkin has often been accused of being much more of a theoretician than a leader of men in action, and there was a good deal of truth in the criticism. His original dispositions before battle seemed reasonable, but once that battle was joined he appeared unable to adapt and change to carry the action to a successful conclusion. Further, he seemed unable to appreciate that his reverse formations were meant to be used in battle, not kept out of harm's way until the battle was lost, possibly because of their non-employment, by which time it was too late to use them.

However it must in fairness be remembered that the instrument to his hand was by no means a perfect one. From the dry

factual reports of the various British officers who were observers with the Russians there emerges a picture of an army
which for a variety of reasons had failed to keep up with the
times and which had in addition tolerated inefficiencies peculiar
to itself. The cavalry in general was described as 'pretty well
worthless', the furnishing of inaccurate reconnaissance reports
being a particular criticism. The Cossacks, with some exceptions in favour of particular regiments, were dismissed as an
'undisciplined yeomanry'. Overall, 'Russian military intelligence
and reconnaissance duties were badly performed prior to, and
during, 1904, chiefly owing to defects in the national character,
which are not likely to be eradicated.' This of course was a general observation, affecting everyone from the highest commander
downwards. On more particular matters, only the quality of the
Russian artillery and their field kitchens received praise. Their
use of their guns was not singled out for commendation,
especially in comparison with the Japanese who were adept at
both concealment and counter-battery work: the Russians' use
of field artillery was no better than their use of smaller arms, of
which it was said, 'The Russians do not understand how to
make the best use of machine-guns'.

Attention to detail was obviously not a Russian characteristic
and this was particularly apparent in matters which touched
the soldiers' welfare. 'Supplies and baggage were not well
organised'; pay, which was just enough to keep a private in
cheap tobacco, did not arrive regularly. Mail, and there was not
a great deal in an army which had a very high proportion of
illiteracy, was dealt with most carelessly, although the personnel
and facilities were available for a much better service. The
soldier received most of his information and news from reading,
or having read to him, one of two newspapers, *The Harbin
Messenger* and *The Messenger of the Manchurian Army*, both
official organs which were so exaggerated in tone as to lose all
credence with even the simplest soldier.

Perhaps, however, welfare services were less important to the
Russian army than others, for, said one observer, 'there is no
more enduring, patient being, I believe, than the Russian
soldier'. He went on, 'He does not grumble or criticise, and
bears all the hardships, many of them unnecessary ones, which

are incidental to a campaign, with great fortitude. He was severely tried in 1904.' The same observer later on in his report said that 'excluding the Cossack, who owing to lack of training perhaps is of very poor stuff, the Russian soldier has many admirable military qualities, actual or potential, but he wants much better leadership. Nevertheless, he is a very dangerous enemy'.

The latter observation was true. The individual Russian soldier was obedient, hardy and brave, a fact that the Japanese were often to underestimate, but he was rarely given an opportunity by his leaders to exercise these qualities. He suffered excessive casualties in almost every engagement in which he fought but 'the heavy losses showed how stubborn and tenacious the Russian soldier is, good leadership and good training being what were lacking'. Time and time again the British observers came back to this question of leadership and training, the latter inevitably being dependent to a large extent on the former.

The effects of bad leadership and poor training were remarked in the Russians' poor rifle shooting and in many other ways, for instance in the comment that 'the endurance of the Russian soldier in marching is remarkable, but better order could be kept. Neglect of this on the part of the officers caused the men to suffer needless fatigue and upset calculations concerning movements.' Russian non-commissioned officers (as Kipling observed, 'the backbone of the army is the non-commissioned man') were recognised on the other hand by the British as being nearly all of high quality: 'there were of course cases of neglect of duty, but one can scarcely blame N.C.O.s for imitating sometimes the example set them by their superiors. The Russian N.C.O.s suffer in fact like the men, from being badly commanded.'

It was Napoleon who said, 'there are no bad soldiers only bad officers', and the deficiencies of the Russian officer corps naturally engaged the attention of the British observers and those of other nations as well.

The career structure was both antiquated and inefficient. Promotion for officers without 'connections' was slow in the extreme, while members of the nobility and Guards officers (frequently the categories were synonymous) raced gaily up the ladder of promotion, avoiding regimental duty as much as possible in the process, but managing to seize upon nearly all the available staff jobs and honorific posts such as those of generals' A.D.C.s, orderly officers and the like. Staffs were in any event grossly overloaded with virtual passengers and hangers-on of all descriptions, none of them remarkable for efficiency even in the few military duties which they had to perform. Guards regiments were commanded by major-generals, with full colonels as battalion commanders; provided that the Guards officer could rise above captain (the rank of major did not exist in the Russian army) he was assured of high rank at a comparatively early age, so that he could be a full colonel at forty. When the Manchurian campaign opened the Guards Corps was full of young senior officers with little or no experience of regimental soldiering. Many were posted to the east to command Siberian and Cossack regiments with which they were totally unfamiliar, with often near calamitous results. Further, the chain of command in the Russian army above brigade and in some cases regimental level was nearly non-existent, and very few officers of the Russian army were capable or experienced enough to command large bodies of men, not in formalised manoeuvres, but in actual warfare.

Officers were certainly brave, often foolhardily so, and, strangely perhaps in view of the numerous defeats and retreats, still confident of their own and their men's invincibility. Indeed, even the cautious and indecisive Kuropatkin, often thwarted as he was by the inadequacies of the staff and command, was recorded as being still supremely confident that victory could be gained solely by the superb qualities of his rank and file. Perhaps the most eloquent observation on the qualities of the Russian officer, because indirect, was made by a British military observer: 'A great struggle, such as the present one', he wrote, 'requires the employment of a large number of reserve officers, and it might naturally be expected that these would, for some time, be less efficient than their comrades on the active list. Yet there was little, if anything, as a matter of fact, to choose between them.' Their general attitude was epitomised in a later sentence in the same report. 'Many of them (both regular and reserve) were no doubt heartily tired of the war, but they had,

I believe, no doubt about Russia's ultimate victory without any special effort on their part.'

This then was the army which was preparing to stand its ground around Liaoyang under its Commander-in-Chief, and which within the fortified position of Port Arthur was awaiting siege under the yet untried, but disturbingly erratic, Major-General Stoessel.

The enemy they both expected was, in the north, the three converging armies of the courageous Oku, the daring Kuroki, and the more easy-going Nozu, and in the south one army commanded by the grey implacable Nogi, all under the direction of the calm, impassive, almost stolid Marshal Oyama, who sat spider-like at the centre of his web.

TEN

'Our men never flinched'

GENERAL KUROKI

In the *Field Service Regulations* issued to, and no doubt studied by, British staff officers in 1904, a booklet which contained much terse, almost Napoleonic, guidance, there occurs the sentence 'Detailed, accurate and timely information about the enemy and the theatre of operations is essential to success in war.'

General Baron Nogi, commanding the 3rd Japanese Army before Port Arthur, was prepared apparently to ignore such good advice. Despite the superiority of his spy and information service he was almost indifferent to the real state of the Port Arthur defences. In 1894 he had commanded the brigade which had charged into the citadel of the town when it had been held by the Chinese. Now he was prepared in effect to do the same thing again, but on a much larger scale. Admittedly, the defences of Port Arthur were, as he no doubt knew, not thoroughly systematised nor in some cases completed; but they were a very different proposition from what they had been ten years before. Russians were very different soldiers from Chinese, and the range and power of both artillery and infantry weapons had increased considerably since 1894.

However, none of these considerations seemed to be of any great significance to the Japanese commander. He said that he was prepared to lose a division in the assault, and his army knew it. War correspondents remarked on the fact that though the 3rd Army had suffered considerably from sickness, mainly beri-

beri, the Japanese private soldier seemed as confident of success, and as prepared to accept sacrifices, as his commander.

The army under his command was divided into three, on its right wing the 1st Division, in the centre the 9th Division and on the left the 11th Division. In reserve were held two independent brigades and six spare regiments (18,000 men) but these were, in contrast to the Russian system, under the direct control of General Nogi himself. The plan to which they would conform was relatively uncomplicated. Wangtai in the centre of the north-eastern sector was the objective. From Wangtai a wedge was to be driven between the fortifications and then a general advance mounted towards the New Town area of Port Arthur. Even if the town were not captured by these means the Japanese were confident of taking Wangtai peak which commanded a view of almost every part of the harbour. From that point artillery fire could be directed on the Russian fleet. In addition, the best artillery positions from the Japanese point of view were to be found in the hills in this sector.

The only subtlety allowed was that the 1st Division's attack should be a feint, possibly to delude the Russians into thinking that their enemy was following the same plan as in 1894, and to enable the 9th Division to advance in the centre to capture the two Panlung forts *en route* to Wangtai. Minor fortifications and entrenchments were to be overrun or bypassed.

It was perhaps the latter instruction which revealed to the full Nogi's intention to ignore the advice set out in the British Field Service Regulations. The terrain round Port Arthur was hilly in the extreme, and totally irregular. Valleys were frequently filled with millet crops over 6 feet tall, or else led nowhere. The Russians had not been either consistent or particularly skilful in 'filling in' the landscape with fortifications, but the point is that they had been filled in, with anything from proper masonry forts to mere barbed-wire entanglements. Everywhere there was an obstacle of some kind which could hold up advancing infantry, so that they became the target for artillery, machine-gun or rifle fire. This was the very antithesis of open country through which infantry could advance at speed. Perhaps the Japanese commander and his subordinates, especially his artillery specialist General Teshima, thought that both obstacles and the Russian garrison could be reduced by preliminary artillery bombardment. This was not possible, but that lesson many World War I generals were not to learn by 1918, after four years of concentrated trench warfare. Even with many more batteries of artillery and a more sustained barrage it is extremely doubtful if the Japanese could have so pulverised both defence works and the men in them as to adjust the odds between dug-in and protected Russians, and their own advancing infantry with no protection save that afforded by chance by the lie of the land.

Although for almost a week there had been relatively small-scale actions between besiegers and defenders, each one tending to bring the Japanese nearer to the main Port Arthur defences, it was not until the morning of August 19th that the real attack began. It opened with a general bombardment by all available Japanese batteries. The Russian guns replied, but were at a considerable disadvantage, as the Japanese had gone to some trouble to site and conceal their artillery pieces in the folds of ground and among the millet crops; whilst the Russians were inevitably exposed in fortresses and emplacements. Among the first casualties on the Russian side were the two 6-inch naval guns mounted in the Wangtai battery itself, most of the crews being killed or wounded and the guns themselves damaged beyond repair.

The first infantry attack was against the so-called Waterworks Redoubt, a battalion of the 19th Regiment moving in single lines of 80 men advancing with three paces between each man. The battalion got to within 250 yards of the Redoubt and occupied an advanced trench abandoned by the Russians. Then came the real task, the advance from that trench under withering rifle fire from the Russians. Of the first 180 men out of the trench only 30 advanced more than a few yards towards the enemy. Elsewhere the Japanese found themselves in the same difficulty. Despite fanatical courage they were simply unable to get sufficient men across stretches of open ground to engage the Russians' real line of defence. Despite the object lesson of the Waterworks Redoubt virtually the whole of Nogi's army went into the attack between August 20th and 23rd, getting what cover it could from the water courses, ravines and valleys and the millet crops. Special squads of men armed with insulated wire cutters attempted to remove barbed and electric-wire entanglements. The Japanese artillery did its best to reduce the defences in front of its advancing infantry.

The Russians replied with every armament they possessed, in some cases field-guns firing shrapnel virtually point blank into the advancing masses, but the majority of Japanese casualties were caused by simple but devastating rifle and machine-gun fire. The ground in front of the Russian lines was already soggy from recent rain, and more rain fell during the nights of the 20th and 21st, so that soon the approaches and the defences were a morass of mud, blood and bodies, the living trying to make their way over the bodies of their dead comrades. During the nights the Russians made considerable use of magnesium flares and searchlights to pick out bodies of troops. By day hundreds of Japanese corpses could be seen littering the slopes leading to the Russian defences. Finally Japanese senior commanders lost touch with their subordinates and company commanders so that subalterns simply led their men in the general direction of the enemy.

Somehow or other, despite numerous counter-attacks by the Russians, the Japanese did manage to capture the two Panlung redoubts, East and West, and to retain them throughout the fighting. However, by August 27th when all significant fighting had ceased, the capture of these two unimportant positions was all they could claim in exchange for casualties amounting to over 15,000 officers and men. It now only remained for both sides under cover of darkness, for there were no truces arranged, to bury the vast amount of stinking, putrefying corpses which covered the open ground between the Japanese and Russian lines.

General Nogi had lost his division, but to no purpose, for he had not captured Port Arthur by direct assault. Having at heavy cost learnt its lesson, the Japanese High Command now realised that Port Arthur would only yield to a prolonged siege and that at least on the defensive Russian soldiers could fight just as stubbornly and bravely as Japanese.

Almost at the same time as the last furious Japanese attacks were petering out in a confusion of slaughter and weariness,

Oyama, realising that there was now no possibility of assistance from the 3rd Army, was making his anticipatory moves towards his first clash with Kuropatkin at Liaoyang, 200 miles from Port Arthur.

As the two commanders-in-chief faced each other, the British dictum about 'detailed accurate and timely information about the enemy' was again relevant, this time to the disadvantage of the Russians. For Kuropatkin, from the beginning to the end of the battle which was just about to begin, was convinced that he was considerably outnumbered by the Japanese. In particular he believed that the Japanese 9th Division, in fact in front of Port Arthur, was with the 1st Army, and that the 8th Division was with the 4th Army, when in fact it was still in Japan. Thus what can only be called Kuropatkin's customary caution as a general was reinforced by a totally false fear of being overborne by simple masses of numbers, when the reality was that he commanded 150,000 Russians to Oyama's 125,000.

The impending battle also had other peculiarities. In addition to being the first time that Oyama and Kuropatkin had each controlled the various sections of their armies, this was also their first real trial of strength on ground chosen equally by both sides. Liaoyang had for a considerable time been the place where Kuropatkin had decided to assemble his main force and collect his reinforcements, and at the same time it was the point at which Oyama had planned to concentrate the converging movements of his three armies. Hitherto there had always been excuses available for the defeats inflicted upon Russian arms. Previously too, such defeats had been passed over either as being of little importance, or as 'planned withdrawals'. Unconvincing as these explanations sounded they did contain an element of truth, in the sense that none of the previous battles could be really singled out individually as being decisive, but there could now be no doubt of the importance of the battle about to be fought round the town of Liaoyang and along the river Taitzu.

The walled town of Liaoyang, with its 60,000 inhabitants and an enormous concentration of Russian war material and supplies, occupied a commanding position on the main railway line running south to north from Port Arthur to Liaoyang, and thence to Mukden and on to Harbin, the junction with the main line running eastwards to Vladivostock. The north–south line was of course Kuropatkin's main line of communication, supply and reinforcement. Just north of Liaoyang flowed the Taitzu river, one of the tributaries of the Liao river which flowed down into the gulf of Liaotung, almost at right angles with the railway. In the dry season the Taitzu was a broad meandering river, varying in width from 70 to 600 yards but in depth being little over 4 feet and consequently fordable in many places. However, rain had fallen almost continuously from August 7th to 17th so that by August 18th the river was a raging torrent nearly 20 feet in depth and a considerable barrier to any army.

Taking therefore the river and the railway line as a cross, with Liaoyang almost at their point of intersection, the Russian armies were concentrated in the south-eastern segment. The armies were divided into two main groups, the southern extending down the railway line under Lieutenant-General Zarubayeff, who had not been noticeably enterprising in previous actions, and the eastern under the command of Lieutenant-General Baron Bilderling, an elderly cavalry martinet with a ferocious white forked beard who had arrived from Europe on July 20th. Between these two major groups there existed a gap of some 12 to 13 miles covered by a cavalry screen.

The Japanese armies could also be divided into two groups: to the east was assembled General Kuroki's 1st Army, while to the south-west of Liaoyang were both the 2nd and 4th armies. In a rather similar way to the Russian, the gaps between the main armies (in this case of nearly 25 miles) was filled and protected by the Japanese 1st Cavalry Brigade and lines of communication were protected by the Guard 'Kobi' (Reserve) Brigade. Just before the battle, reinforcements arrived for both sides: on August 10th the 5th Siberian Army Corps began to detrain at Mukden while almost at the same time the 11th Kobi Brigade arrived from Japan.

The intentions of the two opposing commanders were typical of their national and military attitudes: Kuropatkin was once again determined to fight a defensive action, while Oyama was prepared to take the risk of commencing the attack and concentrating his armies in the face of the enemy. The risk of course was that the Russians might move against any of his armies separately before they could concentrate, but his calculation was that the Russians would lack such enterprise and react to his own moves in their usual sluggish manner. He hoped to push back the Russians from their advanced positions and thus concentrate his own forces in front of their main positions. It was this task which occupied the first three days of the battle, from August 23rd to 26th. The conditions both of weather and terrain at Liaoyang were very similar to those before Port Arthur, so once again the sturdy Japanese infantry advanced in their solid columns through dense fields of millet, sometimes so high as to hide marching soldiers completely, only the heads of the mounted officers showing over the crops to indicate the movement of companies and battalions.

For their part the Russians awaited attack in Liaoyang itself, and their three lines of defensive positions protecting the town stretched for nearly 40 miles, from Anshan on the railway to the south-east to the heights overlooking the Tang river (a tributary which flowed from the south into the Taitse roughly parallel to the railway almost 30 miles away).

General Kuroki's 1st Army was the first to make a move. Its left wing advanced against the centre of the Russian position while to the right three columns stormed the positions held by the Russian left. Now Kuroki was arguably the most able, but certainly the most reckless, of the Japanese generals facing Kuropatkin. Kuroki was a 'pusher' and so the Russian command should have known and made allowances accordingly. However, once again the feeble nature of the Russian command structure was revealed. Kuroki's admittedly furious attacks, especially with the Imperial Guard Division, put all the Russian generals into a panic, lest their whole position be outflanked. Kuropatkin was persuaded to order a withdrawal from the Russian outlying positions closer in to Liaoyang. So almost at the outset the Japanese were allowed to score a moral victory. Once again Russian troops, having been told that they would resist the enemy, were very soon afterwards ordered to retreat. Indeed the situation was even worse than the ordinary Russian private soldier knew, for originally Kuropatkin had planned to attack the Japanese from his most forward positions to prevent the concentration of their armies, possibly even to defeat one army in isolation and advance southwards to the relief of Port Arthur. Certainly this was the course proposed by Admiral Alexieff and favoured by St. Petersburg. It was one to which Kuropatkin had at least rendered lip service when he had talked of the advantages which would be his in August when he would have received his reinforcements. However, there was always a difference of view between Kuropatkin at Liaoyang and Alexieff at Harbin; and there was always also an element of caution and a lack of precision about any of the general's plans and orders, which seemed to guarantee that his actual performance would lag well behind his promises. Perhaps as the man on the spot, cognisant of the deficiencies of the Russian army, he was right not to be too venturesome; but one is left nevertheless with an uneasy feeling that Kuropatkin may have filled his post at the War Office well enough, but that as a field commander he lacked staying power.

By chance most of the foreign war correspondents attached to the Japanese were with Kuroki's army and all gave graphic accounts of the Japanese infantry throwing off their tunics in the sweltering wet weather, and advancing recklessly over the hilly ground towards the Tang. As usual they appeared quite indifferent to casualties. Led by their officers and N.C.O.s carrying the banner of the Rising Sun they frequently outran their own artillery. By the night of August 25th the Russian centre position, which had been held by 60,000 men, had caved in, and the next day and night the artillery emplacement at Hanshaling was stormed and the guns captured. Even Kuroki was stirred by this last operation, for abandoning his usual terse style, he reported as follows: 'The moonlight enabled the enemy to detect our advance and exposed us to a heavy fire. The enemy was also able to roll down rocks from the summit of the hills, whereby many were killed or wounded. Nevertheless, our men never flinched. They scaled the steep hill and charged into the enemy's lines, suffering heavily.'

At about this point General Bilderling panicked and informed the Commander-in-Chief that the river Tang, behind his back, was still rising and that he feared that he and his men would be cut off. What truth there was in this it is difficult to judge. Certainly the Russians to the east of the Tang were being defeated in no uncertain manner. In any event, there were bridges over the river which were soon being used by the Russian infantry, while the cavalry were able to ford the river with few casualties.

The correspondent of *The Times* describing the ending of the first stage of the battle on the afternoon of August 27th, wrote:

At five o'clock the wind caught the curtain which was hiding the landscape, and by a sudden movement tossed it aside, displaying to my gaze a scene worthy of the great wars of the last century. Between two deep rifts in the hills the front of the broad valley containing the Tang ho could be seen. On the far side stood glistening thousands of white tents, and the great baggage train stretching westwards into the hills. Tents were falling fast, and being piled on wagons by the feverish efforts of a host of ant-like figures. Fronting the narrow bridge was a black mass of troops and baggage, and conveying it from different valleys in front of us were long transport trains, besides columns of artillery, cavalry and infantry. The Russian forces were in full retreat.

At this stage Colonel Repington remarked significantly that 'the retreat was conducted in perfect order and evidently planned beforehand'. So by the 28th the Russian forces were on the west bank of the Tang and the Japanese on the east. Once again the Russians were entrenched in prepared positions, the Japanese in the open. Nothing daunted, the Japanese began to advance, wading into the river up to their waists and then their shoulders. Some were swept off their feet by the current and disappeared, many more fell under the hail of rifle fire which peppered the water, but the survivors continued to struggle towards the Russian lines a mile back from the river.

Elsewhere, along the whole of the Liaoyang front, the Russians resisted sturdily but here under the eyes of the foreign correspondents they broke. *The Times* correspondent described their conduct as 'pusillanimous' and later, 'I heard a foreign attaché say when he saw the Russians running that it made him ashamed for white men.' This time the retreat became a rout assisted by as much artillery as the Japanese could bring to bear. By nightfall on August 28th they were established on the eastern bank

of the Tang whilst the Russians were hurrying as best they
could towards the outskirts of Liaoyang.

So far as the two other Japanese armies under Oku and Nozu
were concerned, they certainly profited by Kuroki's victory.
Like him they had been opposed by Russians in dug-in positions and like him they had suffered considerable numbers of
casualties. However, they met tougher resistance and made
scarcely any progress. Suddenly the defeat on the Tang trans-
formed the situation and to their surprise both Oku and Nozu
realised that the enemy were retreating from positions from
which they seemed to be in little danger of being dislodged.
Correspondents with the Russian army testified to the ordinary
soldiers' disappointment and resentment as they retreated,
admittedly in good order, from a battle which they had thought
they were winning. Apparently their Commander-in-Chief
thought otherwise.

On August 29th the second phase of the battle began. Marshal
Oyama planned that Kuroki's army should slow down and consolidate, while those commanded by Oku and Nozu should
co-operate in what was to be essentially a frontal attack upon
the whole Russian position. General Kuroki's army was not to
be entirely idle, however, as his left wing was to co-operate with
Nozu's right, while his right wing was to reconnoitre possible
fords and crossing places of the Taitse. In a very real sense
Oyama was indifferent to the capture of Liaoyang itself, despite
its value as a communication centre, arsenal and store: what he
sought was the surrounding and destruction of the whole
Russian army. Just over thirty years ago the Germans, the
tutors of the Japanese army, had achieved just such a victory
over the French at this very time of year. What Oyama wanted,
and saw himself within sight of accomplishing, was a Far
Eastern Sedan.

Liaoyang was protected to the south in a semicircle by the
Shushan hills, which had been utilised by the Russians as their
line of defence. The Japanese were now advanced up to that
defensive line, so that the town was surrounded to the south
by Japanese armies, the semicircle terminating at both ends
where it met the Taitse which crossed the position laterally.
Below Liaoyang, to the east, the river was unfordable; to the

west towards Kuroki's position this was a matter which would have to be investigated and possibly attempted before the Russian army could escape to the north along the line of the railway towards the Yentai coal mines and thence to Mukden.

Since the main object from Oyama's point of view was the destruction of the Russian army, the processes of encirclement and attack had to be continued simultaneously. If Kuroki advanced too quickly there was always the danger that Kuropatkin, sensing the trap closing round him, would decamp his whole army; so Oku and Nozu had to attack and hold Kuropatkin to the battle in the centre.

Consequently this phase of the battle opened with an all-out attack by the Japanese against the bristling defences of the Shushan hills. Day and night for three days they continued their attack until the slopes of the hills were strewn with Japanese corpses, whole companies were wiped out, battalions halved and some regiments had as many as three successive commanding officers killed in a day. Supporting artillery fire sometimes rained down on the troops it was meant to assist, leading to rumours on the Russian side that Japanese commanders were shelling their own men for not advancing quickly and bravely enough.

The Russians themselves, no doubt aided by an observation balloon, appreciated full well what the Japanese were attempting; but somehow Kuropatkin was never able to use his resources to the full, whether because of a breakdown in communications or because of a reluctance to use his last reserves it is difficult to judge. Finally, on August 31st, the Japanese breasted the crests of the hills and were able to look down at last on Liaoyang. At their feet flowed the Taitse and among the trees and green millet crops could be seen the walls and houses of the city, rising above them its famous pagoda, dedicated to the eight incarnations of Buddha.

To the north stretched the gleaming lines of the railway.

At almost the same time as the men under Oku's and Nozu's command gained their first sight of their objective, Kuroki's right and northern columns crossed the Taitse with the aid of pontoons and began to engage the Russian infantry on the northern side of the river.

On the night of August 31st Kuropatkin gave his orders to evacuate the final positions south of Liaoyang and then the town itself. Perhaps with good sense he decided not to create a minor Port Arthur in the north, and despite the height and thickness of its walls dismissed the idea of attempting to hold out in the town. About 30,000 Russian troops gallantly contested each yard of ground while ammunition dumps, stores and railway equipment were exploded and destroyed, and to the north of the town began what was in fact a race between Russians and Kuroki's Japanese for the railway and the line of communications. It was at this stage that at last the intrepid Japanese infantry to the south of Liaoyang began to show signs of flagging, an occurrence which makes one wonder what would have happened if Kuropatkin had possessed that extra ounce of resolution that might have pushed him for once towards the more dangerous course of standing and risking his armies, rather than the safer one of retreating and saving them.

However 'all the troops destined to take the offensive' Kuropatkin's own words were now, battalion by battalion, pulled out of their positions and ordered to join the slow trudge north. This operation, as a rear-guard action, was carried out in good order, but it is only right to point out that much of its success was due to the fact that the soldiers of Generals Oku and Nozu, having in 50 hours made four general attacks, each one of which had been repulsed with heavy losses, were quite incapable of taking any advantage of the Russians' movements.

The Times correspondent described their condition:

I returned to the bivouac over the battlefield through acres of millet, where the Japanese infantry had been mown down in hundreds. Already twenty or thirty columns of smoke showed where the Japanese dead had been collected for cremation. I visited several dressing stations of the field hospital. All were filled to double their capacity. The victims were cheerful, glorying in their wounds. The hospital arrangements were splendid, but the position was taken at a terrible cost. The casualties of the Japanese five divisions at the lowest computation were not less than 10,000 and probably were more, for owing to the crops many wounded were not found and must have died miserably, while many bodies will never be found until the crops are cut.

The Russian Commander-in-Chief left Liaoyang on September 2nd at eight in the morning, his special train joining those which were conveying military stores and wounded towards Yentai. At the same time his unwounded troops marched to the same rendezvous by the road which ran almost parallel to the railway track.

By September 1st the whole of the Russian army which could march or ride was north of the Taitse. The Japanese, contrary to their usual practice, ignored the bonds of discipline and sacked and pillaged what was left in Liaoyang after the last Russian regiment, the 10th Siberian Rifles, had indulged in an orgy of looting and violence as a last farewell to what they rightly surmised was a hostile Chinese population. The next three days of September were taken up on Kuropatkin's part by a desperate attempt to mount a counter-attack against Kuroki's forces pressing upon him from the east. The Russian hoped both to protect the Yentai coal mines and possibly to roll back Kuroki's troops from his own lines of communications. However, the manoeuvre of swinging round a whole army that had been retreating northwards in column, to an attack westwards in line, was quite beyond the resources of the Russian army. General Orloff, who was given charge of the Yentai operation, failed miserably, and was eventually returned wounded to St. Petersburg in virtual disgrace, although he had been given what was probably an impossible task and a force of inexperienced reservists with which to accomplish it.

By September 4th Kuropatkin had realised that he could not in fact mount his offensive against Kuroki, and that general had realised that with the troops at his command he could not hope alone to defeat or even outflank the whole of the Russian army.

So the battle of Liaoyang petered out on what must be regarded as an inconclusive note. The Russians continued their withdrawal north towards Mukden and Kuroki swung northwards in what was in fact a rather half-hearted pursuit. Behind him Oku and Nozu consolidated their position at Liaoyang, where Marshal Oyama soon took up his headquarters, and counted their booty of 3,000 rifles, a million rounds of small arms ammunition, over 7,000 shells, and a considerable number of artillery pieces. The total of casualties in the three Japanese armies amounted to over 5,000 dead and 18,000 wounded. The Russian losses were 2,000 dead and 13,000 wounded.

Perhaps the last word on the battle lies with the Russian Minister of War. Kuropatkin, in correspondence with him a few days after the battle, objected to the word 'defeat' and received the following chilling reply:

According to generally accepted terminology the side which attains its object, at whatever cost, has won a victory; while the side which fails to do so has suffered a defeat. At Liaoyang our army fought steadfastly with the obvious purpose of repelling the enemy on the Liaoyang position . . . which had been strongly defended for the purpose, and where the whole army was concentrated. In the event, we did not attain the object aimed at . . . were compelled by force of arms to relinquish it. Consequently, we suffered a defeat.

To their Commander-in-Chief the Tsar sent the following message which was read out to all ranks:

I see from your report that you were unable to hold the fortress of Liaoyang owing to the enemy threatening to cut off your communications. The retreat of the whole army in such difficult circumstances and over the terrible roads was an operation excellently carried out in face of grave difficulties. I thank you and your splendid troops for their heroic work and their continued self-sacrifice. God guard you. *Nicholas.*

ELEVEN

'Think at every hour of the defence of Russia's dignity'

GENERAL KUROPATKIN

In Tokyo on receipt of the news of Liaoyang great crowds formed in the streets, bands played patriotic songs and in the eyes of foreign correspondents at least it looked as if for a moment the staid, undemonstrative Japanese were about to imitate their British allies when four years before they similarly had thrown off their customary public reserve and rioted through their capital on hearing of the relief of Mafeking.

Among the uncomplimentary cartoons of a fleeing Kuropatkin and the fire-crackers, there was however a note of disappointment discernible, and not only because many in the crowd were holding aloft paper lanterns originally designed to celebrate the news of the fall of Port Arthur. The official communiqué as well as alluding to the heavy casualties had deliberately avoided any suggestion that the Russian army had been destroyed. The net had been spread but the main catch had escaped. Kuropatkin still possessed an army of 200,000 men, the Port Arthur fleet was still in existence, the port had not fallen and the news of the departure of another Russian fleet from Europe was daily expected. Rightly did the Japanese Emperor's message stress that the end of the war might still be far distant.

After nine months there were considerable grounds for disappointment among the Japanese, whether the ordinary man in the street or one of the inner council of statesmen and soldiers who directed the war. In a way they had experienced too many half victories too early. At all stages, the invasion of Korea and then Manchuria, the landings on the Kwantung Peninsula and the investment of Port Arthur, the Russians had given way; at sea the enemy had suffered losses and avoided battle; and yet the Japanese could not point, either on land or at sea, to one overwhelming victory. It was in their temperament and the relics of the old Samurai warrior culture to think in terms of one all-out effort, indifferent to casualties or consequences, which would result in triumph or glorious death. Theirs was a psychology of extremes, encountered in other brave but melancholic peoples, such as the Norsemen for instance, and it was to manifest itself in their subsequent history. In 1904 it was a matter for chagrin that they could count enormous casualties, point to many acts of almost suicidal valour as well as instances of entirely fortuitous good luck which had come their way, review their meticulous planning and organisation, and yet be forced to acknowledge that despite all their efforts the Russians were still undefeated and could win the war.

Speed was still of the essence of the campaign so far as the Japanese were concerned; Russia could not be defeated nor apparently be worn down by a long war, which in any event the Japanese could not sustain either economically or militarily. The only hope was to inflict upon the enemy in the Far Eastern theatre such signal defeats as to make his continuance of his presence there seem no longer worth while. The Tsar not only in public, but in private conversations, for instance with the British admiral, Prince Louis of Battenberg, at the festivities in connection with the Tsarevich's christening, had evinced his determination to fight if necessary 'to the last soldier', but presumably there were limits. Would the Russians, indeed could the Russians, think in terms of recapturing Port Arthur after it had once fallen?

Still, although the Japanese suffered from depressions and disappointments no one could accuse them of lack of determination. Even during the course of the fighting in and around Liaoyang new developments were taking place in the planning and organisation and conduct of Nogi's 3rd Army at Port Arthur. Plainly the straight infantry assault would not carry the defences, therefore Nogi's men would have to be converted into a siege force, digging, mining and exploding the fortress, emplacement by emplacement, in the time-honoured manner which had not been seen on any large scale since the classic age of siege warfare in the eighteenth century. Colonel Sakakibira arrived from Japan as Chief Engineer, Major-General Teshima concentrated on the command of the siege artillery and the additional Naval Brigade, and under their guidance the 3rd Army began to go underground. If, however, the Japanese were under the impression that the steady prosecution of the siege was to be allowed to proceed in isolation they were in for a rude awakening.

For despite its duration and the casualties suffered, the battle of Liaoyang had been essentially indecisive. Contemporary opinion, in Japan and Russia and in the rest of the world, had expected great results from this clash of the two principal armies, but largely because the popular view of warfare lagged behind the realities actually being hammered out in Manchuria. The previous century had been accustomed to set-piece battles, not exactly on the Napoleonic pattern, perhaps, but certainly of the type set by the Austro–Prussian and the Franco–Prussian wars. Armies marched and manoeuvred and eventually met in battle for a period better measured in hours than in weeks, at the end of which time it was plainly obvious that the defeated general, whether Benedek or Bazaine, was due to hand over his sword to his conqueror. Since 1870 no two major military powers had been at war, and throughout nearly the whole of the nineteenth century there had never been an occasion when two such powers had been engaged together both on land and at sea. Indeed, the strategic considerations involved in balancing the conflicting claims of navies and armies had really lapsed into disuse after Trafalgar.

Now nearly 100 years later the war correspondents and the military attachés and observers in Manchuria were seeing unrolling before their eyes the new pattern of warfare. So, despite the expenditure of men, ammunition, time and energy at both Liaoyang and Port Arthur there were still formidable Russian and Japanese armies confronting each other in the northern and southern extremities of the theatre of war; and in the naval dimension there was a Russian fleet at Port Arthur which had to be watched by the Japanese navy, while in the Baltic a second Russian fleet prepared to join the conflict.

In these circumstances the presence at Port Arthur of five Russian first-class battleships, a number thought to be equal to the total complement of similar vessels in the Japanese navy, was still of immense importance in influencing Russian military thinking. It was even more so for the Japanese who knew what their enemy did not, that they possessed only four first-class battleships, the loss of the *Yashima* having been kept secret. The Russian ships would be in danger of artillery bombardment long before the port itself or its outer defences could be captured, because owing to the geographical position of Port Arthur long-range artillery could be directed on the port if the Japanese were in possession of only one of a number of surrounding heights. The only protection for the Russian fleet came from the actions of the Russian army. So although General Kuropatkin had never been enthusiastic about the possibilities of relieving Port Arthur, one of his duties was to maintain pressure upon the Japanese 1st, 2nd and 4th Armies in order to prevent them from giving any assistance to the 3rd Army laying siege to the fortress.

In fact, of all the senior officers having responsibility for the campaign, whether in Harbin with the Viceroy Alexieff or at Port Arthur or on the War Council at St. Petersburg, Kuropatkin was the least obsessed with the plight of Port Arthur. Like most Russian soldiers he was disappointed with the performance of the navy and contemptuous of its efforts on its own behalf. The recent promotion over the head of his seniors of Captain Wiren to Rear-Admiral in charge of the battle fleet and cruisers, had failed in its object of putting some stiffening into the attitude of the naval authorities at the port.

In addition, he was bound to have very mixed feelings indeed about the military side of the Port Arthur operations. The commandant, General Stoessel, had already disobeyed a direct order and abused his seniority to stay in command. He had then argued that his presence was essential to save the fortress, yet his reports to Kuropatkin on the likely outcome of the siege oscillated with bewildering frequency between quite irresponsible optimism and fatalistic gloom.

Admiral Togo

Above Marshal Oyama
Below General Nogi

Above Emperor Mutsohito
Left General Oku

Above General Kuroki

Below General Nozu

Above Admiral Makaroff

Above Admiral Alexieff, Viceroy
of the Far East

Below Sergius Witte

Below Admiral Vitgeft

Above
Rear-Admiral
Rozhestvensky

Below
General Grippenberg

Above
General Kuropatkin

Below
General Linicvich

The Tsar blessing his troops

Above Japanese infantry
Below Russian infantry

Above Japanese
siege guns bombard
Port Arthur

Below General
Stoessel surrenders
to General Nogi

Above The Russians retreat from Mukden
Below Russian prisoners from Port Arthur

The Tsar and Tsaritsa in 1905, with their daughters and the Tsarevich

Above The MIKASA, Togo's flagship, completed in 1902 by Vickers
Below The TSAREVICH, French-built, completed in 1904 and
    destroyed at Port Arthur

Above Japanese battleship SHIKISHIMA, completed in 1900 on Clydebank
Below The OSLYABYA, Russian-built, completed in 1901, the first Russian ship to be sunk at Tsushima

Above The crew of the ASAMA
Below The crew of a Russian battleship

Above Artist's impression of the sinking of the BORODINO at
Tsushima
Below Rozhestvensky giving evidence at his court martial

At one time the abandonment of Port Arthur might have been considered feasible and advantageous by the Russian Commander-in-Chief, but that time had now passed, the garrison was surrounded and the possibility of a break-out was no longer practicable. Therefore, by a process of elimination of options, the next move was up to Kuropatkin in the north.

That that move took the form that it did may appear rather curious and the only explanation can be found in consideration of those factors which affected a man who was a brave fighting general in the personal sense, but a poor commander of large bodies of troops in battle.

It is deceptively easy for those who have never been soldiers and therefore never tramped over rough ground carrying a rifle and a lot of other kit besides in rain or cold, wondering perhaps if the rations will turn up and where one will sleep that night, to forget, in considering a military campaign, such mundane considerations as terrain, climate, the time of year and the availability of food supplies. These matters are however often much more the stuff of soldiering than grand strategical sweeps represented by arrows on a map, at least so far as the raw material of battles, the private soldier, is concerned. Of course there have been generals who have forgotten or ignored these basics too, as for instance did Napoleon, a strategist and tactician of genius but unlike his rival Wellington a poor quartermaster.

Now Kuropatkin was not of these, whatever his faults as a grand strategist: in this sense he was a soldier's general who therefore never lost the good will of the troops he commanded.

Consequently, he could very easily appreciate that he would soon be approaching the winter season in which it would be almost impossible to make fresh demands upon his troops. At the moment they were suffering no hardships and food and fuel were in plentiful supply. By contrast the Japanese troops were wearied much more than his own by the Liaoyang campaign, and in addition, because of their lengthening supply line, were at the moment not particularly well provided with food, ammunition and military stores. The Russians, despite considerable trouble with hunhutzus, the local Chinese bandits, could live off a peaceful countryside, while the Japanese had to make do in territory ravaged by war. Although they had a high standard of medical care and hygiene the Japanese were also suffering, as were their comrades before Port Arthur, from epidemics of sickness, particularly typhoid. They were also, for the first time in the war, rightly concerned about their comparative lack of man power. By an Ordinance of September 29th, 1904, the Emperor had increased the term of service in the Second Reserve from five to ten years, and in the Conscript Reserve from eight years and eight months to twelve years and four months; by these means it was hoped to provide the field armies with another 46,500 men. The Russians, on the other hand, although still calling up reservist classes, appeared to have little difficulty in swelling the size of their Manchurian army. As an additional advantage, on September 20th the gap in the Trans-Siberian Railway was at last filled, for on that date the Circum-Baikal railway was completed, and by October 3rd trains were beginning to run over the new tracks. No longer would men and supplies have to be transported overland, round the lake, or, as in the previous winter, across the ice. As soon as traffic was running throughout the whole length of the rail network military trains began to arrive at Mukden at the rate of eight to ten daily.

Kuropatkin had arrived in Mukden on September 7th, and had originally shown no evidence of an aggressive spirit. Indeed at this stage he was not slow to observe that Mukden was less well fortified than Liaoyang and he seemed prepared at least to consider its evacuation (despite its prestige value as the capital of Manchuria) in favour of some stronger natural position to the north such as Tienling. However, the consideration of the comparative conditions of his own and the Japanese troops caused him in the next few weeks to take a different view.

The Japanese army appeared exhausted by its efforts and the casualties it had suffered, and now that the three separate armies (1st, 4th and 2nd) were concentrated with Oyama's G.H.Q. at Liaoyang, was in a sense more vulnerable than it had ever been before. Its commanders were also conscious of the nearness of the winter, which would certainly make campaigning more difficult if not nearly impossible, and were no doubt hoping for a period of comparative inaction to consolidate their position.

This is not to suggest that the Japanese army was in any sense idle or neglecting its duty, but engaged as it was in a number of tasks, ranging from improving its supply lines and constructing bridges across the Taitzu to preparing maps of the area from rather outdated Chinese plans supplemented by the reports of their own scouts, it certainly had no immediate intention of pressing further northwards.

The strength of the Japanese army at this time was 120 battalions of infantry, 40 cavalry squadrons, 80 batteries of artillery and 8 battalions of engineers, making a total of between 150,000 and 160,000 men; and for the moment there seemed little chance of any significant increase in these numbers as the reinforcements of reservists coming from Japan came slowly and were used largely to replace casualties. The Russians, on the other hand, were now receiving more and more reinforcements by rail.

The first inkling of any change in the stalemate between the two armies filtered through to Europe in the form of rumours of pending changes in the Russian High Command. One of these rumours, which was in fact true, was that Admiral Alexieff had twice offered his resignation as Viceroy to the Tsar. It would indeed have been strange, in view of the generally uniform lack of success in the Far East, if the Tsar and his advisers had not considered some shake-up of senior officers and no doubt this consideration also helped push Kuropatkin towards the offensive.

Anyhow, for whatever combination of reasons, a number of which were militarily valid, the Russian Commander-in-Chief in his Order of the Day of October 2nd declared that the Manchurian army was now strong enough to begin a 'forward movement'. Thus he again demonstrated the quite incredible indifference of the Russians to all considerations of security, for the contents of his Order were soon known to the Japanese and served to put them on the alert. Immediately they began to watch the Russian army for confirmation, by way of troop movements, of an offensive being mounted. It is unlikely in any event that the Japanese would have remained for ever unconscious of the pending threat, but by announcing his intentions in advance Kuropatkin had sacrificed any chance of surprise

he might have possessed. A week later, on October 2nd, began
the opening moves in what was to be known to history as the
Battle of the Sha-ho (Sha river).

In a curious way it resembled the battle of Liaoyang, but as
if the map had been turned upside down. Once again the main
artery of the two armies was the north to south railway line,
complicated by the elementary road system which was represented by the so-called Imperial Road running from Liaoyang
to Mukden, and the rivers of the area which tended to a pattern
of main course running roughly from the north-east to the
south-west with effluents at right angles. Mukden was just over
40 miles north of Liaoyang and the link between the two towns
was both by rail and road. Running just south of Mukden,
crossed by both the railway and the road, was the Hun river and
almost parallel to it, at a distance of less than 10 miles, the main
course of the Sha, both these rivers eventually joining the
Taitse.

Farther south again were two almost parallel tributaries,
while north of Liaoyang flowed the Taitse itself. Every one of
the rivers between Mukden and Liaoyang was crossed by both
rail and road. To the east the terrain was flat, dotted with small
walled towns, and to the west the ground rose towards a minor
mountain range. Nearly 40 miles to the east of Liaoyang on the
Taitse was the small town of Pensihu from where a road ran
north-east to Mukden. These were the main features of the 40
mile by 40 mile square of territory over which the two armies
were to fight for the next five days.

In his Order of the Day of October 2nd Kuropatkin had
exhorted his soldiers to 'Think at every hour of the defence of
Russia's dignity and rights in the Far East, which has been
entrusted to you by the wish of the Tsar. Think at every hour
that to you the defence of the honour and fame of the whole
Russian Army has been confided.' On October 5th a mammoth
religious service was held at the field chapel in Mukden at the
end of which the Grand Almoner of the Orthodox Church
blessed the Russian Army and its Commander-in-Chief, saying
finally, 'Go with the Cross and in the faith of Christ.'

On a more mundane level the orders and preparations were
perhaps less well organised. What Kuropatkin intended to do

was to advance southwards along the railway line against the Japanese left, to make a vigorous attack upon the Japanese control of the area round the Yentai coal mines, virtually the centre of the Japanese line, and at the same time to work round the enemy's right flank at Pensihu on the Taitse. The strategy was in many ways similar to that employed by Oyama in moving north to the capture of Liaoyang, save for the fact that the Russian army was concentrated at the beginning of the advance as Oyama's three armies had not been. The difference emphasised the contrasting techniques of the two generals, for while Oyama was always content to leave a great deal of independence to Kuroki, Nozu and Oku within his broad general directives, Kuropatkin felt compelled to exercise a much closer control over his own subordinate commanders. In fact he attempted an almost impossible task for one man, the control of an army of 200,000 men with as many as nine senior commanders looking to him for orders.

However, it is fair to say that some at least of Kuropatkin's subordinate generals were not men to whom overmuch independence of command should have been entrusted; and that the Russian military system was too rigid and hierarchical to encourage initiatives by subordinate officers of whatever rank. The fault of Kuropatkin was that in these circumstances he provided little machinery of command whereby his own orders could be communicated. At no stage did he issue a clear overall plan for the intended operation, and no combined orders were given to his various commands, so that each subordinate commander was without a definition of the tasks expected of him. Perhaps an even greater omission was that Kuropatkin, unlike Oyama, did not select some central location for his own headquarters, connected telegraphically with all significant sub-units; instead the headquarters of the Commander-in-Chief accompanied the 4th Siberian Corps, and most orders were transmitted by aides or messengers who frequently took hours in the process. Kuropatkin maintained a reputation as a front-line general, but the battle often extended 20 miles on each side of him, and therefore outside his knowledge or control. Inevitably also in these circumstances Kuropatkin interfered in matters under his nose, or by his presence inhibited nearby commanders, while he was unable to consider problems often more important but further afield.

Three other points are worth noting as being disadvantageous to the Russians from the outset. First, the general plan of attack: as has been mentioned, the east was flat country, the west hilly and mountainous, and both were virtually unknown to both sides. Neither the Russians nor Japanese had anything but the most elementary maps. It was therefore a cardinal and inexplicable error of judgment for Kuropatkin to push his attack to the west where the terrain was likely to provide unexpected problems, especially as in such country he knew the Japanese to be considerably more ingenious and effective than his own troops.

Second, his one known advantage over the Japanese was in cavalry and horse-artillery, yet he made no adequate provision for the creation of a sizeable mobile force with which to attempt his outflanking movements.

Third, and this is in a sense to anticipate the actual course and conduct of the battle, the whole pace of his advance was too slow. The Russian armies were to advance steadily, almost ponderously, pausing as necessary, digging in at the end of the day, reconnoitring the next and then marching forwards again with their face to the enemy. In the previous century these tactics might have succeeded, but in the twentieth century and against such an enemy as the Japanese they were an invitation to swift retaliation. In previous Russian campaigns, in the Crimean War or the Russo-Turkish War, when Kuropatkin was a lieutenant, the enemy might have awaited patiently the Russian onslaught. In 1904, however, Oyama, forewarned in any event by Kuropatkin's rather grandiloquent order of October 2nd, determined to take the offensive himself, as much to push Kuropatkin off balance as for any other reason. As a result, after the preliminary skirmishes and initial shock of contact, by October 11th Kuropatkin was acting offensively with his left, that is to the east of his front, and defensively to his right, while Oyama was also attempting to advance on his left, that is to the west, while on his right he merely endeavoured to stand firm. Thus the two armies assumed a complementary, almost circular, posture, with one significant difference of emphasis. Within a few days of the battle being joined in earnest Oyama had committed practically his whole available force to combat, insisting that his generals achieve their given objectives as stated to them day by day; while Kuropatkin at no time had more than two-thirds of all his combatants engaged with the enemy.

Once again individual Russian units fought with great courage and discipline, but they were more often called upon to demonstrate their dogged powers of resistance in hopeless positions than the dash and verve necessary for the successful attack. Once again Russia's rather elderly generals fell below the standard to be expected in modern war.

In command of the Western Force was General Baron Bilderling, and of the Eastern Force, charged with the main offensive operation, was Lieutenant-General Baron Stackelberg. Neither of these officers had previously shown much evidence of competence or offensive spirit, and there is nothing to indicate that either of them exercised over their own three subordinate generals (commanding approximately 60 battalions of infantry, over 30 squadrons of cavalry and anything up to 200 guns) any better control than that exercised over them by Kuropatkin. It is perhaps significant that the only senior officers to distinguish themselves were the ill-omened Samsonoff and Rennenkampf, but both of these on this occasion were comparatively young men commanding relatively small independent detachments.

For the rest, most of the senior commanders merely demonstrated that in a total force of over 220,000 men neither their previous experience nor their professional training had equipped them for the complicated tasks of command. In many ways perhaps it was not their fault. After the capture of Liaoyang the Japanese had released to the press the contents of some of Kuropatkin's Army Orders and other official documents and correspondence which they had captured. Inevitably there were records of courts martial, of cashierings and dismissals. Some of these records revealed removals from command of colonels and commanding officers, and, especially when the grounds were dereliction of duty or, as in some cases, drunkenness, were seized upon by the correspondents as showing a generally low standard of morale among Russian officers. Certainly the incidence of such dismissals was by no means negligible and later Kuropatkin was to testify in his memoirs to a feeling of dissatisfaction with the quality of his officers, principally those in staff and higher command positions. His judgment was confirmed by the evidence of the foreign observers, but it must also be remarked that the military authors of the German official history of the war were so unimpressed by Kuropatkin's own orders and dispositions for the Sha-ho offensive that they doubted if he intended to mount an offensive at all. Without doubt Kuropatkin's message to Stoessel at Port Arthur to say that he could rely upon his coming to his aid seemed to be wildly at variance with both the military possibilities and the means employed.

The general conclusion must be that the fault lay not with some lack of martial spirit among the Russians, but with the military system which cramped initiative and preferred seniority or social eminence to military competence. The Russian army was incompetent and inefficient for the same reasons that the Russian state was incompetent and inefficient. It was not a matter of democratic institutions – Japan was not a democracy, but a military oligarchy inspired by a religious and patriotic mystique just as much at variance with twentieth-century 'progressive' thought as was the Russian. However, the socio-political considerations are infinite and beyond the scope of this chapter in which it is sufficient to say that at the battle of the Sha-ho it was demonstrated for all the world to see that man for man, officer for officer and general for general, at least in Manchuria, the Japanese were the superiors in almost every way of their Russian opponents.

General Stackelberg's Eastern Force did in the first days make progress, advancing as far south as Pensihu on the junction of the eastern road and the Taitse. However, the Japanese right wing held fast, Stackelberg soon began to feel himself out on a limb and the Japanese attacks on the centre of the Russian armies and along the line of the railway and road link to Mukden quickly began to have their effect.

By October 12th, by furious fighting day and night, the Japanese had driven Bilderling's Western Force as far back as the line of the Sha. The Russian centre still held, but the

Eastern Force was making no progress at all. On the evening of the 12th, Oyama announced in orders to his armies that the Russians were retreating and that he intended to drive them back north of the Sha. General Kuroki was given the task of attempting to cut off the Russian Eastern Force entirely.

On the morning of October 13th Kuropatkin may still have had hopes that though Stackelberg's force was no longer capable of the grand strategic sweep he had first contemplated, it might still be possible for the whole of the Russian army to press steadily southwards. However, such hopes were dashed by frantic messages from Bilderling that he had used all his reserves and now needed protection to avert disaster. Accordingly Kuropatkin gave orders for a general retreat to the north bank of the Sha. During the day and night of the 13th and the day of the 14th the Russian army once again carried out its most practised manoeuvre, the fighting withdrawal. To give Kuropatkin credit where it was due, the operation was skilfully handled. At the same time a reserve of over twenty battalions from the Eastern Force was built up, which seemed to indicate that the Russians were still hoping for an opportunity to counter-attack. Unfortunately for Kuropatkin's plans the snowball effect of the successful Japanese advance began to tell and Marshal Oyama began to form new plans of his own to drive his enemy back beyond the Hun whence he had started. October 15th and 16th were spent by both commanders in reorganising their armies, but soon both were forced to abandon their plans. In the fighting, points and positions were taken, retaken and re-taken again, both sides suffered considerable casualties and both armies were finally exhausted and incapable of further effort. Kuropatkin gave up all idea of a counter-attack, and Oyama abandoned his ambitions to take the fight as far as Mukden if necessary. In his view Kuropatkin must now have abandoned all offensive intentions, at least for the winter. Reluctantly, no doubt, the intrepid Japanese marshal decided to call it a day, abandon the pursuit and put his troops into winter quarters. He saw his mission as blocking for the next few months any possibility of a Russian advance to the south to relieve Port Arthur. Whether Kuropatkin had ever thought in such terms is at least problematical, but he too now allowed his wearied and dispirited troops to form a defensive line south of Mukden. For the first time in the twentieth century two enormous armies dug in along a long front, facing each other, separated by a well-fought-over stretch of territory ranging in width from 2 or 3 miles to as little in some places as 200 or 300 yards. In just over ten years' time it was to be a familiar enough situation, but in 1904 it provoked comment and surprise among the military commentators who still thought of battles as being events with nice tidy beginnings, middles and conclusions.

Overall, there could be no doubt that the Japanese could console themselves with a victory. For the Russians there were few consolations. On October 25th, finally provoked by the news of the Sha-ho the Tsar and his advisers produced their long-awaited military reshuffle in the Far East. Admiral Alexieff was relieved of his responsibilities and recalled to Russia while the Russian supreme commander was henceforth to be Kuropatkin.

That Kuropatkin was allowed to remain in his post, that he was in fact promoted, may seem at first sight rather surprising. Perhaps it was thought that with Alexieff out of the way he would now have a free hand and be able to improve on his record of two defeats in a row. It is more likely however that both he and Stoessel were regarded as being satisfactory enough in stalemate positions, while a new dimension in the war was opened up and a new personality introduced.

This new dimension had been signalised ten days before when on October 15th the Baltic Fleet, re-christened the Second Pacific Squadron, had left Russia *en route* for the Far East under the command of Rear-Admiral Rozhestvensky.

TWELVE

'There must be a mistake somewhere'

THOMAS CARR of the Hull Fishing Fleet

On October 9th, 1904 at Revel (now Tallin) the Baltic Fleet, which had left Kronstadt on August 30th, received its final inspection from its Commander-in-Chief. As such things go, it went well. The Tsaritsa, still recovering from the birth of Alexis, decided at the last minute not to brave the cold winds of the Gulf of Finland, but she had already sent consecrated ikons to the principal ships of the fleet, and there had been gifts of holy water to sprinkle over the guns.

So her husband conscientiously went the rounds, a rather solitary figure, small in stature, dressed in the uniform of a naval captain. Every other European monarch wore the uniform of the highest rank of his armed services, but Nicholas II had some curious quirks. He was by his own choice a 'perpetual colonel', the highest rank to which he had been promoted by his revered father Alexander III, and the naval equivalent of colonel was captain, so a captain he remained. Another example of Nicholas' imperial humility had been his insistence on marching all day in private's uniform and full marching order to try out the new infantry equipment and then filling in a private's pay book, 'Name: – Nicholas Romanoff; length of service – until death.'

These attempts at togetherness, although to modern taste mawkish – and ten years later the Supreme Autocrat was to wear a plain private's uniform with colonel's rank badges – were inspired by the Tsar's sincere belief that with his soldiers and sailors, dedicated to service and 'loyal', he could be truly at home as with no other section of his subjects. Dutifully then

'Captain Romanoff' in his Imperial pinnace went from ship to ship attended by General-Admiral the Grand Duke Alexei Alexandrovich, Admiral Avelan, the Minister of Marine, Rear-Admiral Rozhestvensky and his two junior flag-officers, Rear-Admirals von Felkerzam and Enkvist. The Tsar, using that well-trained attribute of princes, his memory for faces and details, was able to say a few gracious words to each officer, or ask some suitable question about his family or previous service. To the sailors in their serried ranks he gave the customary paternalistic greeting, 'Your health, lads', to receive the customary rolling response as each head swivelled smartly, Russian fashion, to regard the inspecting officer, 'Your health, your Imperial Majesty.'

Then Nicholas mounted to the quarter-deck (some of the sailors observing that he carried himself as if unaccustomed to walking on ships' decks, and wore his captain's cap more like a soldier than a sailor) and there addressed the ship's company. The message was brief and not unexpected. They would all uphold the honour of Russia and the Imperial Navy and 'punish the impudent enemy who had disturbed the peace of Holy Russia'. Finally they were all wished a victorious voyage and 'a safe return, whole and undamaged to your Fatherland'.

Then to the booming of saluting guns, the sonorous notes of the bands playing the Imperial Anthem and staccato Russian 'hurrahs', the Tsar departed for the next ship in line. One of the 'naval architects', commissioned graduates in marine engineering specially attached to the captain's staff of each capital ship, recorded that so dense was the black powder smoke from the 21-gun salutes that it was in fact often quite difficult to see the next ship on the roadstead. Perhaps the sailors could be forgiven on that day, amidst all the ceremonial, for being somewhat blasé about their Imperial master, after all he was not sailing to the Far East, and concentrating their attention upon the one man who from now on was to hold their destinies in his hands. Spare, erect, with his neat dark beard and an eagle eye for an idle salute or a misplaced cap ribbon, Rozhestvensky towered above his Sovereign and the short fat von Felkerzam and the luxuriantly white-bearded Enkvist. Looking at him as he moved respectfully yet dominantly on the Tsar's left-hand side no one could be in any doubt that this was his hour and he was the man.

From this day on the attention of the civilised world was also to be focused on this stern and necessarily lonely figure. Already his name was news. *Punch* facetiously called him 'the Admiral with the terrible name', and every word he had uttered before the fleet's sailing had been industriously recorded by the foreign press. His handsome, if forbidding, features were in all the illustrated papers, and yet, despite the coverage and the part he was to play, he was to remain the least known of men. This was not just because Rozhestvensky was an unknown quantity, as yet untried in battle as a fleet commander, but because the unknown elements in his personality were inextricably bound up with the whole decision to send the Baltic Fleet to the Far East at all.

Unfortunately, the Admiral's previous career provided very few reliable clues as to the make-up of the present man of fifty-six. The son of an aristocratic and reasonably well-to-do family, but of no particular distinction or influence, he had joined the Imperial Navy at the age of seventeen and had early specialised in gunnery and torpedo work, at that time the most quickly changing and developing aspect of the sailor's art. In this chosen field the young lieutenant soon became known as an enthusiastic and able officer.

In many navies, certainly the British, the rising young officer frequently gained some experience of active service while still a midshipman in his teens, but in the Russian service such opportunities were few and promotion slow, so that Rozhestvensky was a lieutenant of nearly thirty before he had his first taste of powder and shot in the war against Turkey of 1877–8. He saw action first in command of one of the early primitive torpedo boats, and then as second-in-command of a small armoured steamer, the *Vesta*, operating in the Black Sea. However, that ship might well have been his last. During the war a delighted Russia learned that the *Vesta*, according to Captain Baranoff, who commanded her, had engaged a Turkish warship of superior strength and had inflicted considerable damage and repelled her. Baranoff and Rozhestvensky both became popular heroes and were decorated and the latter was

promoted as a result. In fact the *Vesta* had fired an ineffective
shot or two and then fled, leaving her adversary unscathed. At
the end of the war the truth was revealed by the British admiral,
Hobart, who commanded the Turkish navy. Then, but only
then, Rozhestvensky wrote to the semi-official St. Petersburg
newspaper *Novoye Vremiya* confirming the truth, but with no
explanation as to his captain's deceit or his own patent connivance. In any other navy than the Russian such a letter would
have made hardly any difference to the inevitable sentences
imposed by court-martial. As it was, and for what reason it is
impossible to tell, Baranoff left the service, but his second-in-
command was allowed to retain both his promotion and his
medal.

His career apparently unimpaired, Rozhestvensky was next
heard of attached to the navy of Bulgaria, Russia's rather unsatisfactory satellite in the Balkans. What such an attachment
was worth in terms of experience it is difficult to gauge, but at
least the Russian was able to concentrate again on his speciality,
naval gunnery. In 1885 Rozhestvensky was sent to the Russian
Embassy in London as Naval Attaché and thus had his first
opportunity of looking at the British and their navy. For the
former, like most Russians, he had little love, but the largest
navy in the world, with a standard of seamanship second to
none, did excite his professional respect. The British officers he
met at this time seemed in return to have some regard for the
tall, punctilious and dedicated Russian. The outbreak of the
Japanese war with China in 1894 found Rozhestvensky in the
Far East, a captain commanding Admiral Alexieff's flagship at
Vladivostock, and presumably a not uninterested witness to
Japan's British-assisted elevation to sea power.

After the war the Captain's career seemed to stagnate as he
moved in the same rank to take command of the gunnery
squadron and school based on St. Petersburg. Perhaps it was
only the flattery of a foreign monarch which finally hoisted him
up to flag rank. On August 6th, 1902 the Kaiser was the guest
of his Imperial cousin at an exhibition of naval gunnery off
Revel. Under the eyes of two emperors and a score of Russian
and German admirals Rozhestvensky staged a superbly successful demonstration, so successful that afterwards some of his

disgruntled subordinates were to allege that the whole thing had been rigged with known ranges and with the towed targets so designed as to collapse at a near miss. However, no navy in such circumstances avoids a bit of preparation so as to show itself at its best. Anyhow, Wilhelm II was fulsomely complimentary to the gunnery captain. That officer having thus come to the notice of the Tsar he became in the autumn a Rear-Admiral, an Imperial aide-de-camp and at the beginning of the Japanese war, Chief of the Naval Staff.

Undoubtedly Rozhestvensky in his manner and appearance had something not possessed by his fellow admirals: an air of decisiveness, command, of leadership and pent-up energy. Perhaps his irascible temper and abrupt manner of speech also added to the image of the ruthless man of action who knew what he wanted. No doubt in comparison with the long-bearded elderly members of the Higher Naval Board or the pusillanimous crew at Port Arthur, such a reputation was not too difficult to acquire, but the fact was that Rozhestvensky did stand out as an obvious choice for the command of the new enterprise.

Witte wrote later, 'The Tsar with his habitual optimism expected Rozhestvensky to reverse the war situation', but perhaps needless to say, 'Rozhestvensky as Chief of Naval Staff at the beginning of the war made a negative impression on me.' Still, Witte's opinion of the abilities of anyone save himself was always modest. The Tsar can be forgiven for favouring Rozhestvensky, especially as his opinion was backed up by the influential *Novoye Vremiya* through the pen of its naval correspondent, Captain Klado, who though still a serving officer both canvassed Rozhestvensky's name as commander and argued powerfully in support of the major decision to send the fleet at all.

For on that matter there were still lingering doubts in many minds, and it is in that context that the Admiral's contradictions of character must again come under scrutiny. Certainly, in the war councils of the Tsar there was considerable controversy as to whether or not to send the fleet to the Far Eastern waters. Some other admirals had indicated by way of expressing their disapproval that they would refuse the command if it were offered to them. Equally certainly Rozhestvensky was consulted and took part in most of the important discussions. What, however, is by no means certain is what official advice he expressed, or indeed if he ever proffered any at all. Reliable witnesses, Ministers, admirals, as well as journalists, testify to both his opinion that the venture was dangerous, if not likely to be disastrous, and the equally strong conviction that it was his duty to lead it in person. What therefore simply cannot be assessed is the extent to which his apparent willingness to submit to orders influenced the Tsar and his advisers to give those orders. If Rozhestvensky had said in clear terms, 'I advise against sending the fleet', then he should have resigned if overruled. If, on the other hand, he said, 'It is foolhardy to send the fleet but if ordered I will take it', then no doubt like the Duke of Medina Sidonia he would have been honourable and blameless. Medina Sidonia, though, was a nobleman and a soldier with as many heraldic quarterings as there were ships in the Armada. Rozhestvensky was a sailor with ambitions yet to fulfil. An uneasy suspicion therefore exists that Rozhestvensky's advice was never quite as clear as it could have been. So he remains a puzzle: an ambitious sycophant hoist by his own petard, a megolomaniac convinced of his own abilities, or a simple sea officer who felt bound to obey his orders whatever his private reservations?

Of course, once the orders were given, and accepted, Rozhestvensky naturally appeared brimful of confidence professionally and publicly, though he would have been less than human, but more discreet, if he had not in unguarded asides revealed that he was not unaware of the problems which lay ahead. To see into the Admiral's mind, and the minds of others, up to the date July 30th, when the final decision was taken, is manifestly an impossibility. On much safer ground, it seems apparent that many of the relevant factors involved in the despatch of a fleet half-way round the world had not been fully considered at the time.

Rozhestvensky was to discover very quickly the immensity of the gap between acceptance of the command and the putting of that command into a fit state to take it to sea. In a period of three months his temper became worse, he worked himself and his subordinates night and day to bring the ships and crews to readiness, and at the same time bombarded an inert Ministry of Marine with requests for men, supplies, services and materials; and even at the end he would have been unseeing and incompetent beyond the wildest allegations of his fiercest detractors if he had been satisfied with his exertions.

In the seventy years which have elapsed since the Baltic Fleet sailed it has become customary to rehearse the defects of the ships, the deficiencies of the officers and crews and the faults of the commander to such an extent that the basic difficulties of the plan have been obscured or ignored. In fact a mixed fleet of battleships, cruisers, destroyers and auxiliary vessels, built for European waters and with different speeds and ranges, had to be navigated something over 21,000 miles through the Mediterranean and the Suez Canal (or else round the Cape of Good Hope), and thence across the Indian Ocean, past Singapore and on to Korea or Vladivostock: there if necessary to fight the Japanese.

It was as if two well-matched heavyweights had been booked for a fight, but before they touched gloves one had to run a marathon before climbing into the ring to face his opponent who had been resting in his corner waiting for him. Yet the boxing analogy represents only Rozhestvensky's strategic problem, as if his fleet merely had to sail and fight. It also had to be supplied with coal and fresh food and water for the crews as well as having to face the possibility of necessary repairs in case of wear and tear and breakdowns. For all these problems Russia was less well equipped than almost any other European nation, for she had no overseas colonies and therefore no bases *en route* at all. Strict rules of international law governed the provision of aid by neutrals to belligerents and the nation in the best position to help was least likely to do so. Great Britain, with a string of colonies and naval bases stretching round the world, was not only not likely to assist in any way the enemy of her Japanese ally, but could be counted upon to be as vigilant as possible in protecting other less powerful neutrals from Russian pressures. France, Russia's ally, was of course also well placed for naval bases though not on anything like the same scale; but she had no wish to be embroiled with

her new ally, Britain, for actively assisting the Russians to
defeat the Japanese. Perhaps she would bend the rules a little,
but Russia could expect no more than that in a conflict where
France's own interests were not in the least involved. If France
had an attitude to the war, it was that she wanted it concluded,
not prolonged. Selfishly her one desire was that Russia would
rid herself of her Far Eastern obligations so as to be able once
more to range herself by France's side in Europe.

Rozhestvensky's fuel and supply problem was eventually
solved by an incredible amount of tricky commercialism on the
part of Frenchmen, Germans and Englishmen, as will be seen,
but at the time of the fleet's sailing it was still the subject of
deals, arrangements and quasi-espionage, any of which might
fail leaving the Admiral entirely to his own devices. Consequently, before they left Revel every ship was in fact overloaded
with provisions and supplies and coal and so remained until
journey's end.

Finally, there was the question of the ships themselves and
the men to serve in them. So far as officers, petty officers and
seamen were concerned, Rozhestvensky's choice was limited,
for despite their second-rate performance there, the best had
already been sent to Port Arthur and Vladivostock with the
First Pacific Squadron. Good experienced crews were also
serving with the Black Sea Fleet, for that station had always
been regarded as a possible danger point in case of friction with
Turkey. Those left in the Baltic and the depots and barracks of
Kronstadt were the least well trained and experienced of Russia's
naval crews. It would be wrong to think that the men who
finally sailed with the Baltic Fleet were only incompetents or
malcontents, although there was a proportion of both. There
were certainly far too many new recruits and old recalled reservists, plus a number of volunteers 'for duration only', who,
although patriotic, also lacked experience. In the process of
rounding up men for what was obviously a dangerous venture,
and one which strained man-power resources, the Ministry of
Marine, if not Rozhestvensky, had an obvious temptation to fill
up vacancies with suspected anarchists or revolutionaries, as
well as normal naval bad characters, trouble makers and de-
faulters; and the Ministry yielded to it. Perhaps it was thought

that a long voyage and active service under a well-known disciplinarian would make men of them. In any event the authorities were pleased to get rid of them and Rozhestvensky had no option but to accept them. Even he was prepared to think that the long passage to the Far East would provide opportunities to improve standards of discipline and training. Unfortunately, he was to discover that such a project was not really feasible without a large complement of good experienced captains and subordinates and these the Imperial Navy simply could not provide.

The ships themselves were divided into six divisions. The First Battleship Division consisted of the *Suvoroff* (Rozhestvensky's flagship), the *Imperator Alexander III*, the *Borodino* and the *Orel*, accompanied by three supply ships, *Anadyr*, *Gorshakov* and *Roland*; and the Second Battleship Division was composed of the *Oslyabya* (von Felkerzam's flagship), the *Sissoi Veliky*, the *Navarin* and the *Admiral Nakhimoff* and the supply ship *Meteor*. The First Cruiser Division was in fact three ships only, Enkvist's flagship the *Dmitri Donskoi*, the *Aurora* and the repair ship *Kamchatka* which was a sort of floating workshop to service the whole fleet; the Second Cruiser Squadron consisted of the *Svetlana*, *Almaz* and *Zhemchug*. Finally, there were two Destroyer Divisions, composed of the *Blestyashchy*, *Bezuprechny*, *Bodry* and *Prozorlivy* and the supply ship *Korea*, and the *Biedovy*, *Buiny*, *Bystry* and *Bravy* and their supply ship, the *Kitai*. The alliterative consistency of these last ships was preserved by the early return to Kronstadt of the *Prozorlivy*.

She was not alone in being judged below standard, as a number of ships, the cruisers *Oleg* and *Izumrud* and the destroyers *Gromky*, *Grozny*, *Pronzitelny* and *Rezvy*, were all deemed unfit to sail on September 26th and were forced under Captain Dobrotvorsky to follow the main fleet on November 3rd. Of these the *Pronzitelny* and *Rezvy* were, like the *Prozorlivy*, finally sent back to Kronstadt.

Now, on paper, and indeed stationary on the water, most of these ships in their new dark grey, almost black, coats of paint, relieved only by the bright canary colour of their funnels, looked most impressive, but some of them were frankly not up to the tasks they were expected to perform, whilst others had defects hidden to the observer but appearing in the captains' reports. Some of the ships were obvious 'misfits'. The *Admiral Nakhimoff*, though included in the Second Battleship Division, was not really in that class at all, being a fairly elderly armoured cruiser, launched in 1885, and recently refitted; the cruiser *Dmitri Donskoi* had also been refitted and refurbished but was too old to be included in a modern battle fleet, having been originally rigged for sail as well as steam; while the *Almaz* was not a cruiser by any stretch of the imagination, but a Commander-in-Chief's yacht on which a bit of armour and a few light guns had been imposed.

Internal and hidden defects were extensive even among the newest of the battleships, the *Suvoroff*, *Alexander III*, *Borodino* and *Orel*, all sister ships of the ill-fated *Tsarevich* at Port Arthur which had been the first of the line. The catalogue of the faults, and their causes, gives a not untypical insight into the state of the Russian navy at the time, and the problems Rozhestvensky had to face even before he got his armada to sea. The *Borodino's* engines needed considerable alterations and of course subsequent trials, for which there had never been time; while the *Orel* had started her service with a serious fire, then a near sinking and then delay at Kronstadt when her propeller shaft was discovered to be coated with emery and brass filings. After this last incident the Senior Mechanic (Engine Room Artificer) was removed for negligence, but as was revealed much later, his crime had in fact been sabotage, in league with others in the engine room to avoid service against the Japanese.

Among the cruisers, apart from those which were simply too old, the *Oleg* also had engine trouble from defective cylinders; perhaps only the new *Aurora* and the *Zhemchug* were really suited to both a long voyage and a battle against modern adversaries.

As a comment on the known state of the fleet there had been official action to help Rozhestvensky, but of such a nature that one is again forced to wonder at both the navy and the Government. Pushed by Klado, the columnist, the Navy Board had pressed Rozhestvensky to accept a number of even older vessels, which had been doing service as coast defence vessels, the idea being that these would inevitably draw the fire of the Japanese thus enabling him to concentrate his more modern ships and guns on sinking the enemy. The fallacies in this argument need not be set out, nor need one ask what the morale of the crews of these decoys would have been. Rozhestvensky contented himself with observing that they were slower than the rest of his fleet, and also burnt coal. Reluctantly the Navy Board conceded his point, and concentrated on trying to obtain some spare South American battleships for him. Hostilities between Argentina and Chile had ceased, and various shady 'agents' reported that Brazil might also be willing to sell. In the event, a lot of money was expended, Admiral Abaza emerged from obscurity to travel abroad, under a pseudonym and in disguise, in quest of ships which might not fire Russian ammunition and would need trained and accustomed crews, which Russia did not possess, to man them. Admittedly, four South American warships were sold, but they became the *Kasuga* and the *Nisshim* of the Japanese Navy, and H.M.S. *Triumph* and *Swiftsure* of the Royal Navy.

Overall, compared with the Japanese, and that was the only comparison which counted, Rozhestvensky's ships were behind the times. Their guns were still fired by lanyard, whilst those of the Japanese, following the practice introduced by the British, were fired electrically. Telescopic gun sights were still being fitted by frantic teams of civilian mechanics when the ships left Kronstadt for Revel and Libau, and alone among first-class navies the Russians had rejected the well-tried Marconi wireless telegraphy apparatus in favour of the products of a less well-known and less efficient German firm. The morale of the officers and men was no doubt affected by what they knew of these disadvantages; but on some ships at least, notably the *Oslyabya*, described by one of her seamen as a 'prison ship', there were tyrannical officers and in consequence doubly disgruntled crews.

The final inspection on October 9th (September 26th in the Russian calendar) at Revel was not, as it turned out, quite as final as might have been expected. The fleet stayed at Revel, with work still being carried out on many of the ships, until October 11th, leaving on that day for Libau, further down the

coast, from whence it sailed for the open seas four days later.
The period from the Tsar's inspection to the final day of
departure, apart from the receipt of a number of encouraging
telegrams and signals from those in authority, was chiefly remarkable for a number of mishaps, revealing the inexperience
of the crews from captains and signalmen, the deficiencies of the
ships, and the building up of tensions and what novelists
once called 'an atmosphere'.

It is impossible to say how and when the atmosphere started,
but certain it is that it was entirely of the Russians' own making
and founded entirely on rumour and fear. The fear was of a
Japanese attack by torpedo boats, not when the Second Pacific
Squadron reached eastern waters, but immediately, at any time
after it had left the protection of Russian shore bases.

Admittedly, the fear in the early twentieth century of all
'big ship men', Rozhestvensky included, was of attack by torpedo boats and later by submarines, and the fear was greatly
exaggerated. The experience of the first six months of Russo–
Japanese naval warfare was ignored, not only by the two com-
batant nations but by every other major naval power as well.
The lesson was that even if torpedoes did reach their mark
(and their range and accuracy was often overestimated), they
didn't always explode, and even when they did, the damage
inflicted was by no means certainly destructive. Paradoxically,
mines which were capable of inflicting fatal damage were underestimated, as was shown by the sinking of the *Petropavlovsk*.
When that ship first rocked to explosions the first thought of
most observers was that it had been torpedoed.

Nevertheless, ignoring the lessons of Port Arthur and the
battle of the Yellow Sea, influenced only by the speed and
secrecy of the first Japanese attack, the Russians were in mortal
fear that their great battleships would be torpedoed before they
could ever bring their guns to bear on the Japanese fleet.

Accepting all this, and some at least of the reasoning behind
the apprehension, it is still very difficult to fathom how exactly
the Russians thought tiny torpedo boats could have made the
journey from Japan to northern European waters unaided and
undetected. To comprehend how a near impossibility became

a reality it is necessary to appreciate the muddle and suspicion which were so much part of the Tsarist administration. For months before the squadron sailed, Russian consuls at seaports all over the world had been alerted to watch for Japanese warships, perhaps disguised as neutrals or as merchant vessels, or under the protection of their perfidious British allies. Not content with the reports of the consuls, which were of necessity probably largely negative, the Russian Government later put into action, and paid for, a whole network of spies and informers who obligingly began to produce more interesting material based on the wildest of rumours of the kind which can be found in any seaport in time of war. If all the reports could have been believed, and some must have been, there was now a whole armada of torpedo-carrying little ships from Norway to the Mediterranean manned by Japanese, and perhaps Englishmen as well, waiting to deliver night attacks upon the Russian leviathans.

As if all this were not enough to fill Rozhestvensky's mind, he had of course a contributory worry, his coal supplies. The squadron was, for want of coaling stations, to coal at sea, by arrangement with the German Hamburg-Amerika line which had contracted to provide colliers at various fixed points along his route, in neutral ports if allowed, but if not, outside the 3-mile limit. The facility when made public had aroused a certain amount of international criticism, led by the British, who disingenuously regarded their own aid to the Japanese as not being an infringement of their own neutrality. Perhaps the final word was left with Kaiser Wilhelm, who saw possible future advantage in helping Russia, for he maintained that the contract should stand, despite cold feet on the part of Hamburg-Amerika at the last moment, and it did. It may not be inappropriate as a final comment on this international muddle to observe that much of the actual coal was Welsh steam coal which reached the colliers by a number of commercial subterfuges!

It was therefore no doubt with a feeling of something akin to relief that Rozhestvensky finally got to sea with his squadron around him on October 16th. Even on these first days, as his great ships, 400 feet long with a 70-foot beam, displacing over 15,000 tons, ploughed through the waves, there were minor incidents to disturb his peace of mind. There were a number of alarms and even warning shots fired as neutral Scandinavian merchantmen came near the squadron; for, because of the fear of torpedo attack, orders had been given that no vessel which had not been previously identified was to be allowed to come too close.

Because of these fantastic precautions, a Danish fishing vessel was driven off with gunfire, though it managed to leave its message from the local Russian consul with a destroyer. If it hadn't been so persistent, on October 18th the Commander-in-Chief of the Second Pacific Squadron might not have learned that on that day the Tsar had been generously pleased to promote him to Vice-Admiral. Long before the squadron had sailed, back in July, Admiral Wirenius had confided to the St. Petersburg correspondent of the *Echo de Paris* that these narrow Scandinavian waters would present excellent ambush sites for ships commanded by the Japanese naval officers whom he knew to be already in Europe. Wirenius was wrong, there were no torpedo boats off the Danish coast, only, to everyone's relief, the first relay of the Hamburg-Amerika colliers.

Two nights later, however, after a day of fog in which the divisions of the squadron had failed badly to maintain contact, station alarm bells rang on the *Suvoroff* and the other battleships to bring the crews to their action stations. Seen clearly in their sweeping searchlights were a number of small vessels dead on the course of the First Battleship Division. At the same time gunfire was heard, shells began to whistle overhead, and discernible to the westwards was a number of cruisers plainly firing at the main battle fleet. Despite conditions of near panic on some of the ships – led by the *Suvoroff* – the *Borodino*, *Alexander III* and *Orel* began to open fire, some on the cruisers, some on the smaller vessels.

Many accounts survive of a totally confused and confusing incident, but perhaps one of the most factual was that rendered on October 22nd by the captain of one of the smaller vessels:

Dear Sirs, While fishing in latitude 55° 18′ north and longitude 5° east on the night of 21st at 11.30 p.m. a large fleet of men-of-war sprang up under our lee, the wind being about SSE; one squadron

passed by the lee side of us, and the remainder, consisting of four
battleships, steamed just across our head, throwing their searchlights
over our fleet. As soon as they got to windward, they began firing on
us, the projectiles flying all round and across our decks for a full
quarter of an hour, some of the shots passing under our mainsail so
unpleasantly near the men who were gutting fish in the pound,
that they cleared out down below, one shot passing right between
them. I very much regret to say that others in the fleet were not so
fortunate as us in escaping hurt; the *Crane* was sunk, the skipper and
third hand killed, and all the rest of the crew wounded, with the
exception of the cook. The skipper of the *Gull* it was who, being
hailed by the *Crane*, (saying that they were sinking), hove up his
gear, got out his boat and went to the rescue of the unfortunate
survivors, the *Moulmein*, the *Mino* and *Snipe*, all having shots pass
through them, the two former vessels being obliged to make sail for
home. I think two or three vessels did not board this morning, but
that may be owing to the thick weather causing them to miss the
fleet. I don't know whether they mistook us for Japanese, or whether
they were practising on us to get their hand in. There must be a
mistake somewhere: they ought to have known that we were only
inoffensive fishermen,

I am, etc.,

(signed) Thomas Carr, 'Admiral'.

Thomas Carr, as will have been gathered, was not an admiral
in the accepted sense, but the senior skipper of the Gamecock
fleet of fishing vessels out of Hull which had been trawling
perhaps the busiest fishing grounds in the world, the Dogger
Bank. His letter was written to the fleet's owners.

Felkerzam's division had passed them silhouetting them in
their searchlights, but that admiral or one of his officers had
presumably read his official sailing instructions which gave
warning of just such hazards in just that position, for the cruisers
had sailed on without incident. The cruisers which had fired
on Rozhestvensky's division had been Enkvist's, both sides
realising after a nearly 15-minute exchange of gunfire that both
were firing on Russian ships.

Incredibly, there were still officers and men of the two
concerned divisions, the Commander-in-Chief included, who

genuinely believed that in some way they had fought off an enemy attack.

It was only when they reached their next stopping place, Vigo Bay on Spain's north Atlantic coast, that some, though not all, began to realise the full enormity of their actions.

THIRTEEN

'The unwarranted action'

KING EDWARD VII

With the battleship divisions anchored in Vigo Bay, while Rozhestvensky argued with the Spanish authorities about coaling, there were opportunities for the officers and crew to go ashore and see foreign newspapers in which the 'Dogger Bank Incident' was front page news.

The undisputed details were that one trawler, the *Crane*, had been sunk and five more hit, while others had suffered lesser damage from fragments from exploding shells. Two fishermen had been killed and six wounded. The cruiser *Aurora* had also been hit five times, one sailor had been wounded and the ship's chaplain had died of his wounds. The torpedo boat scare had started with the *Kamchatka* which had fallen behind in the fog on the night of the 20th. She had telegraphed to the *Suvoroff* that she was being attacked by torpedo boats which 3 hours later in answer to enquiries for more information had miraculously disappeared. In fact, as was discovered later, the *Kamchatka* and possibly a Russian cruiser had fired on a totally innocent Swedish merchant vessel, the *Aldebaran*. The German trawler *Sonntag* had also been in danger, though whether from deliberate or accidental shots it was difficult to say. The Russian cruisers *Aurora* and *Dmitri Donskoi*, and the battleship forces, both off course, had fired on each other, and one or more battleships had fired on the trawlers.

Many of the Russians, however, including apparently the Admiral, were still convinced that there had been torpedo boats concealed among the trawler fleet, although why they should attack the relatively harmless *Kamchatka* first, and then fire not torpedoes but shells was never made clear.

Of course Rozhestvensky's honesty had been shown in a poor light previously in his naval career in the matter of the *Vesta* and the Turkish warship. There can be little doubt that he insisted on the presence of torpedo boats as an attempt to save face. For the same reason, the St. Petersburg government had to accept the version of events contained in his report; and no doubt there were a number of Russian officers and seamen who were able to convince themselves that though the Second Pacific Squadron had inflicted damage on unarmed neutral vessels it had also beaten off some form of enemy attack.

The world press and public opinion was not however convinced. The French tried hard to maintain the delicate balance between the old ally Russia and the new friend Britain, but in the main in France, as in Austro-Hungary and Italy, naval correspondents seemed to agree that the presence of Japanese torpedo boats was very unlikely indeed, especially as the Russian fleet was 30 miles off its own most likely, and therefore expected, course. It seemed clear to all that the commander and captains of the Second Pacific Squadron had committed a colossal blunder. A particularly unpleasant surprise for both Rozhestvensky and the Russian Government and Ministry of Marine was the attitude of the German press. After all, the Tsar and the Kaiser were cousins and on terms of friendship and intimacy, and the latter had congratulated a Russian regiment of which he was honorary colonel on its performance in Manchuria, and had kept the Hamburg-Amerika line to its coaling contract. Accustomed also to a State-controlled press at home the Russians no doubt expected better treatment than they received from, for instance, the *Berliner Tageblatt*, in which Count Reventlow, the naval correspondent, said: 'The officers commanding the Russian ships must be all the time in an abnormal state of mind, and it is therefore not altogether unjustifiable to ask, as the English are asking, whether a squadron led as this squadron is led, ought to be allowed to sail the seas.'

The duty of reading and translating the foreign newspapers to the Admiral fell to his Chief-of-Staff, the sycophantic, aristocratic, polyglot Captain Konstantin Konstaninovich Clapier de Colongue. History does not record Rozhestvensky's reaction to Reventlow's follow-up sentence:

Rozhestvensky is known to be an exceedingly nervous gentleman, who gets into a state of boundless excitement over trifles, and it is all the more strange that he should have been entrusted with a post so unsuitable to a person of his character.

Luckily perhaps for the state of the Admiral's blood pressure other German comments in other newspapers were unseen and unread. Some of these freely stated that he and his officers must have been in a state of near panic or drunkenness, or both, to fire on what were so obviously trawlers with their nets out, or equally obviously, their own ships.

The British reaction was in a sense to be expected, although its intensity surprised both the Russians and the British Government. There was a number of reasons why this should have been so. Throughout the course of the war the British public had been pleased with the achievements of their new ally against the Russians, who were almost universally disliked as tyrants and oppressors. This popular feeling had also been considerably exacerbated by a number of incidents on the high seas when Russian warships and units of their Volunteer Fleet (armed and converted merchantmen) had acted in a high-handed manner towards British passenger and freight vessels suspected of carrying contraband of war to the Japanese. The actions of the *Smolensk* and *Petersburg* issuing from the Black Sea and the actual sinking of the British *Knight Commander* had aroused considerable protest from the London Chamber of Commerce. Although the actions of the Volunteer 'cruisers' had been curtailed, after an exchange of diplomatic Notes and a bit of shadowing by units of the Royal Navy, there remained a feeling in Britain that both Lord Lansdowne, the Foreign Secretary, and Arthur Balfour, the Prime Minister, had been a little too 'soft' in their dealings with the Russians. In matters which affected British commerce on the seas the British public, conscious of the might of the Royal Navy, expected His Majesty's Ministers to be hawks, not doves. In parentheses, it may be noted that the Russians had been equally rough with German merchant shipping, which fact may have influenced the German newspapers in their attitude to what they might otherwise have regarded as purely a British affair.

This time, however, the British public expected something stronger from the Government than diplomatic notes. For the first time there had been loss of life and a lead had been given from the highest authority. The King, Edward VII, though sneered at by the Kaiser's military entourage as 'fat old Wales' and despised by the Tsar's courtiers as being powerless, on a matter which touched the emotive subject of 'those that go down to the sea in ships' felt just about as strongly as the ordinary citizen. He sent 200 guineas, closely followed by £100 from Queen Alexandra, to assist the bereaved families and the injured in Hull, and spoke in a telegram to the Mayor of 'the unwarranted action committed against the North Sea fishing fleet'.

The King was not the only personality to figure in popular calculations. Appropriately perhaps on Trafalgar Day (October 21st) of that year, the 99th anniversary, Admiral Sir John Fisher had been appointed First Sea Lord. 'Jacky' Fisher, as he was known to nearly everyone, was known both to the Service and the public as a reformer and innovator, who also insisted upon the highest standards of competence in all his subordinates. He had the reputation of being 'difficult', pugnacious and a firebrand. It was not in fact war with Russia that Fisher contemplated, but war with Germany, armed with her twelve new battleships. Soon after his appointment he had suggested to the King that the new fleet at Kiel should be 'Copenhagened', without a declaration of war. The King's reply was, 'My God, Fisher, you must be mad.'

The First Sea Lord was obviously not a man to spare the services of the navy in the upholding of British rights.

Needless to say, a number of other people were busy in the crisis. The Member of Parliament for Hull, Sir Henry Seymour King, brought a delegation of fishermen from the damaged trawlers to the Foreign Office to be interviewed and to produce shell fragments to add to the evidence of two decapitated corpses in the Hull mortuary. Lord Lansdowne was summoned from his country house to see the King. The Prime Minister sent telegrams to the Foreign Office and the Admiralty and also made preparations to return to the capital. Demonstrating crowds gathered in Trafalgar Square, outside the Houses of Parliament, and in Downing Street. The Russian Ambassador, Count Benckendorff, was booed outside his Embassy.

On the same day, October 25th, Sir Charles Hardinge, the British Ambassador at St. Petersburg, presented a strongly worded protest demanding an explanation, an apology and an assurance that the officers responsible would be punished. Almost by return, as it were, the Russian Foreign Minister, Count Lamsdorff, called on the British Embassy with the Tsar's regrets to be forwarded to the King and the British Government. This, however, was too much of a conventional expression on the monarchical 'old boy net' really to satisfy anybody. From the Russian Ministry of Marine there was no word.

That same evening, the British Admiralty issued a statement to the British press,

After receipt of the news of the tragedy in the North Sea on Monday 24th inst. preliminary orders for mutual support and co-operation were, as a measure of precaution, issued from the Admiralty to the Mediterranean, Channel and Home Fleets.

The effect of this somewhat cryptic and very careful communiqué was quickly to be seen.

The Home Fleet, consisting of the battleships *Exmouth, Royal Oak, Empress of India, Revenge, Royal Sovereign, Russell* and *Swiftsure*, plus four cruisers *Bedford, Dido, Essex* and *Juno* immediately sailed from Cromarty Firth to Portland. The battleship *Triumph* under repair at Portsmouth was alerted to join them.

At or near Gibraltar the Channel Fleet under Vice-Admiral Lord Charles Beresford, Fisher's great professional rival, composed of eight battleships, *Caesar, Victorious, Hannibal, Illustrious, Jupiter, Magnificent, Majestic* and *Mars*, and sundry cruisers came to a state of alert. Farther afield, the Commander-in-Chief in the Mediterranean, Admiral Sir Compton Domville, began to bring back the divisions of his own command from their courtesy visits to Italian and Austro-Hungarian ports, the battleships *Bulwark, Venerable, Duncan, Cornwallis, Irresistible, Formidable, Prince of Wales, Albemarle, London, Montague, Implacable* and *Queen.*

Four cruisers were immediately detached to shadow the Second Pacific Squadron, while the Homeric catalogue of battleships, cruisers and lesser craft were concentrated at Portland to cover the Channel and at Gibraltar and Malta to cover the Mediterranean, armed, fuelled and manned. The independent Cruiser Squadron was also put on a war footing and the signal to the *Theseus, Endymion, Doris* and *Hermes* about to locate Rozhestvensky's fleet was 'Situation critical – Good Luck.' By the night of October 26th the British had at sea or ready to go to sea twenty-eight battleships to Rozhestvensky's bare eight, and enough gun power allied with seamanship to blow the whole of the 2nd Pacific Squadron out of the water three times over. Nor would the task have been an unwelcome one in the wardrooms and on the messdecks of the largest fleet afloat.

Much of this had to be surmised by Rozhestvensky, but some of it could be guessed at from the presence of British warships which appeared very soon off Vigo Bay. His attitude was one of fatalistic unrepentance: he had sent his despatch, including the mention of two torpedo boats, to St. Petersburg. That it had arrived later than a confusing variety of newspaper reports, perhaps accounting for the Ministry of Marine's silence, he was not to know. Certainly, he himself was not prepared to yield to the might of the British who in his view had provoked the whole situation from the first. Inevitably one asks, did he believe his own story? It is impossible to tell, but from his oracular utterances to his officers one can perhaps surmise that he did realise that his fleet was on its way to becoming a laughing stock. Perhaps destruction at the hands of the Royal Navy would be no more shameful than what might lie ahead.

On October 28th the Russian Naval General Staff published the full text of Rozhestvensky's report in which he referred to the presence of two hostile torpedo boats. Two passages were patently confused and dishonest:

The English press is horrified at the idea that the torpedo boats of the squadron, left by the detachment until the morning on the scene of the occurrence did not render assistance to the victims. Now there was not a single torpedo boat with the detachment, and none were left on the scene of the occurrence. In consequence it was one of the two torpedo boats, which was not sunk, but which was only damaged, which remained until the morning near the small steam craft. The detachment did not assist the small steam craft, because it suspected them of complicity, in view of their obstinate persistence in cutting the line of advance of the warships. Several of them did not show any lights at all. The others showed them very late.

Having met several hundreds of fishing boats the squadron showed them every consideration, except where they were in company of the foreign torpedo boats, one of which disappeared, while the other, according to the evidence of the fishermen themselves, remained among them until the morning. They believed her to be a Russian vessel, and were indignant that she did not come to the assistance of the victims. She was however a foreigner and remained until the morning looking for the other torpedo boat, her companion, either with the object of repairing her damage or from fear of betraying herself to those who were not accomplices.

A few sentences later on there was an expression of regret for 'the unfortunate victims of circumstances', but the principal part of the report was, as they used to say in the law courts, a complete tissue of lies.

Neither the English press nor the fishermen had said anything about the 'torpedo boats of the squadron', which of course did not exist. There was no such thing as 'the evidence of the fishermen themselves' on this subject, and even if there had been, how would Rozhestvensky have known about it? The complaint of the fishermen was not so much that the Russian battleships didn't offer assistance (that was easily provided by the other trawlers), but that neither battleships nor cruisers bothered to find out what damage had been inflicted after they had ceased fire.

The unidentified torpedo boat that remained looking for its companion was sheer fantasy, no fisherman referred to such a vessel and the Russians by their own admission had sailed on.

Was this mystery ship supposed to be Japanese without a Japanese flag, or even a single identifiable Japanese showing himself on deck or on the conning tower? Or perhaps it was supposed to be British, again without identification, visible crew and unhailable by any of the indignant trawler captains.

The only conclusion possible is that Rozhestvensky, in a tight corner, had lied to save his reputation, revealing in a more positive way that streak of dishonesty and lack of moral fibre which he had shown in the affair of the *Vesta*. His explanation of the Dogger Bank Incident, both foolish and dishonest, inevitably also casts grave doubts on the standard of his advice when the sailing of the squadron was being discussed. However, the Russian Government was stuck with his report and short of recalling him or the whole fleet, impossible courses on grounds of prestige alone, was forced to negotiate on the basis that at least there was some truth in what he said. The nationalistic press in St. Petersburg backed him up, but it is doubtful if everyone in authority was prepared to accept fully his version. Some softening in the Russian attitude was discernible after the receipt of his report and the news of the British naval preparations.

In the circumstances another interested party, the Japanese, behaved with commendable restraint. The Mayor of Tokyo sent a tactful telegram of condolence to the Mayor of Hull, and in London Viscount Hayashi, the Ambassador, spoke to the press. 'The story is so ridiculous that it is not worth a denial. I would however, myself, ask a few questions which, perhaps, the Russians may be able to answer.

'How it is possible that Japanese torpedo boats or other small craft could have remained constantly at sea in wait for the Baltic Fleet ever since it was first reported to be on the point of sailing? Is it known by what means such vessels could exist away from bases for food, water or coal? Is it generally regarded as possible that torpedo boats could make the voyage from the Far East to the British coasts without coaling and without their presence being known?'

On October 28th Balfour, the Prime Minister, was due to speak at the annual conference of the National Union of Conservative Associations, the 'Party Conference', which was being held in Southampton. The great domestic issue, and one which was dividing the Conservative Party, was fiscal reform, and the delegates from the constituencies were no doubt looking forward to an authoritative statement from their leader, which would go some way to heal the dissensions which had been apparent the previous year at Sheffield. In the event, the Russian crisis took precedence and Balfour spoke to an emergency resolution on that subject.

Tub-thumping was not Balfour's style. Gentle sarcasm was, but on this occasion his sarcasm was anything but gentle. He began sombrely; and the measure of the intensity of feeling which had grown so quickly in Britain can be measured by the exclamations and cheers which greeted his statement:

'Let me begin by saying that I hope and believe the prospect is wholly of a favourable complexion.'

After the cheers had died down the Prime Minister went on to indicate the gravity of the crisis, which now looked as if it would be resolved. 'If it had fallen out,' he continued, 'that this meeting had been fixed for last night instead of tonight I certainly should not have dared to preface my remarks by any observation of that character.'

When Balfour began to rehearse the events of the incident itself not even his most jingoistic listener could have found fault with either tone or content.

In the story of our fishermen there was much tragedy and no romance, in the story of the Russian Admiral I do not know that there was any tragedy, but I am driven to believe that there was much romance.

By what powers of prevision could hostile torpedo boats know that the Russian fleet would go 30 miles out of its course? I am not only justified, but required, to express publicly my disbelief in the existence of these phantom Japanese torpedo boats, not merely because the nearest of them happens to be 14,000 miles away, but because it is the evident belief of the Russian Admiral that we have been providing them with a base. I enter my most emphatic protest against an allegation to affect our honour as neutrals.

Then Balfour told his 3,000 strong audience, and the frantically scribbling reporters below the Union Jack decked platform, of the reparations which had been offered by the Russian Government. These, he announced, had been regarded as unsatisfactory by Britain, first, because the guilty parties were rapidly disappearing from Europe and European waters, and secondly because of Rozhestvensky's attitude towards neutral shipping 'which makes the high seas a place of public danger'. If Rozhestvensky was allowed to think himself in the right, 'is that a position which it is possible for neutrals to tolerate? Such a fleet would have to be hunted out of existence.'

The Russian Government had now given orders to prevent a recurrence of the North Sea tragedy and the Russian Ambassador had entered into a number of undertakings: that part of the fleet which had been concerned in the incident would be detained at Vigo; the officers who were responsible for the outrage or were material witnesses in the case would not be allowed to proceed to the Far East; and an international enquiry would be held under the articles of the Hague Convention.

Then the Prime Minister acknowledged politely the 'desire shown by the Russian Government that truth and justice should prevail' and even more politely 'the far-sighted wisdom of the Tsar'. Very sternly he told his audience that 'at one moment it was not impossible that the great warlike tragedy which is now going on would have been doubled and the world would have suffered the calamity of a struggle between two first-class Powers'.

Balfour ended by warning that, 'To say that the incident is closed would be too much', and adding, 'I hope I have brought you good news.'

In fact his message sounded much better to his audience of enthusiastic Conservative delegates than events were to bear out. The Russian Ambassador called upon the Foreign Secretary, Lord Lansdowne, the next day, and while accepting a great deal of what Balfour had said objected to the comments about Rozhestvensky, alleging that they were 'an insult to the Russian naval uniform'.

In the next few days a number of telegrams passed between London and St. Petersburg, setting out and commenting upon the conversations and negotiations between a quartet composed of Lord Lansdowne and Benckendorff in London, and Sir Charles Hardinge and Count Lamsdorff in the Russian capital.

The British negotiators were disappointed and angry to find that what they had secured from the Russians was considerably less than the Prime Minister had been allowed to indicate publicly. Vessels of the Second Pacific Squadron were already on the move and some had entered the Mediterranean, but the Russian Government was remarkably reluctant to say that orders had been issued to Rozhestvensky to avoid another North Sea incident. It was a difficult problem for the Russians, for the Admiral's own order had been to fire on any unidentified vessels which came too close to his ships. Obviously a great deal depended on circumstances, and such an order could not be countermanded completely. The only order to Rozhestvensky which would have satisfied the British would have been: 'Do not fire on any more neutral (especially British) vessels.' Indeed one terse Foreign Office telegram to Hardinge put exactly this point of view with some sarcasm:

There are several trawlers from Milford Haven and Fleetwood fishing off Vigo, Finisterre and Oporto. Please inform Russian Government.

However, for the Russians to have sent their Admiral any such order, and to announce publicly that they had so done, would have been implicitly to accept the whole of the British case and brand him as a liar or an incompetent.

Eventually the British had to be satisfied by an assurance from the Russian Government, which was set out in a telegram from Lord Lansdowne to Sir Charles Hardinge,

November 2nd, 1904

Russian Ambassador made the following announcement to me yesterday:

Before the Russian Admiral left Vigo, special instructions were given to him that the Russian fleet, during its voyage to the Far East, is to observe the utmost caution in order to avoid occasioning injury or inconvenience to any neutral shipping which they may encounter.

The following Russian officers have been left behind at Vigo: Captain de Fregate [*sic*] Klado, Lieutenant Ellis, Lieutenant Shramtchenko and Ensign Ott, these being the only officers whose presence the Russian Government considers material for the purpose of the inquiry.

The second part of the telegram was far less welcome than the first, and aroused considerable indignation. Lord Lansdowne considered the situation again 'most serious'. The point at issue was which officer the Russians were prepared to detach

from the fleet to appear before the enquiry. The British wanted
'the responsible officers', that is, those who had presumably
given the orders to fire, and who would, again presumably, be
held worthy of blame and for punishment if the enquiry found
them guilty of negligence. The Russians however held to the
idea that what they should offer were 'eye-witnesses'. Both
claims were in a sense absurd and extreme.

Ultimately in the British sense there was only one responsible
officer, Admiral Rozhestvensky, for he commanded the fleet
and had given it its orders. Marginally, perhaps, Enkvist was
responsible as being in command of a separate detachment of
cruisers. Farther down the scale each captain was responsible
for his own battleship or cruiser which would not open fire
without his implied sanction.

Patently, the Russians were not going to send back admirals
or even captains from a fleet which was sailing to battle. Nor
for a number of reasons would they, or could they, return the
gunnery command chain of the *Suvoroff* or the *Aurora*.

At the other extreme the Russian offer of 'eye-witnesses' was
almost insulting. Almost any officer could have been a witness,
but what value his testimony might have was another matter.
The offer of one captain, but not a captain in command of a
ship, plus three very junior officers, was dressed up to make it
more acceptable by the Russian introduction of another element,
the officers' linguistic abilities in languages other than Russian
which would make them more useful to the enquiry. From their
names it might be inferred that the two junior officers of émigré
stock spoke English and German respectively, but as the enquiry
was bound to be internationally staffed and not without interpreters, such a qualification could hardly be regarded as of
much importance.

Still, as the negotiations continued, the temperature dropped.
Nicholas II had Sir Charles Hardinge to an audience and
exercised, as he could on occasions, his considerable personal
charm. Practical difficulties also arose to work in the Russians'
favour. The Russian fleet could not remain for ever in Spanish
waters compromising the Spanish Government's neutrality;
most of Britain's naval strength was deployed in the Mediterranean and it became obvious that Rozhestvensky's route for

his battleships was round the Cape of Good Hope since it was feared that their draught would be too great for the Suez Canal. There was disappointment in Britain, and a feeling that the Russians had got the better of the negotiations. But at least the International Tribunal would pass judgment and no one doubted that this would go against the Pacific Squadron.

Meanwhile the Commander-in-Chief of that formation was no doubt gaining some satisfaction from the disappearance from his sight of Captain Klado, lately naval correspondent and expert, and a man he regarded as his chief political trouble maker. That Klado released was even more capable of making trouble ashore than afloat, the Admiral perhaps did not foresee. The main fleet was soon on its way to its next stopping place, Tangier, and Rozhestvensky, apart from having to bear some shadowing ships of the Royal Navy, faster and better manned than his own, was able to put the Dogger Bank Incident behind him. The Commission to judge his actions was to consist of five admirals, Russian, British, American, French and Austro-Hungarian, their deliberations were to be lengthy, and their report was not to be published until the February of the next year, by which time he had other much more pressing problems on his mind.

In a sense perhaps the Dogger Bank Incident as an international crisis was a nine days' wonder, but it would be wrong to underestimate the danger of war which did exist. Balfour himself was no 'hawk'. Before the outbreak of hostilities between Japan and Russia he had set out a provisional statement of his views to Edward VII, which contained the following revealing passage,

The interest of this country is now – and always – peace. But a war between Japan and Russia, in which we were not actively concerned and in which Japan did not suffer serious defeat, would not be an unmixed curse. Russia, even if successful, would be greatly weakened.

'For these reasons', he concluded, 'Mr. Balfour would do everything to maintain peace *short* of wounding the susceptibilities of the Japanese people.'

The man who wrote that was not likely to be easily provoked into a war with Russia, which would necessarily include the possibility of war with France as well, for the sake of two dead fishermen and a sunken trawler. Nor, of course, were the Russians, in the middle of one remarkably unsuccessful war, anxious to take on another powerful adversary. However, the Russian attitude of militaristic indifference and dishonesty did provoke a considerable sense of public outrage in Britain, which no democratically elected premier could ignore.

When the storm centre of the crisis had subsided a little, Admiral Sir John Fisher wrote to his wife, on November 1st,

I have been with the P.M. all day. It has nearly been war again. *Very near indeed*, but the Russians have climbed down. Balfour is a splendid man to work with. Only he, I, Lansdowne and Selborne (the First Lord of the Admiralty) did the whole thing.

Discounting 'Jacky' Fisher's customary hyperbole, it was probably not very far from the truth. Only two fishermen and a trawler perhaps, but men had gone to war for less.

FOURTEEN

'War with England would have been welcomed throughout Russia'

SIR CHARLES HARDINGE, AMBASSADOR TO RUSSIA

By late November of 1904 the feelings aroused in both Britain and Russia by the Dogger Bank Incident were dying down and the British, in their legalistic way, were preparing information and evidence for the Commission. For instance, the Government had ascertained from the various nations concerned that on the night in question there had been no French, German or Scandinavian torpedo boats in the area. Later, a Captain Roger Keyes, R.N., who was to achieve fame in a later war and earn the D.S.O. for his attack on the German naval base at Zeebrugge, was preparing to give expert evidence on the performance and capabilities of torpedo boats and destroyers.

On the journey from Vigo to Tangier, which was reached by November 3rd, Lord Charles Beresford's cruisers gained some satisfaction from playing ducks and drakes with the lumbering Russian fleet to such an extent as to provoke a despatch on November 7th from Sir Charles Hardinge to Lord Lansdowne,

My Lord,

On 4th instant telegrams were received . . . announcing that Admiral Rozhestvenksy's detachment of battleships had been followed by a detachment of British cruisers from Vigo to Tangier, a distance of five miles separating the two squadrons of which all ships were cleared for action.

In view of the fact that the negotiations of the terms of the Convention for the submission of the North Sea Incident to an International

Commission of Enquiry were, so far as I should judge, proceeding
satisfactorily, though somewhat slowly, the text of the six principal
articles being accepted the same evening without modification, I
could not but feel that, in the event of the contents of the telegrams
being true, the naval measures in question, which could scarcely be
considered of a friendly nature, were such as to create a very bad
impression in Russia, and, if repeated, might even constitute a
serious danger to the maintenance of peace.

As a matter of fact, this news was the subject of general comment
in St Petersburg and caused, I am informed, great irritation even
amongst those who are not ordinarily ill-disposed towards England.

Obviously, the Royal Navy having been warned that it might
have to use force, and indeed having been massed in such
numbers that 'there would be no dishonour' in the Russians
yielding to it, was a little reluctant to give up. After Tangier,
provocative close shadowing was abandoned, but inevitably the
two sections of the Russian force, especially that sailing
through the Mediterranean, which was regarded as very much a
British preserve, were to find themselves never entirely free of
far from friendly scrutiny by a navy whose every manoeuvre
underlined their own inadequacies and imperfections.

Hardinge's telegram however contained much more of interest
than comment on the conduct of Beresford's captains, for he
related the reactions to the North Sea Incident to the whole
domestic situation of Russia under the stress of unsuccessful
war.

In order to realize the effect of such measures it must be remembered that the mental equilibrium of public opinion in Russia has
been much disturbed during the present year by a series of unexpected events which a year ago would have been thought impossible.
That a small and despised country such as Japan, with a population
described by the Russian press as 'yellow monkeys' should be able
to defeat by land and sea the military and naval forces of the greatest
military power in Europe has been a blow from which the country is
still reeling and from which it will with difficulty recover. That the
Japanese should have been able to achieve these results alone is
regarded by the majority of the population as absurd. The educated
classes consider that, had there been no Anglo–Japanese Alliance,
Japan would never have dared to go to war with Russia, while the
lower classes are firmly convinced that the explanation of the Russian

defeats is to be found in the fact that England is surreptitiously aiding the Japanese and that her officers are to be found fighting in their ranks. Consequently, there is a very widespread feeling throughout this country that England is the real but secret enemy of Russia, and that the simplest means of assuring future peace with a preponderating influence in the Far East would be to attack England in Afghanistan and India, a campaign which no Russian doubts for a moment could result in anything but a complete success for the Russian arms. Thus a war with England would first be undoubtedly popular since not only is victory considered to be assured, but also territorial extension and a large war indemnity, while it is fully realised that there is nothing to be obtained even if after years of struggle Japan is eventually overcome.

The internal condition of Russia is at the same time in a critical state of effervescence. The elements of progress and reform have been captivated by Prince Mirsky's reported liberal ideas, and greater expectations have been raised than are likely to be realised. On the other hand the reactionary party headed by the Grand Dukes Sergei and Alexander Michailovich are greatly disturbed by the prospect of reforms and the propagation of liberal ideas, and a popular war with England would probably be welcomed by them as a means of distracting public attention.

At the same time discontent, poverty and suffering are everywhere rife, and more especially in the districts where the reserves have been mobilised.

The war party, led by nearly all the Grand Dukes and fostered by society and the tchinovniks (civil servants), is very powerful, and owing to greater opportunities they have more chance than others of influencing the Emperor in favour of their warlike view. They are waiting impatiently for a real Russian success, but fully realise that the Russian army has no easy task before it in the Far East, and that the line of least resistance would be in Central Asia. In this way the prestige lost in the Far East might be recovered nearer home.

The navy on the other hand clearly understand the certainty of the destruction of the Baltic Fleet in the event of an outbreak of war with England. For that reason they, though bitterly hostile, would be ready to make any sacrifice to avoid war, and I have reason to believe that if Admiral Rozhestvensky had given almost any other explanation of the action of his ships in the North Sea, he would have been relieved of his command. They also realise that in the event of war with England such as remained of the Russian navy could only find safety within fortified harbours, and that in such a struggle the Russian naval forces would take no part. The public regard the departure of the Baltic Fleet as a forlorn hope, they are confident that it will be stopped on the way by our fleet, and are more or less indifferent to its fate. They do not believe in its arriving in the Far East in time to save the fall of Port Arthur, and they are reconciled to the loss of the fortress, the national honour being saved by the very gallant defence made by the garrison. There is no doubt that in years to come the defence of Port Arthur will be celebrated as a national triumph in the same way that the siege of Sebastopol is now fêted.

These are some of the reasons which, apart from the excitement caused by the incident in the North Sea and the naval preparations made by His Majesty's Government, have for some time influenced the minds of the public, but it has only been during the last fortnight that these ideas have taken concrete form and I can assure your Lordship without exaggeration that on the 27th and 28th of October an extremely bellicose feeling prevailed amongst all classes in St. Petersburg, who were firmly convinced of the truth of the Admiral's telegrams and of the connivance of England in the alleged attacks by Japanese torpedo boats on the Baltic Fleet; I have also reason to believe that owing to the constant misrepresentation in the press of British aims and policy war with England would have been welcomed throughout Russia.

... The Russian Government being at the present moment exceptionally sensitive as to their dignity as a Great Power owing to their reverses in the Far East and to their prescience of the possibly still more hopeless position in which they may find themselves before many weeks are over if a decisive victory is not achieved.

At the bottom of Hardinge's despatch appears this note in Edward VII's handwriting: 'A very interesting despatch and one that raises serious reflections for certain eventualities. E.R.'

Perhaps Sir Charles, like all ambassadors, was over-sensitive to the possibilities of friction between his accredited country and his own, and exaggerated the danger of 'an English war', especially as French diplomats had been as specific as possible in indicating that their alliance with Russia did not contemplate war with Britain, but only with Germany. However, the situation he described inside Russia was indeed developing, even while at Port Arthur the defenders resisted the sapping and mining operations of the Japanese and the Second Pacific Squadron sailed southwards round Africa.

The appointment of Prince Mirsky, Prince Peter Svyatopolk-Mirsky to be exact, mentioned by Sir Charles Hardinge, to the key post of Minister of the Interior on September 5th had occasioned considerable speculation among those who hoped for political change in Russia. He had been a surprisingly liberal Governor-General of Vilna and had resigned from the Ministry of the Interior in 1902 because of his disagreement with the hard-line policies of Plehve.

When that Minister had been assassinated Nicholas II had written in his diary, 'In the person of the good Plehve I have lost a friend and an irreplaceable Minister of the Interior.' Yet rumour had it, and perhaps more than rumour as the ministerial post had remained unfilled for more than a month, that even Nicholas had been shaken out of his complacency by the reaction of the upper and professional classes to Plehve's death. No one, even in official circles, seemed to regret it, but many expressed the hope that his totally repressive policies would have died with him.

For the war, apart from a brief moment of patriotic euphoria in its very early days, had re-emphasised and in some cases increased the yawning gulf which existed in Russia between the rulers and the ruled. Nicholas concentrated his whole attention on the prosecution of the war, and travelled about busily inspecting troops and giving them his blessing as they left for the front. The only task of the patriot in his view, at such a time, was either to fight or to assist those who were fighting. Yet the war was a distant thing, which despite humiliating and unexpected defeats, imparted no sense of urgency or danger to the Russian people. To those who were informed and critical of the Government it merely provided further examples of governmental incompetence. For the mass of the people, it merely provided new burdens to be borne.

In 1904 when the war broke out Russia was only just beginning to recover from the economic depression which had lasted from the turn of the century. In the more advanced economies of Western Europe, war, or even its prospect, often gave a boost to the economy. This did not happen in Russia. Certain obvious industries making war equipment did in fact benefit, but the large textile industry gained nothing from the war, but entered into a period of unemployment. Even in those industries where there was increased work, profits very rarely filtered down to the factory floor and though more work was often demanded wages were kept down to the low pre-war level. In the country, the call-up of reservists did nothing to help a peasant agriculture.

Although the Social Democrats did try to pamphleteer and propagandise the troops, little of their activities penetrated, by the very nature of things, to the armed forces actually engaged in fighting the enemy. It was in the industrial centres of Russia that the danger to the regime existed, as the mass strikes which had taken place in the years 1902 and 1903 indicated. Perhaps the only significant comment upon the war which did register on the army was the increasing number of reservists, especially in remote country areas, who simply refused to report for duty.

Outside Russia proper, but within the Russian Empire, a stronger objection to the war could naturally enough be sooner discerned. For five years Nicholas Bobrikoff, the Governor-General of Finland, had tried to enforce the official policy of Russification upon an unwilling population deprived of its ancient liberties. That Finns should now be called to the colours to fight for Russia made an intolerable situation worse. In June 1904 Eugen Schaumann gunned down Bobrikoff and then turned his gun upon himself. In a posthumous message to the Tsar he wrote of the 'great evil' of government in Finland and elsewhere in the Empire. Nicholas was not impressed and appointed in Bobrikoff's stead Prince Ivan Obolensky, who had made a name for himself as a firm administrator in putting down the peasant troubles in Kharkoff in 1902.

In Poland, the old centre of anti-Russian nationalism, where in fact there had been little trouble for forty years, active opponents of Tsarism, particularly the Polish Socialist Party, were accepting Japanese money to further their aims. In November there were well-organised demonstrations in protest against the call-up of reservists, and in Warsaw the troops had to open fire. Soon the Finnish Party of Active Resistance was imitating the Poles and also receiving help from the Japanese.

Inevitably to one of the Tsar's attitude and temperament these occurrences merely confirmed his conviction that agitation and unrest were provoked by handfuls of men who in peacetime were trouble-makers but who became traitors in wartime. In any event, Russia was used to a certain amount of unrest from her minority nationalities, but this had never tempted nor persuaded successive Romanoffs to grant equality to them or to the religious minorities, principal among them being the Jews.

So far as industrial unrest was concerned the Tsar, and those around him, still had great faith in an experiment which had first been commenced in 1903, so called 'police socialism'. This was basically an attempt, favoured by Plehve when alive, to defuse and keep within bounds unrest among the urban proletariat, particularly in St. Petersburg. The idea was to organise industrial workers, patriotic and of Russian nationality and Christian faith, into branches in which they could have certain benefits akin to those enjoyed by trades unions. Tea rooms, recreational facilities, lectures, concerts and even the establishment of elementary social security schemes were all part of the benefits provided by a benevolent despotism. No doubt in some measure the lot of the workers was improved, but they were forbidden to discuss political matters, or to form themselves into proper trades unions. It is difficult to tell whether Plehve's ideal of the creation by these means of a happy band of patriotic devout workers was ever really achieved, but in April 1904 the first branch rooms were opened of the Assembly of St. Petersburg Factory Workers.

The really active spirit in this organisation was a young Orthodox priest who had started his career as a prison chaplain. His name was Father George Gapon, and certainly at first he sincerely believed in the efficacy of his work. It was he who really persuaded General Kleigels, the Prefect of St. Petersburg, to allow the movement to go forward as an improvement on previous attempts at police socialism, which had been little more than attempts by Government spies to infiltrate into the ranks of the workers.

The new venture Gapon was convinced could succeed, and he insisted on more freedom of meetings and organisation for the workers who joined. Nevertheless, he accepted government financial aid and, though he was in complete charge, agreed to render regular reports on his activities to the Prefect, and submit to constant surveillance by secret policemen. His was an anomalous position from the start, for although a genuine enthusiast he was also in a very real sense also an agent of the Government. The movement had slow beginnings, and took some time to grow from an initial thousand workers to an estimated final ten thousand or more. Nevertheless Russia, and the world, was to hear more of Father Gapon.

At the other end of the scale among the intelligentsia, mainly the middle class of professional men, lawyers, doctors, architects and engineers, there were movements which were directly concerned not with state socialism but positive political reform. The year 1904 was for them an active year and the appointment of Mirsky gave them encouragement. Political parties, all in various ways technically illegal, varied enormously from moderate liberals who often attracted members of the official classes and the nobility, to extreme groups such as the Bolsheviks who regarded everything short of complete, and if necessary bloody, revolution as a mere palliative, if not positively harmful to the cause. Needless to say there was little unity either of objects or means existing among these groups, but all over Russia in 1904 there were men and women, mainly what the police called slightingly 'the intelligents' (not quite the same as the intelligentsia and divided very broadly between liberals and revolutionaries) who were hoping and working for political changes. Outside Russia, principally in Paris and Geneva, were the exiles, Social Democrats and Socialist Revolutionaries, included among them Lenin and Trotsky, who plotted and schemed and pamphleteered and attempted to influence both their fellow countrymen and sympathetic foreigners.

The most respectable organisation actively working for reform was the moderate Union for Liberation which held its first congress in January 1904. Most, if not all, its members were prepared to work through the only available official means, the rural zemstva and the urban dumas, to establish the framework of democracy based on universal suffrage. These liberals had all been heartened by Mirsky's appointment and by the minor concessions which the Tsar had made to mark the birth of the heir to the throne. These grants, corporal punishment was

abolished in the army and navy and removed from the competence of peasant courts, and the restrictions on Jewish freedoms
were reduced, were little enough and given 'of grace', but the
fact that they happened at all led many active reformers to think
that 1904 might well be the year in which Russia at last began to
move away from autocracy.

In any country other than Russia it might have been assumed
that the moderate liberals had the best chance of seeing their
ambitions achieved. It might also have been thought that the
Government, aware of unrest, and apparently willing to make
concessions, could have come to some agreement which could
have been implemented at the conclusion of the war. Unfortunately, Russia being Russia, neither of these assumptions was
wholly correct.

The Tsar and officialdom were solely concerned with the
prosecution of the war. Anyone who sought to distract them from
that task was at best a nuisance, at worst a traitor. The fact that
large sections of the populace, both influential and ignorant,
were almost entirely indifferent to a war in which they had no
interest, was incomprehensible. That the minority nationalities
were in a state of considerable unrest was taken for granted, and
certainly at first not regarded as being of any special significance.
That some people were prepared to use the war as an opportune
moment in which to work for concessions was regarded as
merely evidence of their disaffection and lack of true Russian
patriotism, and as no indication of the genuineness of grievances
or the unpopularity of the war. Perhaps the more discerning,
although silent upon the subject and inactive, did foresee that
some sort of crisis lay ahead. But the form of that crisis probably
none could have predicted; and that a pattern was to be set
which was to repeat itself in a graver crisis and in a greater way
ten years hence none could even have guessed.

At home in Russia in the autumn in the political and social
fields there was, as has been shown, considerable activity. But
in the actual theatre of war there was something of a delusive
calm. In the north, the onset of the winter season was soon to
have its effect on both Japanese and Russians, and a condition
almost of stalemate was to develop; but round Port Arthur the
apparent calm was soon to prove itself an illusion.

The two theatres will of necessity have to be considered separately, a division which is made more acceptable by the fact that Kuropatkin, now the supreme commander, answerable only to the Tsar, never did, throughout the tenure of his command, appear to appreciate the interdependence of the one upon the other.

For four months after the conclusion of the battle of the Sha ho, the main Russian forces remained more or less stationary, and for some weeks in many sections of the line which was now establishing itself scarcely a shot was fired. To describe the line as establishing itself was as near as one can get at the truth, for no general orders were issued to the Russian soldiers that they should dig in and fortify, although this is what they nearly all proceeded to do. This form of amateur 'do it yourself' activity was also noticeable on the Japanese side.

Immediately after Sha ho the Russian morale was definitely low. Observers described a mood almost of hopelessness which overtook the soldiers. No doubt in time the occupation of constructing minor fortifications became a form of therapy, but the original motive was probably self-protection both from the danger of shell and rifle fire and the approaching winter. The line of trenches, dug-outs and rifle pits was certainly not planned at anything above regimental level, and consequently the results did not provide anything like a proper defensive line, let alone a springboard for future advances. Sufficient at the moment that with a variety of whatever materials they could find, the soldiers should make themselves reasonably safe and comfortable.

Losses had been much heavier among the Russians than the Japanese. At the beginning of November regiments were still under strength at less than a thousand men, and the overall infantry strength of the Russians in the front line was down to 940 officers and 90,500 men with something like 960 field and mountain guns. In the artillery reserve many guns were still under repair. This then was a period of recuperation and eventual reinforcement. On both sides men were being brought up, not in any great haste, to replace casualties; while out of the actual firing line necessary supplies were being replenished and the auxiliary services replaced and reorganised.

These tasks were especially necessary as the first snow fell in Manchuria on November 5th, and within a month the temperature was down to zero Fahrenheit, and the ground was frozen hard for a depth of several feet. Both Japanese and Russians were now in need of warm clothing and lined boots in order to avoid frostbite, and appropriate food to resist the cold. The Japanese, whose skill in designing appropriate summer and winter clothing had impressed all military observers, were soon well equipped. A light summer uniform with hooks and eyes instead of buttons had been brought to Britain by a Scots volunteer nurse and was eventually to fascinate that enthusiast of military tailoring, Edward VII, and be praised by the *British Medical Journal*.

The Russians on the other hand were still, according to their Commander-in-Chief, even at the end of December 300,000 pairs of felt-lined boots short of requirements. It was however at this period a shortage of food which most concerned them, and inevitably brought irritation and depression in its train. Much of the shortage was not the fault of the Russians themselves, but was accounted for by the attitude of the Chinese population. The Russian supply line had always been subject to depredations by the roving bands of hunhutzus, and these had now increased in intensity, demanding more and more troops to act as railway and depot guards. China was technically neutral in the conflict between Russia and Japan, but there was little doubt where the sympathy of the ordinary Chinese in Manchuria lay, given the choice between soldiers of Oriental and European race. No doubt the native inhabitants of Manchuria were less than enthusiastic about invading armies of whatever nationality, but they had none of the Koreans' traditional hatred of the Japanese, and were not averse to seeing their former Russian overlords in difficulties, especially at the hands of people who bothered to acquire some familiarity with their language, and endeavoured to cultivate good relations with the civilian population. The Japanese too were punctilious in matters such as paying for food acquired locally.

In consequence the Japanese encountered little local difficulty and in many cases were able to gain useful information as

well about enemy movements. The Russians, careless or indifferent, fared far less well, and found difficulty in obtaining food
supplies. Inevitably as winter drew on the local population, like
peasant populations the world over and since time immemorial,
began to hoard their own food supplies and deny them to an
army for which they had no love and which cynically they judged
to be the losing side.

It was in this period that, in the hope of gaining greater
efficiency and effectively absorbing the drafts of replacements
coming through from the north, Kuropatkin indulged in an
absolute orgy of reorganisation. The General was of course
now free from the irritating influence of Alexieff, who had
returned to St. Petersburg to find himself, apparently to his
surprise, an object of press criticism and popular disapproval,
but it is doubtful if even now Kuropatkin had a completely free
hand, especially in the matter of the appointment of senior
officers under his command. It is difficult otherwise to explain
the successive plans and orders issuing from his headquarters,
some of which cancelled others which in point of fact had not
actually been put into effect.

As far back as the time of preparation for the Sha ho offensive
there had been a scheme to have two Manchurian armies, one
commanded by a newcomer, General Grippenberg, the other
commanded by Kuropatkin. The Tsar's letter to Grippenberg
appointing him, which had contained the sentence 'Your many
years of experience, your warlike exploits and your wide experience in warlike training of troops give me full assurance
that you, following the general directions of the Commander-in-Chief, will successfully lead to the attainment of the
object of this war . . .' had aroused intense speculation in St.
Petersburg. Sakharoff, the Minister of War, had been curt with
Kuropatkin after Liaoyang; was Grippenberg being groomed
to replace Kuropatkin? The Commander-in-Chief referred to
was Alexieff, but everyone seemed to know that his days were
numbered.

In the event, the Sha ho offensive began without a Second
Manchurian Army, although some of the units of which it was
to be composed, principally the 6th Siberian Army Corps, did
arrive in time for the battle; and General Grippenberg remained

in St. Petersburg. After Sha ho, and now without the presence
of the Viceroy, Kuropatkin began his own scheme of reorganisation, planned to take account of the reinforcements on the way.
This scheme, however, was abandoned within a matter of weeks,
and the final solution emanated presumably from the War
Council. Kuropatkin was confirmed as Commander-in-Chief,
and Stackelberg and Bilderling, neither of whom had distinguished themselves when commanding respectively the Eastern
and Western Forces, were demoted to corps commanders. All
the Russian forces were now to be divided into three armies, the
1st Manchurian Army, under General Linievich, the 2nd under
General Grippenberg and the 3rd under General Baron
Kaulbars.

The choice of subordinate commanders was a strange one.
General Linievich had up until this moment been Governor of
the Pri-Amur Command which stretched towards Vladivostock.
He was renowned as a fierce disciplinarian of the old school, but
his duties and those of his command had been throughout the
course of the war almost entirely confined to reconnaissance.
He had considerable experience of the Far East, stretching back
to the Boxer Rebellion, but he was elderly and had never come
into collision with the Japanese army. Grippenberg and Kaulbars were in a sense perhaps even more unusual choices, for
both were to come out direct from Russia where they had been
throughout the war. Both were in their sixties, indeed Grippenberg was sixty-six and had recently suffered a mild heart-
attack; both had previously held military governorships in
European Russia, and both had had their last experience of
active command in the Russo-Turkish War, twenty-seven years
ago. None of these elderly officers, much bemedalled, bald but
fiercely moustached or bearded, seemed to be in any great
hurry to take up their commands. Linievich arrived on November 10th, Grippenberg on December 13th, and Kaulbars only
on December 15th.

The soldiers they were to command, no doubt to Kuropatkin's
relief, were capable of making better time to their duties so that
by the beginning of December a whole new army corps, the
Eighth, had taken up its positions. Russia might be short of
young experienced generals, and felt-lined boots, but she had no

shortage of men. From Mukden Kuropatkin could now survey any army steadily increasing in size, which it was hoped by the end of the year would consist of 321 battalions of infantry, 171 squadrons of cavalry and over 1,000 guns, plus ancillaries such as sappers and service troops. When these units were up to strength Kuropatkin would have 225,000 infantrymen alone at his disposal.

As early as November 25th the Commander-in-Chief had set out his views and requirements by telegram to the Tsar. They form an interesting estimate of the Russians' own view of their chances of success. Essentially, Kuropatkin stated that he had no intention of remaining permanently on the defensive. He was prepared to take the offensive when his units, especially infantry, had been made up to strength. When this had happened and companies were again at their full strength of 150 men, he would have ready 320 full-strength battalions to pit against his estimate of a Japanese strength of 220, or at the most, 240 battalions. In other words, Kuropatkin was prepared to order the three Manchurian armies to advance so long as he had a superiority of 225,000 infantry against 170,000–190,000, that is, the Russians could only think of success so long as they had at least 35,000 more men in action than the Japanese.

Now Kuropatkin was not so foolish as to think, nor indeed in his despatches had he ever suggested, that lack of numbers was his principal problem. The very reverse was the truth. Yet in Russia, through the medium of official propaganda and the government-guided press, the impression was always given that the Japanese achieved their victories only by virtue of overwhelming superiority in numbers. The picture of gallant Russian rearguards at last overborne by hordes of little yellow fanatics was one which understandably had its attractions for Moscow and St. Petersburg journalists. The truth was somewhat different. The Japanese certainly had superior leadership from general to subaltern, but they did seem to be almost entirely indifferent to casualties. In most engagements, large and small, they committed all available men, whilst Russian generals, including Kuropatkin himself, held back their reserves which were often never committed to battle at all. Often the only part played by troops in reserve was to wait until they received the order to retreat along with the rest of the army.

Still the myth of Japanese superior numbers did have paradoxically an advantage for the Russians. At no stage did the Commander-in-Chief encounter any official reluctance to send him the replacements and reinforcements he required. To this extent at least he had no excuse.

Nor did he have an excuse for his failure to appreciate what the Japanese were trying to do, so far as their overall conduct of the land war was concerned. On their side of the fence, shortage, of men was beginning to tell. Already the conscript classes of 1905 and 1906 had been called to the colours, and there was only one regular division left in Japan earmarked for home defence. All other units in formation or about to be formed would have to be composed of Kobi-men, or reservists. However Oyama in the autumn asked for the one remaining regular formation to be sent to his command. Bearing in mind that his information about Russian strengths was always better than their knowledge of his, he might well have been expected to send the division to redress the balance in the north. Characteristically he did not, and it was given to General Nogi.

For once again Russian military thought was revealed as being static and unenterprising. While Kuropatkin was reorganising and calling for situation reports from his subordinate commanders, as if he had all the time in the world, Nogi's army opened their second general assault upon Port Arthur.

FIFTEEN

'We need not be disturbed about the fate of Port Arthur'

GENERAL KUROPATKIN

Between July 26th and October 26th the Japanese of Nogi's army had lost 293 officers killed and 7,849 N.C.O.s and men, the figures for wounded being 817 officers and 22,224 men. At the cost of over 30,000 casualties, more than three-fifths of the total Russian garrison, they had learnt that it was virtually impossible to live above ground before Port Arthur. The lesson that determined men armed with rifles and supported by artillery and reasonably well dug in, could inflict totally insupportable casualties on an enemy advancing in the open had been made plain as far back as the American Civil War, though it had been slightly obscured in the Franco-Prussian War. Since then, rifles and artillery had been improved and the machine-gun had come into its own, thus increasing the odds in favour of the defence. Still, the lesson seemed not to have sunk into the military mind. It was to take very nearly four years of a much larger conflict ten years later, and an unprecedented number of casualties, before the lesson was fully learned.

At Port Arthur, certainly, foreign military observers tended to attribute the enormous Japanese casualty rate to Japanese fanaticism and recklessness. Undoubtedly the Japanese rank and file possessed a courage of a high order, and their commanders a quite incredible determination. Nevertheless, it would be wrong to attribute the heavy casualties of the attackers exclusively to their personal characteristics. Given that they were determined to take the fortress as quickly as possible, almost any other nation would inevitably have lost almost the same amount of men, because of the very nature of the task before them.

No fortress is impregnable, and Port Arthur was by no means perfect. In many ways it was still incomplete at the time of the siege. Again, there was hardly any consistency in the nature of the defences constructed. A great deal was done during the progress of the siege to improve protection, particularly from artillery, but as a defensive position it still had many defects, particularly in the sense that some sections were much weaker than others. What it did possess was the advantage of depth, often haphazard and inconsistent though the defence works were in siting and construction. All the same, from the attackers' point of view once one obstacle had been taken, another existed beyond it.

Thus the Japanese, although in the time between their first assault and October they had gone to ground, constructing trenches and parallels leading up to the defences, and lost many men under Russian fire in the process, were still no nearer a position of potential break-through. There was no one fortress or entrenched line which they could point to and say 'If we carry that we have the key to the fortress.'

Provided the Russians continued to show the same skill and courage in resistance as hitherto, a process of steady attrition was the only possible plan of action.

For the Russians there had only really ever been two courses open: abandonment or resistance. It was rumoured that the day after war broke out General Dragomiroff, the Grand Old Man of the Russian Army, had given the Tsar his personal opinion that Port Arthur should immediately be evacuated. But apart from his lone voice no one else had seriously suggested such a course, when it could have been practicable. By the autumn of 1904 General Stoessel could obviously wipe out of his mind any possibility of relief by Kuropatkin's armies from the north. A Russian victory emanating from Mukden was only likely to relieve pressure on Port Arthur. Therefore to succeed, Stoessel had to hold out until Rozhestvensky's Second Pacific Squadron arrived in Far Eastern waters. That the paradoxical situation had been reached whereby naval personnel and naval guns were

now helping to defend a fortress which had had as its primary
purpose the protection of the fleet was no longer of importance.
Indeed it was now becoming difficult to see how precisely
Rozhestvensky's fleet could 'activate' the warships immured in
the inner harbour of Port Arthur. That two fleets combined
would have a considerable advantage over the Japanese was
beyond doubt, but it was beginning to look as if the main function of the Second Squadron, now on its way, would be to sever
the connection between the Japanese mainland and the theatre
of war.

With the Second Pacific Squadron actually at sea, obviously
time pressed more heavily on General Nogi to put the warships
at Port Arthur out of action by capture or destruction. So his
second general assault, both from his own point of view and
that of the more belligerent Japanese newspapers, was not
behind time.

The actual assault was not launched until October 26th, but
in the months of September and October there had been a good
deal of activity, and some successes, as a preliminary. The sapping and mining which the Japanese had carried out had been
with the object of bringing their troops, under cover, as close as
possible to the Russian defence line. The basic pattern of all the
defences, from the point of view of the besiegers, was, first, a
deep ditch almost 10 feet deep, though sometimes twice that
depth, and anything from 20 to 30 feet wide. On the further side
of the ditch there would be an earth and masonry wall with
loopholes for firing. Frequently, this parapet would be completely roofed over with concrete and iron plate reinforcements,
forming an enclosed gallery for the defenders. Sometimes this
pattern of ditch surmounted by a reinforced parapet would be
repeated behind the first, forming a second line of defence and
retreat if necessary. At stages in most defence lines there would
be specially constructed emplacements for small-calibre quick-
firing guns or machine-guns. Guns of heavier calibre were for
obvious reasons of range held further back, preferably on raised
portions of the ground, either natural or man-made, so as to
give them a greater field of fire and observation. It was a
criticism of the Russians that their ratio of heavy guns and
howitzers to quick-firers was too high. Heavy guns were difficult

to conceal, so they quickly became themselves targets for long-range Japanese artillery. Howitzers for high-angle fire, to 'drop' shell on an enemy, were of obvious use to the besiegers to pierce through concrete or iron roofing to Russian galleries and trenches, but of less use to the Russians who were contending with forces moving towards them on a level plane.

The above summary is of necessity both elementary and general. Some Russian defences, especially those of the permanent fortresses in the line, were much more complicated: sophisticated structures of reinforced concrete elaborately constructed so as to give fields of fire in different directions, and provide living quarters and ammunition and food stores for the men who served in them. On the other hand some defences were little more than ditches with behind them a reinforced trench providing a series of rifle pits. In latter-day parlance some of the permanent fortifications were almost of the Maginot Line type, on a small scale, while other sections of the perimeter were protected by little more than the open trenches associated with the 1914–18 War. The Russians had not been particularly wise in devising the defences of Port Arthur. Too much money had been channelled off to make Dalny a model civil port, and too much attention had been lavished on the seaward defences to the neglect of the land side. Many of these decisions had indeed been taken during Kuropatkin's tenure of office as Minister of War. He it was who had said in 1903, 'We need not be disturbed about the fate of Port Arthur.'

No doubt these were words which the Commander-in-Chief would now have not been too anxious to recall. But the defenders since the outbreak of war had certainly endeavoured to make good the deficiencies. Working both to their advantage and disadvantage had been the terrain which on the one hand provided, from its hilly nature, many natural obstacles, while on the other hand the hard rocky soil in some places made the rapid digging of entrenchments virtually impossible without the use of complicated engineering equipment.

Whatever the strength of the defences finally to be stormed, the first object of the Japanese in the early autumn had been to get as close as possible under cover so that the length of the final rush was as short as possible. Consequently, they had constructed a network of trenches, one main trench with successive 'parallels' at right angles, approaching those defences it was intended to attack. Curiously, they made little distinction in their plans between permanent and impermanent fortifications—not through lack of observation or reconnaissance, as for one period they were aided by the services of a captive balloon, but more perhaps through sheer lack of experience of siege warfare. At many stages during their digging operations the Japanese actually went completely underground, intending to undermine the ditches and the defence works. Although such operations intrigued reporters and historians, especially as they attracted counter-mining operations by the Russians, there is little evidence to show that many days of painstaking digging, blasting, and mining, plus the occasional sensational subterranean explosion, really affected the course of the siege one way or the other to any great extent.

By conventional means, lengthy artillery bombardment followed by repeated infantry assaults, the Japanese succeeded during September in capturing successively the Waterworks Redoubt and the Temple Redoubt, and overrunning the far weaker defences of Namako Yama, a long narrow hill from which two 6-inch naval guns had bombarded the Japanese lines.

The Waterworks and Temple Redoubts were almost directly north of the town centre of Port Arthur, being respectively east and west of the Lun river which flowed almost due south of the town into the harbour basin. Namako Yama was farther east, north-east that is of the town, and very little distant from 203 Metre Hill, the highest eminence in the area, and one which commanded the whole town and harbour area. On September 20th this hill itself was attacked, and though three separate and almost suicidal attacks, in which the Japanese lost nearly 2,500 killed and wounded, were made, all were repulsed by Russian machine-gun and rifle fire from the crest, and field artillery from neighbouring positions.

The failure to capture 203 Metre Hill was a tremendous disappointment to the Japanese, and minor gains in the next few days round about the Waterworks and Temple Redoubts did little to compensate for the failure. The capture of the Waterworks Redoubt did have one subsidiary effect in that the Russians, fearing (quite unjustifiably as it turned out) that the Japanese intended to poison Port Arthur's water supply, closed their end of the pipeline, thus confining the garrison and civilian population to the use of wells within the fortress which gave an adequate but not abundant supply. To the inhabitants of Port Arthur this was but a minor irritant of little importance beside the fact that food itself was becoming short. Rationing was now imposed, and though there were considerable stocks of grain to sustain life, meat, butter, eggs and fish were all in short supply. Horse flesh was now the staple meat and rice was used in place of green vegetables. In the last month, too, the Japanese had tightened up their naval patrols, intercepting practically all the Chinese junks which were still prepared for profit to take the risk of selling food to the garrison.

However, there was as yet no positive shortage of food, and the cases in hospital of soldiers, sailors and civilians suffering from dietary illnesses were still comparatively few. The Russian situation in this respect contrasted very favourably with that of the Japanese who had 5,000 sickness cases in July, increasing to 10,000 in August, dropping again to 5,000 in September. Of these 20,000 patients no less than 16,000 were suffering from beri-beri due to deficiencies of diet, whilst the remainder were chiefly typhoid and dysentery cases. Indeed the Japanese, who had started the war with medical services warmly commended by British military observers, with considerable experience of eastern diseases, were beginning to show the strains imposed by a very high rate of battle casualties. Where once all had been efficiency and sanitary neatness, now dressing stations were crowded with bloodstained and filthy stretchers constantly in use to carry dead and wounded burdens. Even the Japanese soldier himself, by inclination and training a scrupulously clean individual, was through necessity now deprived of his customary daily bath or 'stand up wash'. Bloodstained bandages not used for the first time were beginning to be noticed and swarms of flies which brought in their train the diseases of the camp and the battlefield began to make their appearance.

Still the determination of General Nogi slackened not one whit, despite the loss of one soldier son at Nanshan and now another at Port Arthur. As a comment on his second family bereavement he said that he too would count it an honour to give his life for the Emperor in such an important cause, and there could be no doubt of the truth of his assertion. Equally too, the officers and men under his command were still prepared, shouting 'Banzai' and waving the Rising Sun banner, to throw themselves at the enemy. Having lost one entire siege train to the Russians at sea, they were now encouraged by the arrival of six 11-inch howitzers, taken from Japan's home defences, as replacements. These enormous siege guns were emplaced to the north-west and with the assistance of observers on Namako Yama were very soon put to use.

The first shells fell fairly haphazardly on the town. Some of the actual shells failed to explode but the arrival of these heavy projectiles with enough force to destroy a house fully justified General Stoessel's proclamation calling for calm among a confused and frightened civilian population. Very soon though this sporadic bombardment came to an end as the Japanese began to concentrate upon much more worthwhile military targets.

On October 2nd the battleship *Peresvyet* was hit by at least twelve shells and on the 7th the *Poltava* was set on fire. The next day the *Retvizan* made a solitary attempt to escape the shellfire, but once out of the inner harbour and into the roadstead was driven back by patrolling Japanese torpedo boats. A few days later serious damage was done to the *Bayan*. From now on, although the warships shifted position and sought shelter, almost daily hits were registered on one or more of the vessels, as well as on buildings in the Old Town which lay in the line of fire from the howitzer positions to the harbour. The toll of damage steadily increased as throughout October the Japanese received considerable reinforcements to their batteries firing into the harbour area, notably twelve more 11-inch howitzers and two 6-inch naval guns. These additional guns joined in the general bombardment which continued, although with no particular pattern, save for the concentration upon the warships, until the eve of October 26th.

On that day the Japanese artillery was ordered to commence a bombardment of the Russian forts and trenches which was to continue day and night. For six days two Japanese infantry divisions, the 1st and 9th, attacked two Russian forts, Singshu and Ehrlung. At the same time the 11th Division concentrated on another fort and battery at Chikuan. All three Russian positions were in the north-western sector, almost due north of the Chinese Quarter of Port Arthur, and were interlinked by a number of minor defence works. The battle raged for six days and nights, often at such close quarters that the Russians found that their rifles were less effective than grenades and even stones, and burning paraffin-soaked rags which they rained down on the heads of their attackers. For the Japanese emerging from their trenches were able in most cases to get only as far as the protective ditches fronting the fortresses. Once there however, there they remained, the ditches and the parapets soon being littered with corpses and wounded men. So many were the bodies and so intense the danger in front of the fortresses that the Russians frequently saw Japanese soldiers attempting to make parapets out of their dead comrades, desperately trying to use them as improvised sandbags.

Eye-witnesses and participants on both sides have tried to describe these six days of almost continual fighting, but have been able only to put down the events as they happened in their own sector. For the overall plan after a few days, fighting disappeared, and individual regiments and companies could only concentrate on their own particular action. Finally, after a loss of nearly 4,000 men, many of whose bodies remained unburied, strewn across the defences they had striven so courageously to storm, the Japanese simply gave up, out of sheer exhaustion. After terrible losses they had managed to force themselves into three minor fortifications, but the main object of their attack remained untouched. Japanese outposts now hung on by the skin of their teeth in constant danger within anything from 100 down to 40 yards of the north-western salient of the Russian defences, but the defence line remained intact.

Behind it the Russians, soldiers, sailors and some civilian volunteers, who had exerted themselves almost beyond endurance, were themselves suffering casualties and exhaustion, but had succeeded in repelling attack. Yet another lesson had been demonstrated, which was to remain unlearnt for nearly ten

years: that it was almost impossible to destroy fortified and
dug-in positions by artillery fire alone; that to the surprise of
the attackers, after colossal bombardments defenders were still
capable of rising phoenix-like from the smoke and rubble, not
only to fight back, but to win the day.

Precisely at noon on November 3rd, the birthday of the
Emperor of Japan, the naval guns fired a salute of a hundred
and one guns but with live ammunition, directly into the town
of Port Arthur.

Oddly enough, the Mikado's birthday in 1904 was also the
tenth anniversary of the accession to the throne of Nicholas II,
an event which was celebrated off Tangier by toasts of cham-
pagne in the wardroom and vodka on the messdecks of Roshest-
vensky's fleet.

Tangier as a stopping point was important in a number of
respects. Felkerzam's division had sailed there in advance of
Rozhestvensky's while he and his battleships had been virtually
detained there by the Royal Navy. The politicians and diplomats having agreed in principle to the International Commission of Enquiry Rozhestvensky sailed on, but it was only off
Tangier that he finally rid himself of the British cruiser squadron
which had done its best to turn the progress of his division into
a rogue's march.

Battleships, cruisers and destroyers now being reunited, they
were soon to be divided again. Felkerzam, with the two old
smaller battleships *Sissoi Veliky* and *Navarin*, plus the destroyers,
was to make his way eastwards through the Mediterranean and
thence via the Suez Canal into the Red Sea, and then southwards to Madagascar. The four 'Suvoroff'-class battleships, the
Oslyabya and the remainder were to make the journey round
the Cape of Good Hope.

In many ways it was a curious arrangement, and is not fully
explained by commentators who have taken up the reason
advanced by Rozhestvensky to the fleet. This was that the
draught of the four 'Suvoroff' battleships was too great for the
Suez Canal, but that the *Sissoi Veliky* and *Navarin* were perhaps
not modern enough to weather a possibly rough passage round
the Cape. In point of fact the four largest battleships could have
passed through the Suez Canal, although care would have been

necessary. If the *Sissoi Veliky* and the *Navarin* were unfit for the long arduous Cape voyage, what of the smaller vessels including the hospital ship *Orel* and the repair ship *Kamchatka*, which were ordered to sail with Rozhestvensky?

The Commander-in-Chief was not a man to communicate a great deal to his captains, his temper was bad, and it was to get worse. Consequently, it is almost impossible to judge the real motives for many of his decisions. It is just possible that he still feared some attack by the Japanese in collusion with the British. Perhaps therefore it would be safer to divide his forces and keep at least his strongest ships away from that British preserve, the Mediterranean, and away from areas such as Egypt, the Suez Canal and the Red Sea, all dominated by their powerful navy. Whichever was the route chosen, Madagascar, where the two fleets were to rendezvous, was the only place where the French, his only friends, were prepared to give real assistance. Round the Cape route he would naturally avoid all British African territory, but could perhaps hope for some co-operation at French ports, but none from ports held by Portugal, 'Britain's oldest ally'. The shorter route through the Mediterranean and the Suez Canal would obviously have used far less coal, but perhaps again he thought the British would interfere by putting some sort of pressure on the Hamburg-Amerika colliers if they showed their presence in such sensitive areas.

Nevertheless, for whatever combination of reasons, and few of Rozhestvensky's decisions were free of complications, the squadron was ordered to divide. As a sort of comment on the whole proceedings, when leaving Tangier the supply ship *Anadyr*'s anchor fouled the telegraph cable linking Tangier with Spain. When the anchor came up, so did the cable. From the flagship came the impatient order to cut the cable. This was done, and the telegraphic link between Africa and Europe via Spain was severed for some days. Once again, Rozhestvensky was bidding fair to becoming a world laughing stock, and once again his temper was not improved. At Dakar, the first stopping place after Tangier, reached on November 16th, Rozhestvensky's division had its first baptism of coaling in the tropics, a process which with a little more experience in even hotter climates they were to christen 'the black fever'.

Though later the temperature rises as the fleet sailed southwards were to make the work even more unendurable, Dakar was certainly no gentle foretaste of what was to come. First, the French authorities were not as co-operative as might have been expected, thus putting Rozhestvensky in a foul temper for a start, and secondly the colliers through some misunderstanding of their orders had turned up with 40,000 tons of coal, well in excess of requirements so that each Russian ship was forced to take on board 50% more than its usual supply. The operation, with a prize for the first ship to complete, took well over 24 hours. Soon every ship and every man was black with coal dust. After the bunkers were filled, all available space was crammed with the extra coal stored in bags, and when the bags broke, simply stacked in living quarters and gangways. Inevitably, there were accidents, and the hospital ship took on board a number of sailors suffering from heat exhaustion, or who had been injured by falling coal. Lieutenant Nelidoff, son of the Russian ambassador in Paris, fell down dead on the deck of the *Oslyabya*.

The next stopping points for the fleet were, in order, Gabon, Libreville, Great Fish Bay and Angra Peguina, the first two in French territory, the third in Portuguese Africa and the fourth in German South West Africa. Then came the 3,000-mile trip round the Cape to Madagascar.

At Gabon the French Governor had apparently received no instructions from Paris, one way or the other, with regard to the reception of the battle fleet of his country's principal ally. Tactfully, the fleet stayed outside territorial waters, but the ships' crews were allowed to enjoy a day's shore leave in what to them was an incredible tropical paradise before they returned to the black drudgery of coaling. The stop at Libreville on December 1st was noteworthy perhaps for the ceremony of crossing the line and the first occasion since the fleet had left Kronstadt when the Commander-in-Chief was actually seen to smile, as he watched the schoolboyish antics of his officers and men.

At Great Fish Bay the reception was very different. The Portuguese Governor had received instructions. The colliers had arrived a day before the fleet on December 5th and so he was doubly forewarned. Courageously, considering the reputation of the Russian navy and the Second Pacific Squadron in particular, he came alongside the mighty *Suvoroff* in a minute gunboat whose sole armament was one three-pounder gun. In Rozhestvensky's cabin he told the Admiral that he and his fleet must leave the bay otherwise he would take action. No doubt wondering what such action might be, Rozhestvensky first argued and then refused. The Governor left and coaling commenced in fact outside territorial waters. The action threatened by the Governor in his gunboat could only be to contact the nearest British warship and as he sailed off the Russian flagship hoisted a contemptuous signal of farewell.

At Angra Penguina, reached on December 11th, there promised to be worse trouble than at Great Fish Bay, for though the British had ceded the colony to Germany, they had retained two offshore islands and were disposed to make difficulties. In fact, all went well due to the friendliness of the German Governor who, whether on orders from Berlin or not, went out of his way to be helpful. Brushing aside the protests of the irate British he went on board the flagship and enjoyed Russian hospitality and was obviously prepared to assist in every way he could. In fact his conduct was some consolation for the rigours of coaling not only in the tropics but with a rough sea. Angra Penguina was much worse than Dakar, for added to the heat and the dust and the back-breaking toil was the hazard of collisions between warships and colliers. The ships' launches were used as lighters to transport coal, attempts were made to work at night with the aid of searchlights, again there were accidents and casualties and for the first time in two months positive refusal by some sailors to carry out the orders of their officers.

It was only because of the delays in the coaling operation that the fleet was still at anchor when the Governor came on board the *Suvoroff* on December 15th to give the Commander-in-Chief of the Second Pacific Squadron some news of the war in the Far East. At Port Arthur the Japanese had captured 203 Metre Hill.

Whether from true or feigned ignorance Rozhestvensky asked to be informed of the significance of that particular event, and it was explained to him that the hill commanded the whole of the harbour. With observers in position there, the Japanese heavy guns and howitzers could destroy what remained of the First Pacific Squadron which Rozhestvensky was sailing to join. What effect this news had on the Admiral it is impossible to tell, but certainly he appeared unmoved. A day later his ships departed from their hospitable haven for the difficult passage round the Cape.

For some days thereafter Rozhestvensky and his ironclads disappear as it were from history to emerge at Madagascar. During this period their only problems were to be the elements, plus a rumour that off British South African territory there might well be an attempted attack by Japanese torpedo boats, as always with the co-operation of their ally. Perhaps in retrospect the refusal of such rumours to die a natural death provides the Admiral and his captains with some excuse for their panic-stricken behaviour off the Dogger Bank.

More important, though, than mythical torpedo boats now was the ultimate destiny and purpose of the whole Pacific Squadron. It now looked as if any battle with Togo's fleet would be fought with no assistance from the fleet already in the Far East and possibly without even the advantage of Port Arthur as a base. From Tangier to Angra Peguina Rozhestvensky had endeavoured to practise his fleet in manoeuvres and deployment. The results, confusion and incompetence, had not been encouraging and had given more grounds for Rozhestvensky's scarcely veiled contempt for a number of his captains and officers. Increasingly throughout the voyage he had withdrawn into a shell of taciturnity which in turn made communication even more difficult and confidences impossible.

At the same time, a number of the ships had given further evidence of mechanical defects which had been apparent even before they sailed and these, taken together with the obvious failures of seamanship, had lowered morale throughout among crews already suffering from alternating bouts of hard work and cooped-up boredom.

The battle was still a long way off, but only the unthinking could regard the prospect with anything like equanimity.

SIXTEEN

'Port Arthur will be my grave'

GENERAL STOESSEL

The capture of 203 Metre Hill, south of 174 Metre Hill, and $2\frac{1}{2}$ miles from the Harbour Basin, although Rozhestvensky affected indifference, was a fearful blow to the defenders of Port Arthur.

The capture itself had come as the culmination of yet another Japanese general assault, this time shifted from the north-eastern front to the north-western. Nogi's third large-scale attack had begun on November 26th. Before that date, however, throughout most of the month there had been considerable preparations which some of the foreign observers both before and after the event regarded as presaging a 'new' form of attack. In fact this was hardly the case. There was no new easy approach to the problem of Port Arthur. Nogi, ten years before time, was faced with almost exactly the problem which faced British and French army and corps commanders on the Western Front once the German line had stretched 'from Switzerland to the sea' and any chance of mobility had disappeared.

Artillery seemingly, however heavily concentrated, could not destroy a defending force completely, so that the infantry could then walk in. Infantry on its own faced with natural obstacles plus prepared positions simply could not live long enough to make headway. All the tactical devices dear to generals' hearts such as feints and outflanking movements were either inapplicable or of no effect. The defenders need not take up any initiatives, in fact they were probably better off if they did not. All they had to do was sit back and wait. So long as they had sufficient food, water, ammunition and endurance, and their morale did not break, they were seemingly invincible.

The only advantage that Nogi did possess over Fock and Haig and the senior commanders in the next Great Power conflict was that his enemy at Port Arthur was surrounded. Stoessel could not receive reinforcements of men or material. There must therefore be a limit. Imperative orders from Tokyo demanded that Nogi should try again whatever the sacrifices, and though it was easier to give such orders in Tokyo than put them into practice at Port Arthur, the little grey-bearded general determined to try again.

Curiously in a way, his first assault, attempting to treat a siege like a field action, as if the fortifications did not exist, had come nearer to success than his second – perhaps because of the element of surprise, and because the Russians were less well prepared for the savagery and persistence of Japanese infantry attacks. However, there could now be no going back. His troops, those that had survived, had lost their freshness, and it is doubtful if even their splendid morale could have borne the prospect of another open attack. Accordingly, he did what he could. The trench systems leading up to the Russian defences were increased in number and complexity. Extra protection was provided and the trenches and parallels widened and improved so as to facilitate the movement of men, ammunition, light guns and casualties. More mines and explosives were brought up to the very limits of the excavations in the hope of creating gaps in the Russian fortifications.

Reinforced by an extra division of infantry, from the martial area of Hokkaido, fresh, enthusiastic and of a high reputation for patriotism and discipline, bringing his total attacking force to nearly 100,000 men, on November 26th he tried again.

The fighting in the next ten days was no different from that on the previous occasion save in its intensity and desperation. The Japanese were determined to capture 203 Metre Hill, known to them, confusingly, as both Nineisan and Royosan; and some of the neighbouring hills and knolls had to be taken in the process, so that they could bring their artillery to bear on the main objective and at the same time deny those positions to the enemy. Equally, the Russians were determined to resist, and should ground be lost counter-attack to regain it. In one sense a new element was introduced into the military techniques practised, as for the first time the Japanese applied their experience of mining and tunnelling to the capture of hill features. The eighteenth century had seen this sort of warfare applied to the besieging of fortresses, but nearly always on level ground. Hills in that and the succeeding century were carried by storm. Now, the Japanese tunnelled their way laboriously and frequently near suicidally uphill to capture a feature on which the Russians expended numbers of men well in excess of the original garrison, throwing in reinforcements until the feature was at the last surrounded.

On the Japanese side volunteers were frequently called for and major-generals led small bands of desperate men, 'forlorn hopes' they would have been called a century or more ago, who were told bluntly before they started that they were not expected to survive the day.

Round the peaks of the hills and of 203 Metre Hill especially, Japanese, Russians, and, later, foreign observers, all remarked that they had never seen so many dead men collected together. Even the sober pages of the British Official History uses the expression 'mediaeval' to describe the fighting, referring to the fact that despite modern personal weapons and a crushing artillery barrage in the last stages, men were fighting hand to hand with grenades, bayonets and even fists.

The corpse and rubble strewn peak once taken, it was the turn of the Russians to fight uphill. At least two principal counter-attacks were set in train which despite heavy losses failed to reach the summit. Finally, on December 5th, the Russians conceded their losses.

Apart from 203 Metre Hill, the Japanese had gained a considerable area mostly consisting of fortified hills about 2 miles to the north-east of Port Arthur new town. The Russian losses in killed and wounded were nearly 3,000 men while the Japanese had lost in eight days' fighting over 12,000 killed and wounded, many of the latter in the freezing cold weather joining the ranks of the dead as they froze unattended where they had fallen.

The capture of 203 Metre Hill was important in at least three different ways. First, perhaps, it served to vindicate the reputation of the Russian soldier, for though he had finally been forced to yield, no one in future could doubt his courage and tenacity even against such an opponent as the Japanese. Second, with its capture a great section of the Russian defence line, north-west round to west, was now exposed to both artillery fire and close investment by the besiegers. Having originally started in the north-east, the whole Japanese front of attack had by necessity swung over towards the west. The third factor was the decline in morale on the part of the defenders. Hardly anyone in Port Arthur could fail to appreciate the significance of the loss which had now occurred. Almost everyone knew with a grim foreboding what would now happen. It was only a matter of waiting to watch the fleet destroyed before their eyes.

Almost immediately after its capture a Japanese party commanded by a naval lieutenant ascended to the summit and dug themselves in behind sandbags as best they could. The lieutenant was connected by telephone ground line to the commanders of the artillery batteries. On December 7th the bombardment of the sitting ducks began.

Vainly the Russian crews tried to position their vessels in places of protection or reinforce the decks with sandbags and the like. It was all a waste of time. At short range, 11-inch howitzer shells falling from a considerable height at a steep angle dropped like aerial bombs on the ships, tearing through the decks and exploding well inside the hulls. With the smaller cruisers and destroyers the shells frequently pierced the decks and exploded only on reaching the skin of the hull, sinking them immediately.

During the next three days one by one the great battleships foundered and sank in the harbour, many of the masts and superstructures remaining above the surface as their keels struck the bottom, mute reminders of what once had been. The four battleships, *Poltava*, *Retvizan*, *Peresvyet* and *Pobieda*, two cruisers and a number of destroyers were all sunk. Only the *Sebastopol*, of the big ships, remained afloat, and von Essen, her captain, at least made an attempt to save her by taking her to the harbour mouth out of reach of the hail of howitzer shells. There he was immediately attacked by flotillas of torpedo boats which were on watch for just such an occurrence. In blinding snowstorms the fight between the Japanese small craft and the last Russian battleship continued for three days, only ending when von Essen sailed a badly damaged and listing ship into the deep water of the harbour where eventually she was to be scuttled.

So ended the somewhat inglorious history of the, fully entitled, First Squadron of the Russian Pacific Ocean Fleet which, since Rear-Admiral Skrydloff's recall to St. Petersburg, had been commanded by Vice-Admiral Bezobrazoff, from May to October, and from October until the end, Rear-Admiral Jessen. All three officers had been stationed at Vladivostock and had therefore been deprived of an opportunity of even sighting the ships under their nominal command. The ships themselves now lay ruined in Port Arthur harbour, never having properly engaged the Japanese fleet, although their crews had fought and died gallantly on land to defend the fortress.

The day after the destruction of the fleet a Council of War was held at Port Arthur. General Stoessel was absent, having been slightly wounded by a shell splinter, and in his absence no decisions were taken, although the general situation of the garrison was reviewed. The meeting of the Council, however, provides an opportunity to examine both the responsibilities and personalities of the senior naval and military officers who, under Stoessel, conducted the defence of the port.

Functions had been ill-defined from the beginning of the siege, and recent developments had done nothing to improve the situation. Apart from anything else there was a plethora of senior officers. Rear-Admiral Wiren had been promoted from captain over the heads of his seniors such as Prince Ukhtomsky and Gregorovich and was now the senior naval officer. He was a determined, vigorous officer who had nevertheless failed to galvanise the ships' captains into any sort of constructive action. Discussion rather than decision had always seemed the order of the day in the ranks of the senior officers of the Russian navy after the loss of Makaroff, and now Wiren had little authority and no fleet. His sole remaining command was the sailors and marines from the sunken ships, nearly 9,000 men, who still formed a considerable part of the actual fighting force.

Unfortunately, however, the rivalry between the two services, army and navy, had been exacerbated by the repeated failure of the fleet to take to sea and engage the Japanese. The soldiers blamed the sailors for their present predicament, and the sailors pointed scornfully to Kuropatkin's failure to relieve the fortress by land. Despite the navy's considerable contribution in men and guns in the last few months, accusations and sneers had often led to blows and ugly scenes between soldiers and sailors, and this lack of co-operation between the two services was by no means confined to the junior ranks.

Consequently Wiren, despite his personal determination to fight to the end, exercised little influence among his equals in rank and certainly none over Stoessel himself. On the army side, technically Lieutenant-General Smirnoff should have been regarded as second-in-command to Stoessel, but his position was anomalous, for, as has been seen, he was the officer who had originally been entrusted with the whole conduct of the defence as 'Commandant of the Fortress'. Dishonestly, Stoessel had managed to wrest the overall command from him, and now Smirnoff was, as it were, bound by his acquiescence.

Even more curious was the position of Major-General Fock who had possessed a command before Port Arthur had been closely invested. Ever since the men of his division, the 4th East Siberian Rifle Division, had been absorbed into the garrison, he had been almost a supernumerary. Nevertheless, the hierarchical system of the Russian army plus the favour of Stoessel ensured that Fock should not be ignored. In any event, it became obvious that he had no intention of being ignored for his behaviour was even more curious than his lack of any precise authority. The General took it upon himself, although presumably not without some sort of agreement from Port Arthur's commander, to circulate a series of 'notes' or memoranda, setting out his personal views on the conduct of the siege, the chances of success or relief, as well as the conduct and shortcomings of a number of officers not under his control. In any military command such conduct would have been incredible, in a fortress suffering already from the fierce attacks of the enemy and all the stresses and strains of a desperate siege, his behaviour was inexcusable, especially as he was generally

regarded as a 'mouthpiece' of the Commander, and his observations were cast in the most depressing vein possible. In a not
untypical example he had compared Port Arthur's situation
with that of a man suffering from a mortal lingering disease.

As an agreeable contrast to this military Cassandra was his
opposite number, Major-General Kondratenko, originally the
commander of the 7th East Siberian Rifle Division, which like
Fock's command had also been absorbed into the garrison. If
Fock can be regarded as being in Stoessel's camp, Kondratenko
was equally firmly a supporter of Smirnoff. Together in the
summer and early autumn they had inspected the defences of
the fortress and with the enthusiastic help of Major-General
Byeli, the commander of the fortress artillery, had encouraged
the men to improve their positions, and protect the gun emplacements. With the beginning of the siege proper and the
concentrated Japanese attacks Kondratenko had really come
into his own, his tall black-bearded figure being seen almost
everywhere giving orders, advice and encouragement. He was
one of the few general officers who constantly exposed himself
in the front-line trenches. He was also particularly active in the
Russian counter-mining operations designed to explode and
destroy the Japanese trenches and tunnels, as they advanced
towards the Russian positions, on at least one of these occasions
insisting on exploding the charges himself. Truly, if such an
expression be appropriate, Kondratenko was for the defenders
'the life and soul' of the siege.

In all, there were twenty-one senior military and naval
officers entitled by rank, major-generals and rear-admirals, and
colonels and naval captains with special appointments, to take
part in the deliberations of the Council of War, but apart from
those mentioned, and Colonel Reis who was Chief of Staff to
Stoessel and effectively his *alter ego*, few seem to have contributed a great deal, being content merely to attend and receive
their orders. It may well be said that there was little else they
could do at the moment.

In some famous sieges in the past the garrison had been able
to sustain itself with the hope of a relieving force coming to the
rescue. Any hope that Kuropatkin, with his three Manchurian
armies, was likely to carry out that function had long since

disappeared. At first, the news that Rozhestvensky's fleet had left Russia had been regarded optimistically, but time had dimmed the prospect of relief by sea. Anyhow, no one at Port Arthur knew where he was, somewhere off Africa presumably, but now that the Port Arthur fleet had gone to the bottom would not Rozhestvensky sail on to Vladivostock? Really, the only function of Port Arthur was to engage Nogi's army and thus prevent it joining Oyama's three armies in the north. The nearest parallel in Russian history, and it was not an encouraging one, was with the siege of Sebastopol in the Crimean War where the garrison of that fortress had held out against the British, French, Sardinians and Turks simply out of a determination not to give in and yield to an otherwise victorious enemy.

Outside the Council of War the garrison had fought, and still fought, with great bravery. Colonels and more junior officers of regiments had done wonders to redeem the reputation of the Russian officer corps. Their men had shown that given reasonable leadership they could fight the toughest adversaries imaginable and not be found wanting. Yet there was a limit, there must be a limit. Already the hospitals were full of well over 10,000 sick and wounded. Surprisingly, still, the occasional blockade runner would get through the tight Japanese cordon. The most recent had been a small British ship, the *King Arthur*, bringing a number of delicacies including smoked hams, as well as 800 tons of flour. But the contribution they could make was minimal. Already there was a raging Black Market in foodstuffs, meat (other than horseflesh) and mostly pork, selling at nearly £1 for a pound and eggs at over £6 for a dozen. The military stores were still reasonably full of stocks of grain, but men could not be expected to fight day and night on such a basic diet. Already they were showing symptoms, such as a high incidence of sickness and sleeping at their posts, which were attributable to their inadequate diet. Perhaps even more serious was the consciousness that for the Russians there could be no replacements for casualties, nor replenishments of shells, grenades and rifle ammunition.

Ultimately, then, the choice in the mind of every senior commander must have been – should Port Arthur surrender, or fight to the last man, and embrace the fate presumably envisaged by Stoessel when he had said, 'Port Arthur will be my grave.'

The choice was finally of course that of one man, the commander, Major-General Anatole Mikhailovich Stoessel, and in considering his motivation one comes up against a not unfamiliar problem in dealing with both the Russian army and navy, the quality of the man at the top. Just like Stackelberg and Bilderling, Witgeft and Rozhestvensky, Stoessel had risen through the grades of his profession, gaining what distinction there was to gain in time of peace, seeing some active service, in his case fairly recently during the Boxer Rebellion, and presumably distinguishing himself sufficiently to be chosen for the higher ranks. Yet he was manifestly unfit for the post he held. His disobedience to orders and his method of displacing Smirnoff showed that like Rozhestvensky his honesty could not be relied on. The fact that Kondratenko and others had been forced to take over the task of preparing the defences and encouraging the troops by personal example showed that like Stackelberg, Stoessel was afflicted with the militarily dangerous maladies of inactivity and complacency. His conflicting series of forecasts and reports to Kuropatkin on the state of Port Arthur reveal him either as an incompetent or else as someone whose mental stability must have been questionable.

Charitably, it might be said that after nearly five months of siege Stoessel could well have been suffering from strain and battle fatigue. Against this, however, can be placed the fact that his failings and inconsistencies had been noticed by some of his senior officers, themselves subject to the same strain, to the extent that there was some talk at least in the Smirnoff 'camp' of removing him as unfit for his command and replacing him by the fortress commander. Probably because of Smirnoff's own strong sense of duty and discipline, however, such talk came to nothing.

With any other commander than Stoessel obviously Port Arthur's resistance, unless some miracle occurred, must come to an end. That it did come to an end in the manner it did was attributable to one cruel stroke of fate and the personality of Major-General Stoessel.

After the capture of 203 Metre Hill and the destruction of the fleet, the Japanese heavy guns began to fire on the town and the harbour installation. In the process they also inflicted damage on one military hospital, but in all probability by accident, for some at least of their shells were erratic. At the same time the infantry and sappers continued their work of attempting to undermine and destroy the permanent fortifications both to the north-east and north-west. Slowly and steadily, almost foot by foot, if the Japanese were not carrying the Russian defences at tremendous cost to themselves they were damaging and destroying them. They were behaving in fact as if they were faced with some gigantic impassable natural feature through which a road had to be blasted and which only incidentally happened to be defended by artillery, machine-guns and rifles. The Russian reply, which showed few if any signs of weakening, was to attempt to destroy the burrowing Japanese by mines and explosives and if this was unsuccessful to defend the heaps of rubble and masonry remaining. As an indication of the nature of these operations it may be mentioned that relatively untrained officers and men on both sides were now dealing with explosive charges of anything from 100 to 1,000 lb. of dynamite, almost as if all their lives they had intended to be not infantry, but quarrymen. It was during one such operation, on December 15th, centred round the fort of Chikuan on the north-east front that Port Arthur suffered its most grievous loss. An 11-inch shell landed directly on the casemate of the fort burying under the fall of enormous masses of concrete Major-General Kondratenko and officers of his staff, including his faithful aide, Colonel of Engineers Rashevsky. The loss was irreparable, for no one occupied in the heart of the troops or the regard of his brother officers anything like Kondratenko's position. He alone was exempt from the jealousies and bickerings which afflicted the War Council and he alone was capable of sustaining the morale of the rank and file.

After his death, Major-General Fock was appointed to be, under Stoessel, the commander of the land forces. From the death of Russia's most active, and at the age of 47 youngest, general, a steady decline in the fortunes of the garrison of Port Arthur can be traced. As more than one participant remarked, the soul had gone out of the defence.

Steadily, as the old year ebbed away and the cold weather

became more intense, the great Russian fortresses, the corner-stones of the defence, Erhlung, Chikuan and Sungshu, fell to explosion and assault. The Japanese were now fast approaching the situation when no part of the fortress would be screened from their observation and their artillery fire. With the carrying of the last of the principal defence lines just before the New Year, ironically enough the reinforced old Chinese Wall, the Russians found themselves in the same position as besieged garrisons before and after them. As at Sedan, as at Dien Bien Phu, they were surrounded by an enemy which occupied all the available high ground around them, and who could now anticipate and restrict almost their every movement.

Days before that situation had been reached, however, Stoessel, Fock and Reis, who formed a pessimistic cabal among themselves, must have decided that despite all the Commanders' previous brave words, resistance to the end was not to be con-templated.

On December 29th a Council of War was held at which, despite the deterioration in the situation, the senior officers present by a considerable majority declared themselves in favour of continued resistance, being no doubt reinforced in this view by the reports of Major-Generals Byeli and Nikitin that there was no shortage of gun and rifle ammunition. How-ever, despite their decision, Stoessel, probably in connivance with Fock and Reis, must have made up his mind, for on the same day he despatched to the Tsar in St. Petersburg a telegram which as well as some theatrical phrases such as 'Great Sovereign. Forgive. We have done all that was humanly possible. Judge us but be merciful' included the more precise 'By the capture of Fort No. 3 (Fort Ehrlung) the Japanese have become masters of the whole north-east front and the Fortress can only hold out for a very few days. We have hardly any ammunition. . . .'

Without waiting for any reply from St. Petersburg, Stoessel, certainly now with Fock's and Reis' knowledge, sent a letter on January 1st under a flag of truce through the lines to General Nogi, written in English. The purport of the letter was contained in one sentence,

Therefore in order to avoid needless waste of life, I desire to open negotiations for the evacuation of the fortress.

Almost at the same time a thunderstruck Admiral Wiren received orders that he had only a short time in which to ensure that all ships and harbour installations were completely destroyed. Meantime Major-General Fock, very quick off the mark indeed, was having some difficulty in persuading subordinate commanders in the outlying fortresses and emplacements that when he ordered them to destroy and evacuate, he meant it, and that he was giving them direct orders which had to be obeyed. Although firing still continued from both sides the rumours quickly spread through the garrison, confirmed very soon by the roar of explosions as Fock's orders were carried out. A surprised and furious General Smirnoff, who had not been consulted, found himself in the position of realising that things had gone too far for him to think of taking over command. Released after months of endurance and tension, soldiers and sailors began to ignore the bonds of discipline and emerge from their entrenchments, still bewildered, still doubting.

The Japanese, relaxing not one bit, steadily and methodically moved into the evacuated and deserted positions, where if it was necessary they dug themselves in in case of further fighting.

Their precautions were however unnecessary, there was to be no more fighting. On January 2nd, by which time the last rifle shots had died away from even the most distant outposts, Colonel Reis, empowered by Stoessel as chief negotiator, and accompanied by a posse of staff officers and interpreters, met with a similar team led by General Idichi, Nogi's Chief-of-Staff. The Japanese had a comprehensive draft of their surrender terms set out in detail, they had been written some months ago. The Russians haggled a bit, their main request being that the garrison should not be made prisoners of war. This Idichi flatly refused, though he indicated that some concessions would be made in the case of officers. At 9.45 p.m. on January 2nd, 1905 the terms of surrender were signed by Idichi and Reis.

General Stoessel then gave orders for the destruction of war material to cease. In Port Arthur that night large numbers of Russian troops threw away their arms, drank anything they could find and began to embark on full-scale looting expeditions through the streets of the town which they had defended for 154 days and nights.

In the next few days small detachments of Japanese began to enter the town, having just taken over all the remaining fortresses and trenches. The Russians themselves restored order among their own ranks, though General Stoessel asked for, and was given, a Japanese guard detachment for his own headquarters. General Nogi himself did not make a formal entry into the town until January 13th, accompanied by contingents from every regiment and unit which had played a part in the siege.

Before his ceremonial entry, which was a quiet and restrained affair, other detachments of the Japanese army had entered the town in a disciplined and orderly manner which came almost as a disappointment to some war correspondents who no doubt had contemplated headlines announcing rapine and outrage. The Japanese officers charged with the task of collecting together and assessing all the booty, from prisoners of war to half-submerged battleships, found some of their figures somewhat surprising.

Although some guns were damaged and many rounds of ammunition defective for one reason or another, they found that they had captured more than 600 guns of various calibres and nearly 34,000 shells, plus 35,000 rifles and over two million rounds of small arms ammunition. Nearly 3,000 live horses were captured and on average about a month's supply of rations for these horses and nearly 33,000 men. The only real deficiency was salt meat and live cattle, although there was enough tea and salt and nearly enough dried vegetables to have lasted for the duration of another siege.

In the various hospitals there were 15,000 sick and wounded, and of those Russian combatants found fit to march into captivity there were 878 officers and 23,491 men.

It was perhaps this last figure that the Japanese found most surprising, for they had been led to believe, and no doubt applying their own rigid standards of military honour expected, that there would be no more than 10,000 fit men in the fortress. The Russians had in fact lost nearly 6,000 men killed and over 20,000 wounded. The Japanese price for Port Arthur was over

14,000 killed and missing, 36,000 wounded and over 30,000 sick in hospital.

A few days later the Tsar and the Emperor of Japan received almost identical telegrams expressing admiration for the conduct of their troops and asking for their consent to the award to both General Stoessel and General Nogi of the highest military distinction of the German Empire, the Order 'Pour le Mérite'. The author of the telegram was of course Kaiser Wilhelm II.

SEVENTEEN

'*Serious disorders took place in Petersburg*'

TSAR NICOLAS II

The news of the fall of Port Arthur flashed around the world and produced a variety of reactions. In Britain and France press comments had a curious similarity, despite the fact that Japan was the ally of Britain and Russia of France. While Britain was naturally pleased with her ally's performance, considerable space was devoted to the courage and endurance of the besieged. France, though sympathising with the defeat of a 'friendly and allied nation' made honourable mention of the bravery of the besiegers. Both countries were much impressed by the restraint shown by the Japanese in occupying the town. The German press, perhaps because the Kaiser had got in first with his telegrams and decorations, seemed to hand over comment to their military correspondents, and the principal journals gave considerable space to discussion of strategy and tactics, ammunition and armaments. Perhaps the most interesting reaction came second-hand by way of foreign correspondents, mainly British, in places such as China, India and Persia. The reaction was one of surprise, not unmixed with pleasure. The greatest European land power had had wrested from it the last bastion of its colony in the East, which with Dalny had been intended to rival Hong Kong or Singapore, a colony protected by a large army and a considerable fleet. This had been achieved not by another European power, but by a small Oriental nation of whom many Chinese, Indians, Afghans and Persians had hardly heard twenty years ago. The fact that all these people had for generations lived in awe of Russia added to the effect of the news, and a number of journalists reported that influential Chinese were now saying that Japan had shown the way to others who for too long had been subjected to the domination of the West. The fact that Japan by her victories was herself becoming a colonial power was not mentioned and perhaps not fully appreciated.

After the news of the capitulation itself the details of the supplies still in Port Arthur at the surrender began to be reported. The conduct of the Russian officers who took advantage of the Japanese offer of parole and so returned in comfort to Russia instead of choosing captivity with their men aroused a great deal of unfavourable comment. The Japanese had granted the concession at the request of the Russians, and perhaps out of a sense of what they thought was fitting in the circumstances. It is likely, however, that they had not expected many officers to take up the offer, which necessitated that they give their word to take no further part in the war. In fact a large number of the officers, led by General Stoessel, left Port Arthur with the wives, children and non-combatants, leaving their men to fend for themselves in Japanese prisoner-of-war camps.

Soon the newspapers were beginning to criticise Stoessel and then to chip at his reputation as a hero. Few however were as yet as outspoken as the Peking correspondent of *The Times* who three weeks after the surrender ended a splendid diatribe in the following way:

> All accounts agree that no man who ever held a responsible command less deserved the title of hero than General Stoessel.
> Those who have witnessed the condition of the fortress, contrasting the evidence of their eyes with the astounding misrepresentation of General Stoessel, had their sympathy turned into derision, believing that no more discreditable surrender has been recorded in history. Had the Kaiser waited until he had received the reports of the German and other military attachés, he could never have conferred the Order 'Pour le Mérite' upon General Stoessel.

In Japan itself the news of Nogi's final victory was received quietly. Too often in the past the fall of the fortress had been anticipated for there to be any great public rejoicing now. The figures from the enormous roll of casualties also had a muting effect upon the nation which, however high its patriotic spirit, was becoming increasingly conscious of its vast sacrifices of manpower.

General Stoessel was to arrive, neither commended nor criticised, by way of Japan in a Russia which was numbed by yet another defeat. On the day of the announcement of the fall of Port Arthur, soldiers had been seen to weep openly in the streets. While Port Arthur had held out there was some hope, some consolation in the feats of bravery and endurance reported in the press. Now there was nothing. For many the war was over, the Empire in the East had collapsed, and what Kuropatkin could do in Manchuria or Rozhestvensky achieve with his fleet was almost an irrelevance. There was considerable doubt expressed as to whether he would now continue with his voyage. The decline in Russia's fortunes in one year was even expressed in the Tsar's New Year message to his troops.

In January 1904 he had telegraphed the customary,

May God bless Russia with peace and prosperity in the coming year,

but in January 1905 a more solemn note was struck,

With all Russia I believe that the hour of our victory is approaching, and the Lord God will bless my beloved army and navy with renewed strength to crush the enemy and to support the honour and glory of Our Fatherland.

Certainly at two widely separated points on the globe the Tsar's divinely inspired optimism was not reflected. In Madagascar two Russian fleets had arrived in its steamy heat in time to celebrate Christmas according to the Russian calendar. Rozhestvensky's division had survived a considerable battering round the Cape to arrive at Ile Sainte Marie and then to move on to Diego Suarez. Felkerzam's division had had a much easier passage, the only real crisis occurring when some of the crew, drunk and naked, had scandalised the streets of Cannae during shore leave in Crete. It had now apparently arrived at Nossi Bé, 500 miles away on the other side of the island. The cause for the two rendezvous was finally explained when the two admirals met, but the information was of the type designed to send Rozhestvensky into another of his famous rages. Felkerzam, because of his route more in touch with St. Petersburg than Rozhestvensky, had been ordered to Nossi Bé to refit and recuperate at his leisure, because there was another fleet on its way, the Third or Reinforcing Squadron, which was soon to leave Libau. The Higher Naval Board in its wisdom had decided that Rozhestvensky needed more ships, even if they were the more elderly vessels he had once rejected, and that it was worth his while to await their arrival, even if it meant an eight to ten weeks' delay in reaching the Far East.

Almost at the same time Rozhestvensky learned of the fall of Port Arthur, and the consequent complete destruction of the Russian fleet there. Now, Russia had no naval base in the Far East nearer than Vladivostock, and Rozhestvensky would have to face the whole of the Japanese navy which now had no other task but to sit and wait for his arrival.

Rozhestvensky's situation was now almost indescribable. On every side there were frustrations and disappointments. Almost every day a despatch boat was sent to the nearest telegraph station to send or receive messages to and from St. Petersburg.

Almost as if cut off from the world he and more than 10,000 Russian sailors lay off an African island. The French authorities, protested to by the Japanese for a breach of neutrality, had a duty to bother him with periodical visits from a cruiser. To conform with diplomatic niceties, some part at least of the combined Russian fleet had to be either in motion or outside territorial waters when the cruiser arrived. On shore officers and sailors sought relief from the boredom and the heat in Nossi Bé and the neighbouring, not inappropriately named, Helleville. Native traders made profits and native women and native alcohol caused fights and disturbances. The hospital ship was full.

Telegrams from St. Petersburg confirmed that two cruisers which had been left behind as unready were now on their way, plus the Reinforcing Squadron composed in essence of one old battleship and some coast defence vessels, heavily gunned but elderly, unmanoeuvrable and slow. Rear-Admiral Nebogatoff was in command, which in a sense made the command line-up even less impressive. Of Nebogatoff, Enkvist, Felkerzam and Rozhestvensky himself, none had seen recent active service, none had commanded a naval formation in a battle, and Felkerzam was ill and confined to his ship.

Seeking relief in action, Rozhestvensky put his ships and crews to exercises. Their gunnery, especially on the part of the *Oslyabya*, was not as bad as might have been expected, but ammunition had to be conserved because there would now be no new supplies until they met the Japanese. Although Rozhestvensky could not know it, gunnery practice results were not much better in the Japanese navy, or, for that matter, in the British navy. His fleet's deficiencies in manoeuvring, in keeping station, in turning to order, however, were painfully obvious. On almost every exercise battleships and cruisers narrowly avoided collision. Truth to tell, he hardly commanded a fleet, but an assortment of not very well matched vessels, each one answerable to a captain of very limited experience.

Off Madagascar a depression settled over the whole of the Russian fleet. The Admiral raged at his officers, but, to his credit, not at the lower decks. No one in the Ministry of Marine seemed to appreciate his difficulties. Rumour went round the fleet that he had tendered his resignation, but that it had been refused. News filtered through of civil unrest and riots in Russia, more disturbing to a fleet which contained many reservists than to one entirely composed of regulars. It is perhaps no wonder that overcome by exhaustion, or suffering some form of nervous breakdown or stroke, the Admiral retired to his cabin for some days to emerge worn and pale, dragging one of his feet when he walked.

The news from Russia perhaps accounted in part for the Government's seeming indifference to Rozhestvensky's reports and requests. In St. Petersburg at the moment the war was forgotten, although its lack of success, culminating in the news of the surrender of Port Arthur, had played a considerable part, if only as a catalyst, in bringing about the present situation.

It has been seen already how in the previous year agitation for reform of the political system had grown at an alarming rate. Curiously perhaps, such agitation, by way of speeches, meetings and the 'banquets' which were in fact disguised political gatherings, was almost entirely confined to the educated middle class: curiously because although this was obviously the thinking part of the population this was not the class which had suffered most either politically, socially or economically, nor was

it a class which had been affected to any noticeable extent by
the economic depression exacerbated by war. That class was
the peasantry and the urban workers. It is easy to see, therefore,
how a short-sighted Government, and the Tsar's advisers were
beyond belief myopic, could console itself with the thought
that though despised intellectuals could agitate, and at times
subject nationalities demonstrate, the great mass of simple
workers and peasants were loyal to their 'Little Father',
Nicholas II.

To a large extent the latter analysis was true. There was a
large fund of loyalty to the sovereign but in 1904 and 1905 there
were many, and Father Gapon was among them, who were
beginning to make a distinction between a patriarchal but
distant Emperor and his advisers – 'the Grand Dukes', lumped
together with some justice as purblind autocrats, and a number
of oppressive governors and prefects and indifferent Ministers.
From this distinction there grew the feeling encouraged by
Gapon, that if only the workers could get through to the Tsar,
past his insulating horde of Ministers and officials, soldiers and
policemen, then he would listen to their grievances and right
them. Gapon's encouragement of such a project was as far as
can be judged sincere and he now dominated eleven branches of
what could be called 'his' Assembly of St. Petersburg Factory
Workers. This meant nine or ten thousand factory workers and
a following of many thousands more, perhaps fifty thousand
men and women, comprising more than half the manual workers
in the capital.

However, it was to the intelligentsia's precise and articulate
demands and not to the workers' plight that the Government
decided to yield in 1904. In December of that year an Imperial
Ukase was issued which contained many of the proposals which
Prince Mirsky had urged with threats of his own resignation
and which the intelligentsia had been pressing for months. Not
untypically, the reforms were a rag-bag of concessions: the
removal of some of the 'disabilities' imposed on national and religious minorities, a move towards a freer press, the ending of the
virtual martial law which governed so-called 'protected' areas,
and the establishment of a scheme of State insurance for low-
paid workers. All worth while, but totally in consonance with

official thinking, these measures were regarded as a sop to achieve peace and quiet. The demand which really mattered and which the Zemstva and Duma members hoped would lead to some measure of democracy at a national level – that there should be elected members to the State Council – was ignored. So the liberals were not satisfied, although in the Government's view they should have been. They had been given a present and now they were expected to behave. In the last weeks of December political meetings and demonstrations were again made illegal although the police did not yet think it wise to enforce the law too rigorously. Many moderate liberals were disillusioned and were now coming to the conclusion that the Tsar and his circle would not yield to reason, but only to some form of force. Inevitably, if slowly, they began to see common cause with the out-and-out revolutionaries.

For the moment, however, the middle-class reformers were quiescent. Doubtless, the Tsar and his advisers breathed a sigh of relief, but if they were satisfied their satisfaction was to be short-lived. The Tsar was not to be allowed to return to his preoccupation with the war in the Far East for some time.

Christmas was quiet in St. Petersburg, and so was New Year's Day. The Tsar and his family moved out of the capital to the Alexander Palace at Tsarskoe Selo, 15 miles away, presumably to relax from the cares of statecraft.

The only cloud, the size of a man's hand, was a strike at the Putiloff Armaments Factory, originally over the alleged unjust dismissal of four workmen, but beginning to embrace more general complaints. Gapon was not unnaturally busy among his charges, but in the eyes of officialdom this was all to the good, that after all was his job. It is difficult to say precisely how the Putiloff strike grew, no doubt partly by accident and partly by design. The question 'whose design?' is equally impossible to answer. Sufficient is it to say that there was ample cause in the condition of the workers and the machinery was to hand in Gapon's assemblies. It is doubtful if he could have been the sole organiser and inspiration, but certainly by his speeches and activities he appeared so to be. The strike spread from the Putiloff works to the Franco-Russian Shipbuilding plant and then to other factories. Soon there were 25,000 workers out asking for better wages and improved working conditions. It was in fact an indictment of officialdom that no one, neither Prince Mirsky, the Minister of the Interior, nor the Grand Duke Vladimir, Commander of the St. Petersburg Military District, seemed to take any notice of what was fast becoming a general strike throughout the whole industrial district of the capital. Yet representatives sought and obtained an audience with Witte, who told them that he had no jurisdiction over the subject of their complaints, and sought but were refused a meeting with Mirsky.

It is not clear when the strikers, led by Gapon, decided on a peaceful march to the Winter Palace to put their grievances to the Tsar. However, when the proposal became public knowledge, officialdom began to stir itself. Troops and police were drafted into the capital and General Vasilchikoff of the Imperial Guard Division was placed in charge of operations.

Mirsky and the Tsar were both informed of the march and the troop preparations, but at no time did anyone seem remotely to consider the possibility that the Tsar might actually come into his capital and receive if not all the workers then perhaps a delegation. Nor as a kindness did anyone think of informing Gapon and his organisers that the Tsar was not in the Winter Palace but 15 miles away at Tsarskoe Selo.

On Sunday January 9th (by the Russian calendar) the streets of St. Petersburg filled with two bodies of people, both lacking in clear instructions and objectives. In the industrial district thousands of men, women and children gathered, peaceful and orderly, holding up ikons, religious flags, the Russian flag, and pictures of the Tsar and Tsaritsa. As they began to march they sang hymns, and policemen cleared the way and kept back the onlookers, who bared their heads and crossed themselves as the religious symbols were carried past.

As they began their march from the south of the city, in the centre round the Winter Palace and the great Palace Square, the other body, the *élite* of the Russian army, the Semenovsky, Pavlovsky and Preobazhensky regiments of Foot Guards, and the Horse Grenadiers of the Guard on their jet-black mounts, were taking up their positions.

The workers were organised into converging columns and

the subsequent history of each column, one of which was led by Gapon, was tragically similar. When each column reached the neighbourhood of the Palace the police ordered it to halt. In nearly every case the workers disobeyed and continued peaceably on. Then the cavalry moved in to break the heads of the columns. Finally, the infantry fired a volley over the heads of the crowd and then a second into the packed masses of men, women and children, some of whom were already fleeing when they saw what was about to happen.

The disturbances which followed continued confusedly throughout the short cold wintry day and into the evening. Finally, Vasilchikoff decided to clear the streets of everybody, strikers, bystanders and the merely curious. There were difficulties in some areas now with workers and students enraged by the troops' actions and in some places barricades were put up and minor battles fought, but by nightfall order had been restored and the only inhabitants of the streets were patrolling soldiers. The official casualty figures were 94 civilians dead and 333 wounded, of whom 34 died in hospital. The police casualties were two dead. These, however, were official government figures of bodies and wounded collected. Many more dead and wounded, some of whom may have died subsequently, were undoubtedly removed by the strikers themselves.

That night the Tsar wrote in his diary,

A grim day! As a result of the desire of the workers to go to the Winter Palace, serious disorders took place in Petersburg. In many parts of the city troops were compelled to fire; many were killed or wounded. God, how sad and grim.

In the long and reasonable petition which the workers had hoped to present to the Tsar there were only two direct references to the Japanese war: in the preamble where the phrase 'government by bureaucracy has devastated the country, has involved it in a horrible war, and is leading it further and further into ruin' occurs; and later, among the many requests, there is to be found 'termination of the war in accord with popular demand'. For the rest, the petition is devoted to the remedying of social, political and industrial grievances.

Nevertheless, the Ministry of War was soon announcing that

'Anglo-Japanese provocateurs' had fomented the strikes in an effort to cripple the Russian armaments industry. How many people actually believed this in Russia it is difficult to tell. What is certain is that very few realised that what soon came to be called 'Bloody Sunday' was the beginning of a new disillusionment with the Tsar among the hitherto inertly loyal masses, and that while Russia was at war she was also in a state of revolution.

Although the war and its complete lack of success had helped to spark off a revolution, the news of 'Bloody Sunday' and its aftermath, suitably doctored and censored in all available Russian newspapers, did not have any immediate effect upon the armies in Manchuria, save perhaps to deepen its disillusionment with the war and the sense of helplessness. Rozhestvensky's fleet, more literate and educated, and more recently in Russia, took more notice as personal recollections testify. Yet both bodies of men were subject to the bonds of discipline, far from Russia and facing or about to face a powerful enemy. In the nature of things they had little choice of action, but it would not be too fanciful to regard the 1905 Revolution as symptomatic of many ills in the Russian system and to contrast, as a purely military consideration, the declining morale of Russian soldiers and sailors with the burning zeal and patriotism of the Japanese.

At the same time the news of the Winter Palace massacre was reported widely in newspapers in Europe and the U.S.A., and shifted opinion, both official and public, firmly against Russia even in those countries, such as France and Germany, which had hitherto been friendly or benevolently neutral.

Meanwhile, as Russia and Japan entered their second year of conflict, there existed in Manchuria, centred round Mukden, the largest army Russia had so far assembled in her history. Curiously, perhaps, at the head of the three Manchurian armies there were respectively, a general of Polish Catholic ancestry, Linievich, a Lithuanian Protestant, Grippenberg, and one of German stock, Kaulbars. At their head, and considerably younger than any of the other three, there was the only true Russian, Kuropatkin. Temperamentally, too, he was divided from his subordinates. Linievich was cold, proud and distant, Grippenberg melancholic and either a hypochondriac or else genuinely in poor health. Kaulbars looked like a blimp and was a swashbuckling extrovert. Kuropatkin had much more of the good soldier's temperament; although he was often too cautious in his actual conduct of a battle, he did possess a sort of incurable optimism. He had not yet celebrated a victory, and in the early stages he had been forced to defer to Alexieff, the gubernatorial sailor. The deficiencies of the Russian staff and command system meant that delegation was almost impossible, but he never gave up. Now, in 1905, in his newly acquired German motor car, the first general to use such a conveyance, he toured his armies, encouraging all who saw him and never losing the confidence and affection of the rank and file.

The fall of Port Arthur had presented him with a double-sided problem. The loss of the fortress had at last rid him of an obligation to pay lip service to the idea of its relief. Quite obviously no one, not even in far-off St. Petersburg, now expected him to try to regain it. At the same time a considerable part of Nogi's army, battle-toughened veterans all, would now be released to join Oyama's forces facing his own. Already there were reports of Japanese units leaving Port Arthur behind them and moving north. The Second Pacific Squadron would presumably some day turn up in Far Eastern waters but only to head for Vladivostock. Some Russians feared that the next move of the Japanese would be to advance on that port, but that danger was somewhat remote, as it was extremely unlikely that the Japanese would wish to embark upon a second Port Arthur.

Kuropatkin's dilemma was therefore very similar to that which was to face generals on the Western Front in the First World War. He had a considerable army and what they did not always have, the promise of unlimited reinforcements. Behind him stretched the Trans-Siberian Railway, which had not succumbed to attacks and raids from hunhutzus, even though they were now encouraged, and in some cases led, by Japanese officers and agents. Under the direction of Prince Khilkoff the railway had improved its service and could now be relied on as a constant source of supply of men and warlike material. Troops were now increasingly in demand in Russia itself as civil disturbances spread to Poland and Finland, but the Russians' problem had never been shortage of manpower and so far reinforcements for the East had not been affected. Therefore Kuropatkin had plenty of men and a relatively stable fortified front, and the question was, what was to be his next move? The temptation must have been to stay on the defensive and simply wait and see what the Japanese would do next.

Perhaps Kuropatkin would have been a wiser general if he had done just that and thereby posed the problem to the Japanese, leaving them to decide the difficult questions such as how much farther north, and at what further cost, they wanted to advance.

However, it is all credit to Kuropatkin that, even at this stage, he still tried to wrest the initiative from his opponents and for once impose his will upon them.

Accordingly, he began to formulate plans to take action against the Japanese before their full strength was concentrated with the addition of Nogi's army from Port Arthur.

It is a sad comment on Kuropatkin's reputation as a general and upon the condition of the Russian army that though he had a superiority in numbers, and the plan, as will be seen, was reasonable enough, contemporary commentators expressed surprise immediately after the event that he should even have contemplated such action. There would seem to be little doubt that the plan was Kuropatkin's own, but nevertheless as soon as the combination of news and rumours leaked out that he was taking the initiative a number of military observers and correspondents, including Sir Ian Hamilton, assumed that his object was not military but political. They suggested that St. Petersburg had commanded him to create a diversion in Manchuria which would take the Russians' minds away from the increasingly desperate domestic situation. If this were so the results were to prove disappointing, but the theory was an unlikely one, as was its 'embroidery' that the recently arrived General Grippenberg was the bearer of these instructions and was also the man given the duty to see that they were carried out.

However, this is to anticipate. Kuropatkin's plan was to discover the Japanese strength, and if reports indicated that Nogi's army had not yet arrived, to strike a blow before it did so. The method chosen was the cavalry raid, hallowed by examples such as Stuart's success in the American Civil War, and particularly well adapted to the situation in Manchuria where the Russians possessed a superabundance of that particular arm.

The situation of the Russian Manchurian armies was that the right was occupied by Grippenberg's army, the centre by Kaulbars and the left by Linievich. On Linievich's left, to the east, there was Rennenkamp's cavalry while on Grippenberg's right to the west there was posted Major-General Mischenko's cavalry force. It was this latter formation which Kuropatkin decided to put into action.

The object of their attack was to be Yingkau, the port of Niewchuang near the mouth of the Liao river. This had now become the site of a considerable Japanese supply depot joined by a branch line to the main railway from Port Arthur, through Liaoyang, to Mukden. This line would, it seemed likely, be used by Japanese reinforcements from the south so that at one and the same time Mischenko could destroy and observe.

Accordingly on January 8th the General rode off across the Hun river from the main Russian position south of Mukden at the head of six thousand cavalrymen, mostly Cossacks, accompanied by six batteries of horse-artillery. Mr. Francis McCullagh of the *New York Herald* accompanied this picturesque force and cabled home a report of its activities.

The performance was unfortunately well below the appearance. Japanese intelligence was again good, and though Mischenko was striking at a poorly defended area there were soon troops to oppose him. Wisely, perhaps, the Japanese did not oppose cavalry with cavalry but sent up infantry reinforcements by rail. Mischenko never reached Yingkau and only slight damage was done to the branch line. Soon his dashing cavalrymen were in retreat from prosaic rifle-firing infantry, and some part of his division was forced to violate neutral Chinese territory to the west in order to return safely. Casualties were few, but the strike had failed. The information that he brought back to Kuropatkin, that Nogi's 3rd Army had not reached the other Japanese armies north of Liaoyang, could no doubt have been obtained by other means and as it turned out was perhaps of doubtful value.

Thus a good plan failed in its execution and revealed the Russians as being not particularly skilful in an area of military activity in which they may well have thought they exercised superiority. At the same time Mischenko's raid proved to be but a curtain raiser to two related battles which were to decide Kuropatkin's fate as a general and indeed the fate of the Russian armies in Manchuria.

Mischenko's information that the whole of Nogi's army had not yet arrived where it would be expected to find its place, on the Japanese left, provided a considerable temptation for Kuropatkin. He was, as has been seen, a cautious general, certainly when the actual battle was joined; but he must by now have been oppressed by his own retreats and failures and therefore almost unable to discount what appeared to be the presentation of an opportunity to score a victory. Undoubtedly his present superiority in numbers encouraged him towards such a course. It is also possible that a marked deterioration in the weather may have led him to hope that Russian soldiers, more accustomed to such conditions, would have an advantage over their opponents. So the Russians were ordered to leave their well dug-in and protected lines before Mukden and move into the attack.

Naturally as the Japanese weakness was assessed to be on their left the lead in the attack was made by the Russian right under Grippenberg. It was that general's first essay in commanding an army in Manchuria, and in that sense his baptism of fire. On January 26th he advanced one of his divisions across the frozen Hun river as heavy snow was falling and so made the first move in a three-day battle which was variously called Sandepu and Heikoutai after two small Manchurian villages 36 miles south-west of Mukden.

The conditions soon became such that one of the British observers, not given to hyperbole, said in his report, 'Rarely, if ever, have troops fought under such terrible conditions.' During the night the temperature fell to nearly 45° of frost while during the day it was rarely less than 15°. For the Russians the climate must have been bad enough, but for the Japanese, hastily rushed to stem the tide, truly appalling. Throughout the whole battle the prevailing wind, which at times was almost at gale force, blew directly in their faces as they struggled to make progress towards the north-east.

Steadily the Russians increased the pressure until they had committed seven divisions while the Japanese were hardly able to assemble four, one of which was their 8th Division which had seen no previous fighting of any seriousness, having only arrived in the theatre of war in October of the previous year.

Finally, on the second day of the battle the Russians succeeded in capturing Heikoutai, but not, despite tremendous efforts, Sandepu. Into this small walled village of about a hundred thatched buildings, on the direct orders of Marshal Oyama, the Japanese poured the infantry of their 5th Division supported by artillery. It was at this stage that some sort of disagreement developed between Kuropatkin and Grippenberg. The latter, despite no particular marked success so far, wanted to go on and to do so demanded considerable reinforcements. Kuropatkin refused to commit more troops and on January 28th ordered his subordinate to retire. At about the same time Oyama determined that the Russians must be driven back over the Hun river and his troops succeeded, though in the Marshal's words 'all the columns of the attacking parties expected annihilation', in recapturing Heikoutei.

Grippenberg then, according to his own account reluctantly, obeyed his orders as did his men who, he was to write later, 'retired unwillingly with tears in their eyes'. By the next day the battle was over, the Japanese having a total of 9,000 killed and wounded, while the Russians had the appalling total of nearly 20,000 killed and wounded, plus 400 prisoners lost to their enemy.

These were the worst losses, proportionate to the men involved and the time engaged, of the whole war, many of the wounded being in fact men suffering from frostbite, and many others who might otherwise have survived, dying of the extreme cold.

From the Russian point of view nothing at all had been achieved while the Japanese had merely, but at considerable cost, confirmed their superiority in command, organisation and fighting prowess. Perhaps, however, the most revealing light shed on Russian military methods and standards was in the sequel, as far as it concerned the two generals Kuropatkin and Grippenberg.

On January 20th Grippenberg reported to Kuropatkin and asked to be relieved of his command. He also telegraphed to St. Petersburg asking to be relieved on grounds of ill-health. Asked by the War Council for his real reason he stated his disagreement with his Commander-in-Chief and promptly returned to Russia, having held his command of the 2nd Manchurian Army for only a matter of seven weeks. With the snow of Manchuria off his boots Grippenberg's conduct became more curious. In St. Petersburg he was received in private audience by the Tsar and but a few days later gave an interview to a reporter of *Novoye Vremiya*, saying flatly that a victory would have been within his grasp if Kuropatkin had not refused him reinforcements.

Now generals had been known to disagree with their superiors in the past, and they were of course to do so in the future, but for Grippenberg thus to reveal the dissensions of the High Command in the middle of a desperate war was inexcusable. Even worse perhaps was the nature of the divisions he revealed. Who was right, Grippenberg or Kuropatkin, hardly mattered, but it was plain to all that a battle in which an enormous number of Russian soldiers had suffered death and wounds in virtually sub-arctic conditions had been fought under a mammoth misapprehension on the part of either the Commander-in-Chief or the general commanding one of his armies. Kuropatkin had planned a raid in force presumably, but Grippenberg had seen his action as the beginning of a battle which was to pull in many more Russian troops and turn into a general action involving not only his army but that of his eastern neighbour General Kaulbars as well.

There were of course other interpretations of the now publicly aired dispute, and variations and rumours chased each other round St. Petersburg and inevitably within the Manchurian armies where Bilderling, having once been demoted, was now promoted to fill Grippenberg's place. Unfortunately for the Russians no one could gain credit from the battle nor the arguments which followed it. Following close upon the growing criticism of Stoessel's conduct at Port Arthur, and coupled with reports of increasing civil disorder at home, the picture pre-

sented of Russia to the world in early 1905 was of a nation
bedevilled with incompetence in high places.

This view of their enemy, it is needless to say, did not pass
unremarked by the Japanese.

EIGHTEEN

'It is essential that the enemy be dealt
a heavy blow'

MARSHAL OYAMA

Now it was the turn of the Japanese to be tempted: tempted by the thought of outright victory.

Throughout the course of a year of warfare, they had been universally successful. Time and time again the Russians on land and sea had shown themselves to be slow in reaction and incompetent in execution, often no doubt well beyond the reasonable expectations of the Japanese themselves. Only at Port Arthur, despite the premature final surrender by Stoessel, had the length and quality of the resistance come as a shock to generals who had originally thought in terms of taking the stronghold by the first general assault.

The new year was obviously a time for the Japanese to assess their progress, and think in terms of future action. Once again they were to give little regard to Russian performance on land and over-emphasised the dangers likely to arise when once again there was Russian naval force in the Far East. In one sense perhaps they were right; some of their own successes at sea had contained an element of chance and luck – Makaroff and Witgeft had both been removed at a stroke – the result of a naval battle was far less predictable than a land battle. The Second Pacific Squadron, without Port Arthur, could hardly avoid battle and who could tell what might happen in an encounter between two fleets which, at least on paper, seemed almost equally matched? One or two accurate shots from the 12-inch guns of the *Suvoroff* or her sister ships and the whole balance of seapower in Japanese waters could be reversed.

At the same time the Japanese had gone almost as far as they could in expenditure of money and men. Their military reserves were called up to the limit and Japan itself was virtually denuded of fighting troops. Economically too she was at full stretch, and the financial position of Russia, despite her internal and external difficulties, was still considerably better than her own. There were signs too that European banking houses, even those controlled or influenced by the British, were beginning to look a little askance at Japanese ambitions. What is more Russia could not be totally defeated: Japan had swept Korea free of Russians but Kuropatkin could retreat many more miles into Manchuria and Russia itself would be unaffected. Yet still there was the temptation to try for an all-out victory on land, an attempt not to push back the Russian army but to destroy it, to inflict a Canae or a Sedan before Rozhestvensky appeared in the war theatre.

Throughout the war Japanese intelligence was good, save in one respect – the state of the Baltic Fleet. For the very good reason that though there were Japanese spies, or other nationals spying for Japan, in Port Arthur, in Korea and Manchuria, there was none at Kronstadt.

Nevertheless, in the early part of the year there were two matters, both well publicised, which though perhaps only straws in the wind should have given the Japanese some better indication than they had of the quality of the Russian fleet and the navy of which it formed a part.

On February 26th the five Commissioners – Vice-Admiral Sir Lewis Beaumont, Vice-Admiral Dubassoff, Admiral Baron von Spaun of Austria-Hungary, Rear-Admiral Davis of the United States Navy, and their French president, Vice-Admiral Fournier – published their conclusions on the Dogger Bank incident. Diplomatically it was a superb and welcome whitewashing operation, no doubt to the intense relief of both the British and Russian Governments.

By now of course with the passage of time much of the steam had gone out of the affair. At the time a scheming Kaiser, always anxious to wean Russia away from her French alliance and form some sort of combination against Britain, had fed an enraged and half-persuaded Tsar a number of 'authoritative'

rumours and falsehoods, all leading to the conclusion that as far
as the British and Japanese were concerned 'there has been
foul play'.

Far from accepting the Kaiser's version the Commission
decided 'that they lack precise evidence to identify on what
objects the ships fired, but the Commissioners unanimously
recognised that the boats of the flotilla committed no hostile
act, and the majority of the Commissioners being of the
opinion that there was no torpedo boat either among the
trawlers or on the spot, the fire opened by Admiral Rozhestvensky was not justifiable'.

The report was a long one, but this was the most important
sentence. Excuses were then found for Rozhestvensky's behaviour
although there was disapproval of his failure to give aid to the
trawlers or even report their plight. In many ways the report was
a masterpiece as it did manage to do justice to the British claim
while sparing, as far as it could, Russian susceptibilities.

As a result, the claim of the British Government for £65,000
compensation for the Hull trawlermen was promptly paid by the
Russians.

For the Japanese the report should have held a definite
interest, particularly in what might be called the small type,
where the Commissioners dealt with what they decided had
been the real cause of the incident. The cruiser *Aurora* they
found had been hit by a number of 47-mm and 75-mm projectiles which could only have come from a capital ship,
probably the *Suvoroff*. Further, it seemed likely that the *Aurora*
and perhaps other cruisers had in fact engaged in a gun duel
with the battleship division. In addition it was only when the
Dmitri Donskoi identified herself that Rozhestvensky ordered
the cease-fire.

Even from the terse officialese of this report the Japanese
should have formed some preliminary evaluation of the state of
the fleet that was sailing on its way to meet them in battle, and
drawn some consolation from the apparent state of both its
gunnery discipline and its general morale.

At no stage of course could Togo and his admirals afford to
ignore the threat posed by the Second Pacific Squadron, but
there was also another indication available in the early part of

1905 of the fact that, at the very least, the Russian navy was not free of the defects which afflicted the Russian army.

Before giving his evidence before the North Sea Inquiry in Paris as the designated principal witness, Captain Klado, the sailor-journalist, had returned to St. Petersburg where he had engaged in some strange activities for a serving naval officer.

Almost immediately he had given a lecture on naval policy in the house of Admiral Birileff, the Commander-in-Chief at Kronstadt. This he had followed up with a series of articles in *Novoye Vremiya* criticising the Ministry of Marine and arguing that more ships should be sent to reinforce Rozhestvensky's fleet. The Ministry retaliated with an Order of the Day accusing Klado of misrepresentation and sentencing him to arrest. Klado denied the accusation by a letter to the paper and demanded a court martial. Soon there was a 'Klado movement' with meetings and demonstrations. The Ministry backed down, withdrew its accusations and Klado, an honest man and something of a popular hero, departed to give his testimony to the Commission in Paris.

With Klado in Paris, Admiral Birileff then took up his pen and through the columns of the *Novoye Vremiya* announced to the world that reinforcements were on their way. The reinforcements were all old ships: the *General Admiral Apraxin*, the *Admiral Seniavin*, the *Admiral Oushakoff*, all coastal defence vessels, and the *Vladimir Monomakh*, a cruiser launched in 1882. In addition the slow old battleship the *Imperator Nicholas I*, launched in 1889, was also being prepared for the voyage to the Far East.

Birileff at the same time assured a no doubt now confused Russian public that Klado's allegation that Rozhestvensky's fleet was weak was mistaken.

Back came Klado from Paris by way of newspaper interviews and a letter to the Russian paper accusing Birileff of trying to lull his countrymen into a false sense of security. This incredible newspaper battle between a serving naval captain and his superior continued for some time unchecked by any discipline, any action. As a result ships which Rozhestvensky did not want and had rejected were sent to join him under Rear-Admiral Nebogatoff. At the same time Klado frankly criticised Rozhestvensky's fleet and poured doubt on its chances of success, chances hardly increased, it might have been thought, by sending a number of ancient ironclads to its assistance. It is difficult to analyse Klado's motives, or indeed to support the logic of his arguments. Even more difficult is it to visualise the state of a navy in which both he and Birileff could have acted as they did.

Klado's articles reached Rozhestvensky and his officers off Madagascar and needless to say did nothing to raise morale. At the same time the content of the articles and the report of the paper war between Captain and Admiral was widely covered in the world press.

Again, the Japanese were provided with some very clear illumination on the state of the Russian navy.

Perhaps Togo was heartened by the confusion of his enemy, it is not known, but perhaps by February when Nebogatoff's hastily assembled flotilla of ill-assorted vessels was despatched it was of little immediate importance to him; for on the 23rd of that month the Japanese launched an all-out offensive in Manchuria and began what was to become the largest land battle of the whole war.

It will be remembered that one of the main purposes of General Mischenko's raid had been to ascertain whether the Japanese 3rd Army under Nogi had yet got itself clear of Port Arthur and joined Marshal Oyama's forces in the north. As at that moment it had not, it was obviously to Kuropatkin's advantage to attack as soon as possible while he still possessed a considerable numerical advantage. Perhaps in any other army than the Russian this is what he would have done. Indeed at that stage for Kuropatkin to have decided not to attack would have been to admit that even with the advantage of numbers Russian armies could not take the offensive against Japanese. Now Kuropatkin did not admit defeat, he was still an incurable optimist and not lacking in offensive spirit. Yet two factors militated against an immediate offensive while the Japanese armies were still relatively disorganised, and both were products of what might be called the Russian military character.

The two factors also had a chicken-and-egg relationship, it was difficult to know which came first.

The Russian troops before Mukden were strung out along a

front of nearly 90 miles. Reading from west to east first there was the army of General Kaulbars with its farthermost western (i.e. Russian right) cavalry wing straddling the Hun river, which flowed north-east to south-west past and to the south of Mukden. Then came Bilderling's army, its western wing about 15 miles due south of Mukden at right angles to the railway and the Mandarin road. Then came Linievich's army with its eastern wing commanded by General Rennenkampf, forming the extreme tip of the Russian line in the mountainous country near Shinking nearly 70 miles from Mukden. It was a long line and one with very little depth, the central reserve of troops being held behind its centre. It was essentially a defence forma-tion, and it had grown almost of itself. Russian soldiers, junior commanders, and even generals seemed bound, if not expressly forbidden, to take up a defensive position. In consequence the Russian armies were in the worst possible position should their Commander-in-Chief wish to mount an attack which would mean inevitably a concentration of troops either to outflank or drive through the Japanese. The other factor, which may well have been related to the first, was the delay after Kuropatkin had decided that he wanted to attack. Literally for weeks the higher command of the three Manchurian armies dillied and dallied making up its collective mind as to what it intended to do and how to do it.

Unfortunately for Kuropatkin, in that time the Japanese did not stand still. Even while Nogi's army made the utmost haste despite appalling weather and primitive road conditions to appear across the Hun facing Kaulbars' ring wing, significant developments were taking place at the other end of the Russian line.

In the second week of February Marshal Oyama held a Council of War in Liaoyang to consider his next move and though considerable Russian troop movements were reported to him it was thought at this time that these merely indicated a strengthening of the Russian defensive line and not prepara-tions for an offensive. Thus at almost the same time, and with-out the other suspecting, both Commanders-in-Chief, Russian and Japanese, were preparing to take the offensive.

Kuropatkin has been criticised for delay and the poor

disposition of his troops, but the Japanese plan did not display
any great military originality. They had however one surprise
in store for the Russians: instead of four Japanese armies,
including Nogi's, there were now five, for a new general had
appeared on the scene, Kawamura, who had under his command
one regular division and a Kobi division plus a Kobi brigade
and one extra regiment (i.e. three battalions). Kawamura took
the right of the Japanese line to the east opposite Rennenkampf.
Thus the Japanese line-up was, from west to east, Nogi's 3rd
Army, Oku's 2nd Army, Nozu's 4th Army, then Kuroki's 1st
and finally Kawamura's 5th or Yalu Army.

The Japanese plan, as will be seen, did involve one element
of surprise. Following what were now becoming the rather old-
fashioned concepts of their German instructors, Oyama and his
commanders, instead of thinking in terms of a wide outflanking movement either to right or left in order to sever
Kuropatkin's very narrow supply line of railway and road,
decided upon a form of attack which should have reminded at
least the British observers of the Zulu War. For the Zulu impis
in their heyday had been very fond of a formation called the
'horns and head of the buffalo'. The 'head' in the centre,
charged, but at a steady pace; while the 'horns', the right and
left wings, accelerated round the enemy's flanks. The effect upon
the enemy, if he did not possess superior weapons or the
superb fighting qualities of the Zulus themselves, was confusion,
demoralisation and destruction.

This then, in simplicity, was Oyama's plan: for it to succeed
he once again relied upon the endurance and courage of his
own troops, and his object was the destruction of the Russian
armies. On February 20th, Oyama issued his orders and
summed up his general intention in the following way: 'The
object of the battle is to decide the issue of the war. The question
is not one therefore of occupying certain points or seizing tracts
of territory. It is essential that the enemy should be dealt a
heavy blow . . .'; he ended by stressing that pursuit, at which on
previous occasions the Japanese had not excelled, must this
time be continued for as long and as far as possible.

On February 23rd, therefore, 207,000 Japanese armed with
1,000 guns and, significantly, 254 machine-guns, began to

attack 276,000 Russians armed with 1,200 guns and 54 machine-guns. The overall plan as has been seen was simple, the only subtlety was the built-in surprise. The first pressure was to be exerted by the newly arrived Yalu Army which was then to be assisted by its next-door neighbour, Kuroki's 1st Army. This however was only a feint because the main attack was eventually to be delivered by the army commanded by the conqueror of Port Arthur, General Nogi, on the Japanese extreme left.

Admittedly, this feint and switch of pressures was of no great complexity, but by chance it did create the maximum confusion among the Russian forces. For Kuropatkin had planned his offensive on his right, against Nogi's positions, and when he found that his own attack had been pre-empted and on his left, he began to transfer troops from his right to his left. No doubt a more far-seeing general would have persisted with his own attack especially as the terrain to the east was flat and made easy going while to the west the country became increasingly mountainous and difficult.

Nevertheless, the attack by Kawamura's army, consisting as it did partly of the 11th Division veterans of Port Arthur, and virtually inexperienced reservists, was no walk-over. The Russians, taking advantage of mountain defiles and passes, fought back furiously, and the drifting snow which swept the battlefield soon covered hundreds of Japanese dead.

By February 27th, however, two changes in the battle had taken place. First, the Russians, because of Japanese successes to the east, had given up their own offensive in the west, which was to have taken them towards the old battlefield of Sandepu. Kuropatkin now found once again that his plans prepared before a battle had to be abandoned once battle was joined. His offensive would have to be sacrificed as troops were rushed from west to east, using the branch line railways which the Russians had constructed. Almost at the same moment as the Russians became fully involved with their reinforcements in the east Nogi's 3rd Army and Oku's 2nd began an enveloping movement in the west.

Kuropatkin had thus been caught by Oyama's elementary ruse. Naturally enough the principal blame must fall on the

Commander-in-Chief himself, but some portion of it must also fall upon his subordinates, especially his cavalry commanders. In the next war, ten years hence, the tasks of reconnaissance and observation were to be in a large part taken over by air forces but in 1905 those functions were firmly the duty of cavalry. In this respect Kuropatkin was badly served. He had 16,000 horsemen as opposed to the Japanese 7,300, and even though they were badly disposed, one-third under General Grekoff being in the west while Rennenkampf had two-thirds in the east, they should have been able to supply Kuropatkin with better information than in fact he received. As it turned out, despite their numbers, the Russian cavalry were almost entirely inactive throughout the whole battle, either as fighting men or scouts.

From February 27th to the evening of March 7th there were virtually three battles taking place before Mukden. To the west Nogi's army was extending itself round the Russian right with considerable success, while in the east Kawamura's 5th Army made little progress, but suffered considerable casualties against the stubborn resistance of Linievich's 1st Manchurian Army, probably the best commanded of the three Russian armies, and now considerably reinforced by troops from the east. In the centre Kuroki, the most vigorous and skilful of all the Japanese generals, found himself thwarted by excellent Russian defences and forced to indulge in large-scale slogging matches with heavy and medium artillery.

The conditions for the troops engaged, as at Sandepu, were of the worst. Temperatures were well below freezing, and heavy snow made living conditions almost unbearable. Perhaps for the first time in the war foreign observers noticed signs of strain in the Japanese army. Its proven efficiency in previous battles was beginning to break down. In the east Japanese formations were without maps, and they were trying to advance into territory about which they knew little or nothing. Throughout the whole length of the front, borne down by the burden of casualties, lack of proper supplies and the killing weather conditions, the Japanese medical services found themselves simply unable to cope.

However, two qualities sustained the Japanese: once again

the fanatical courage of their private soldiers and the determination and mutual co-operation of their general officers. On the Russian side courage was by no means lacking in the ranks, but the three generals, Kaulbars, Bilderling and Linievich, did little or nothing to assist each other, while Kuropatkin's control virtually disappeared in the confusion.

Even then, despite the talents or deficiencies of generals the fighting soon degenerated into hand-to-hand encounters with rifle and bayonet and hand grenade.

As *The Times* correspondent in the centre with General Oku put it:

Warfare reverted to a primaeval scrimmage where brute bravery and fox-like cunning on the part of individuals or groups won the day.

On March 5th and 6th the front was almost static, but soon, it was apparent, one side or the other had to break. On March 7th Kuropatkin gave the order for a Russian withdrawal in the centre and on his left in the hope of concentrating his forces for the defence of Mukden.

It was a forlorn hope. Encouraged by the first sign of the collapse of Russian resistance each Japanese commander, and his troops, was given a new lease of life. Kuroki was at last able to give assistance to the hard-pressed Kawamura on his right, and together they forced Linievich back from his hill positions. Nozu being allowed to advance closer to Mukden could now help Oku to close in on Bilderling, who began to withdraw some of his forces through and beyond Mukden. The relentless Nogi, assisted in his turn by Oku's victories against both Bilderling and Kaulbars, began to take ground to the north and north-west of Mukden, finally reaching and wrecking the railway line which ran northwards out of the town.

Kuropatkin's situation was now desperate. His communications were cut and he was in danger of having his armies surrounded. For 48 hours the Russians resisted and tried to defend Mukden, but on the evening of March 9th their Commander-in-Chief gave the order for a general retreat to Tiehling, nearly 40 miles to the north.

As it turned out, so pressing now were the Japanese attacks that the Russians had to fight their way north out of a bottleneck to safety. The Russian rear-guard fought hard and sacrificed itself in the process, but on March 10th the victorious Japanese entered Mukden. For the next six days the Russians moved north, some formations in utter confusion, others conducting an orderly fighting retreat.

The Japanese, for all their commanders' hopes, were unable once again to administer the *coup de grâce*. The crushing pursuit was beyond them. Once again a look at the casualty figures provides their excuse, for their casualties in killed and wounded were 70,000, against the Russians' 20,000. One-third of the Russian casualties were listed as 'missing' on the retreat, while the Japanese killed outnumbered their enemy's dead by almost two to one.

At the end of the longest and most savage battle in modern history, the Japanese had won a spectacular victory, but a Russian army still existed to the north. Sixty thousand rifles, sixty field guns and an immense quantity of booty from the base at Mukden had been captured, but the army had escaped. Inevitably, even for a people as stoical and self-sacrificing as the Japanese had proved themselves to be, there must have been the question in many minds as to where and how the final blow might be struck.

The Russian opinion of their defeat can best be gauged by the fate of one man. Mukden was the last battle for Kuropatkin as Commander-in-Chief.

NINETEEN

'Let every man do his utmost duty'

ADMIRAL TOGO

On the same day that Kuropatkin was relieved of his overall command of the Russian armies and at his own request given the subordinate command of the 1st Army, under Linievich, the new Commander-in-Chief, Rozhestvensky's ships left Nossi Bé for the last leg of their journey to the Far East.

Before they left Madagascar the Admiral and his officers and men had learnt of the colossal and seemingly final defeat of their compatriots at Mukden.

Ahead of the Russian fleet stretched the long haul across the Indian Ocean and as it proceeded it made history, for this was the first time that a modern battle fleet had undertaken such a lengthy journey, miles from land, relying on no port but refuelling at sea. News reports in the world press and rumours of all sorts abounded as to where exactly the squadron was, while for a space of three weeks Rozhestvensky again became a sort of Flying Dutchman disappearing from the sight of man. The journey was an arduous one for the crews, once again faced with the task of frequent coaling in a tropical climate, and a number of mishaps and engine breakdowns. Nevertheless, it is possible to argue that the solitude was not unwelcome to Rozhestvensky for he had not waited at Madagascar for Nebogatoff's Third Squadron and it is quite possible that he hoped that it would never catch up with him. On March 24th Nebogatoff had reached Port Said and was therefore, considering the age of the ships he commanded, making rather better time than the Ministry of Marine could reasonably have estimated. However,

Nebogatoff's whereabouts were as unknown to his future Commander-in-Chief as were Rozhestvensky's to him.

On April 8th, however, the world once more knew something of the Second Squadron's movements, for on that day many of the inhabitants of Singapore went out in launches and small boats to get a better view of the Russian fleet sailing past at a steady 8 knots about 6–7 miles out from the shore. Those who managed to get near to the fleet noticed that all the ships trailed great masses of underwater vegetation just below the water-line, and that their decks were stacked with coal despite the fact that as they passed Singapore they were accompanied by a tiny fleet of colliers. The fleet was in sight from the shore for nearly three hours until it disappeared towards the east, each ship belching out great clouds of black smoke from the soft coal being burnt.

Singapore was of course a British colony and the fleet did not enter territorial waters, but a source of much speculation among the Russians for the rest of the voyage was the question of what information on their progress was known to the Japanese. It was assumed, quite wrongly, that in such a matter the British would be in league with their allies and do their spying for them. In fact the Russian apprehensions were unjustified for it would appear that the Japanese knew little more about the fleet sailing for their waters than could be picked up from casual press reports, or from occasions when, as at Singapore, the warships appeared for all to see.

Togo's policy at this time, and he hardly had an alternative, was very much a matter of wait and see, though he sensibly used the time on his hands to prepare his ships and men for the coming battle. After refitting, the battleships and cruisers put in a considerable amount of target practice wearing in the gun barrels and getting the gun crews used to the new British telescopic gun sight which had been fitted in most of the vessels.

On April 12th Rozhestvensky arrived in Kamranh Bay in French Indo-China, almost his last landfall before sailing into Japanese waters. Then occurred one of the many almost inexplicable events which marked the whole passage of the Russian fleet. For Rozhestvensky stayed put, occasionally changing his anchorage, so as not to offend France's neutralist susceptibilities, for a month, thus allowing Nebogatoff to catch him up. As he had apparently left Madagascar so as to avoid the Reinforcing Squadron it seems strange that he now waited off Indo-China. It is possible that he received imperative orders from St. Petersburg to do so, but it is also possible that he simply changed his mind. Whichever was the case, the picture of the overall command and organisation of the two fleets revealed was hardly an impressive one.

On April 27th Nebogatoff was reported off Penang and on May 5th he in his turn passed Singapore. On May 8th Nebogatoff's ships sailed into Kamranh Bay, and their commander was at last able to board the *Suvoroff* and report to the Commander-in-Chief.

This event, with whatever inner reservations it is impossible to imagine, Rozhestvensky celebrated by a General Fleet Order. After the expected compliments to the Third Squadron and his own, his choice of subjects was not uninteresting and gives one some sort of glimpse into a mind never easy to read.

The Admiral began by telling his fleet that it now had a superiority over the Japanese in battleships, but he was quick to warn them against any over-optimism on that account. For the Japanese had more fast ships, and more torpedo craft; they had floating mines which they were likely to cast overboard in the path of Russian warships; and finally, and this was something of which Rozhestvensky had absolutely no evidence, they had submarines.

Accordingly, the fleet was told that as well as concentrating on the accuracy of their gunnery they must also not miss 'floating objects' and 'periscopes sticking out of the water'. As if all this were not enough, the Russians were then told of the long fighting experience and excellent gunnery practice which their enemy had enjoyed: the Japanese too were 'devoted to their throne and country; they cannot bear dishonour, and die like heroes'. The only consolation for the now combined Russian fleet was in the last words of the Order and this was both presumptuous and ambiguous: 'The Lord will strengthen our right hand, will help us carry out the task of our Emperor and with our blood wash away the bitter shame of Russia.'

On May 14th the Russian fleet left Honkohe Bay, its last

landfall, and after coaling at sea on the next day, headed northwards. It is an appropriate moment to review Rozhestvensky's command, the course it was to follow, and its plans for battle.

The Admiral's first task had been to absorb into his own fleet the additions which owing to Klado's journalism had been wished on him, under the command of Nebogatoff. These being the elderly battleship *Nikolai I*, an old armoured cruiser, the *Vladimir Monomakh* and the three coastal defence ships, *Admiral Apraxin*, *Admiral Seniavin* and *Admiral Ushakoff*, plus seven auxiliary vessels to add to his own train of ships which were superfluous to a battle, the task was an impossibility. So Rozhestvensky simply formed a Third Division which consisted of the *Nikolai*, in which Nebogatoff flew his flag, leading the *Apraxin*, *Seniavin* and *Ushakoff*. The Commander-in-Chief in the *Suvoroff* led the First Division of the most powerful ships, the *Alexander III*, the *Borodino* and the *Orel*. The Second Division, commanded by Felkerzam, was however something of a compromise because the flagship the *Oslyabya* was modern, and under the strict discipline of its Captain perhaps the best run ship in the fleet; and its companions were older and less efficient, the *Sissoi Veliky*, *Navarin* and *Admiral Nakhimoff*. The eight cruisers formed a separate division under Rear-Admiral Enkvist flying his flag in the *Oleg*. The rest of Rozhestvensky's total of forty-five fighting ships were made up of light cruisers and destroyers. This was the fighting part of the fleet, but in addition there were the supply ships, some of which would be needed at Vladivostock. Some the Admiral rid himself of by sending them off towards Shanghai, but others he felt he had to keep with the squadron, which meant that they had to be protected and that their speed, or rather the speed of the slowest, something like 9 knots, dictated the speed of the whole fleet. So, from the beginning the armada was slow and, from its lack of homogeneity, unwieldy.

The next problem was what was its course to be to Vladivostock, battle or no battle. There were actually three alternatives – the Korean Straits, the Tsugaru Straits and the Soya Straits even farther north. The basic difference was that the Korean Straits meant passing up the western coast of Japan, whilst the two alternatives would mean sailing round the eastern coast. The Tsugaru and Soya Straits were shorter routes to Vladivostock, and perhaps if Rozhestvensky had intended to avoid battle these would have presented an advantage. However, their passage would also have meant coaling off Japan, and possibly risking the danger of mines. Rozhestvensky chose the Korean Straits which meant in many ways the most obvious choice, and the one which would bring the Russian ships closest to the Japanese navy's base at Mozampo. The pros and cons could be rehearsed almost endlessly, but perhaps the real, and from its nature, the unanswerable, question, was whether Rozhestvensky was courting battle or not. It is obvious from his utterances that he knew the risks, but at the same time he had revealed a streak of fatalism and pride in his character. It would have been consonant with his mental make-up to have scorned 'sneaking' past the Japanese coast. In addition, of course, he must have realised that just to get to Vladivostock without touching the Japanese fleet would serve very little purpose at this stage in the war, save perhaps to create another Port Arthur situation.

So the Russian fleet was committed to steering a course through the Korean Straits, past the island of Tsushima.

The final point was what were its plans for battle? Rozhestvensky had under his command three rear-admirals, Felkerzam, Nebogatoff and Enkvist, each commanding a division, in addition to the captains in command of each vessel. At no stage did their Commander-in-Chief summon them to a conference either to hear his orders or to put their own comments or questions. The only orders his subordinates received were by way of the printed Fleet Orders, and perhaps because there was no two-way traffic of ideas these remained very general indeed. Details were not filled in, and there was no attempt to agree emergency changes of plan. It has been said that Rozhestvensky, with the experience of a long voyage full of mishaps and bunglings behind him, had but a poor opinion of his subordinates and considered consulting them a waste of time. If this were so his omission was even more inexcusable. If he had had first-class junior admirals and experienced captains perhaps he could have relied on their initiative and skill, but if not it was surely up to him to give them guidance. Further, he had on countless occasions seen that signalling between ships in the Russian navy was well below standard, even in the course of relatively uncomplicated manoeuvres. In the middle of a fleet action the standard would obviously be lower, so he could not hope to direct the movements of three divisions from the flagship. Therefore it was his plain duty to keep signals to the minimum by issuing very full orders before battle was joined.

In the event, Rozhestvensky neither gave such orders nor allowed his divisional commanders a free hand, so that a distinctly disorganised mass of ships sailed towards the enemy.

Perhaps, however, the most fantastic example of this lack of preparation and communication occurred on May 23rd when Rear-Admiral Felkerzam, who had been ill since Madagascar, died in the night on board the *Oslyabya*. Presumably fearing that the death of his second-in-command would further depress the spirits of the fleet, Rozhestvensky the next day ordered that his death should be kept secret and his admiral's flag remain flying on his flagship. Incredibly also Nebogatoff, next in line of command, was not informed so that if in action the Commander-in-Chief were by chance disabled or killed all captains save those on the *Suvoroff* and the *Oslyabya* would look for command to an officer who was laid out dead in his cabin.

By May 26th Rozhestvensky had sent some of his transports away from the fleet in an attempt to confuse the Japanese, and perhaps lure some of their warships away from his own. The ruse was in the event unsuccessful, and it was almost his only attempt at any kind of subterfuge. He would no doubt have been wiser to order his whole fleet of auxiliaries away from his battle fleet, but he did not, and proceeded towards the Korean Straits in a cruising formation consisting of two lines of battleships and cruisers protecting the remaining auxiliaries, with his destroyers acting as a protective screen.

The Russians were now nearing what must obviously be the area of maximum danger, and even at this last moment it was still impossible to fathom what was going on in Rozhestvensky's mind. All the Russian ships were ordered to cease wireless telegraph signals and the destroyers were ordered in close to the main fleet, as if the object were to escape the attention of the Japanese. Yet at the same time the fleet was slowed to about 8 knots and eventually stopped so that the passage of the Straits would be made on May 27th in the daytime. In fact, so curious were Rozhestvensky's actions that after the event there were theories that he did not want to fight on the 13th (by the Russian calendar) or else that, impelled by some excess of patriotism, he did want to fight on the 14th which was the anniversary of the Tsar's coronation.

Whatever the Commander-in-Chief's intentions, and indecision may have been the only explanation of his lack of consistency, it was by now apparent throughout his fleet that action could not be far off because throughout the day Japanese cypher signals had been intercepted. As daylight faded the last signal hoisted on the *Suvoroff* was 'Prepare for action. To-morrow at the hoisting of the colours, battle flags will be flown.'

And at this moment the Russians knew more about the Japanese than the Japanese knew about the Russians. Admiral Togo, with his three divisions of four battleships, Admiral Kamimura's six armoured cruisers and Uriu's light cruisers still at anchor at Mozampo 75 miles from Tsushima, must have been very near the point of doubting his own judgment. Admittedly, with very little information to go on, he had decided that Rozhestvensky would take the Korean Straits and had made his dispositions accordingly, and his scouting forces armed with squared maps of the sea area were stretched across the Straits considerably to the south of Tsushima island. The outer line consisted of four armed merchant ships supported by two old cruisers, the *Akitsushima* and the *Idzumi*. Behind them were Rear-Admiral Dewa's four light cruisers with Rear Admiral Kataoka's division of four elderly battleships in the harbour of Tsushima itself. The last news that Togo had received of the Russians was of their being off the mouth of the Yangtse on May 25th. Now Rozhestvensky's slow progress disconcerted and worried him, for when night fell on May 26th there were still no reports of the sighting of a single Russian ship.

At 2.45 a.m. on the moonlit but misty morning of the 27th Captain Narukawa of the merchant cruiser *Shinano Maru* was to end the uncertainty and tension which existed in both fleets. His first sight was the navigation lights of what proved to be on closer investigation the Russian hospital ship *Orel*. Still undetected, he moved closer then to distinguish beyond the *Orel* the dim shapes of the darkened Russian warships.

Immediately he signalled 'Enemy squadron sighted square 203 apparently bearing eastern passage.' As his signal was radioed north alerting the Japanese fleet, the wireless operators on the Russian warships detected a change in the signals they had been receiving all day. These were no longer the desultory exchanges of scouting forces keeping in touch, but the same signal, identifiable despite the language difference and the use of code, repeated urgently again and again. Whatever Rozhestvensky's intentions his fleet had been detected and the next day would see the test of battle.

At 6.34 a.m. after confidently signalling his Emperor 'I have just received the news that the enemy fleet has been sighted. Our fleet will forthwith proceed to sea to attack the enemy and destroy him', Admiral Togo took his battleships and cruisers to sea.

From about 7 a.m. of that morning the impending clash took on a formal air of inevitability as Japanese merchant and light cruisers began to appear and proceeded to shadow the Russian fleet at a distance of 5 miles to starboard, reporting its every movement. Surprisingly they were not driven off by the Russians nor was any attempt made with the wireless transmitter of the *Ural*, a converted merchantman, the most powerful in the fleet, to jam their many signals. At 10 a.m. however Rozhestvensky ordered his heavy armoured ships into battle formation of line ahead, with his cruisers, transports and auxiliaries and destroyers to starboard. Now Rear-Admiral Dewa's squadron arrived on the scene, having already missed the Russians once by steaming too far south.

Upon this addition to the shadowing force coming within less than 8,000 yards, the battleship *Orel* opened fire, to be followed by others. Rozhestvensky immediately ordered them to cease fire. He then ordered his fleet to sail at 8 knots.

So in this slow, almost stately manner, the two sets of antagonists proceeded slowly to the north-east in poorish misty weather with a heavy rolling sea. At 11 a.m. the Russian crews were piped to dinner and in the wardrooms the officers drank the health of the Tsar and his consort on the anniversary of their coronation.

Soon after this Rozhestvensky ordered his only real tactical disposition of his whole fleet. The mist had thickened, hiding him from the view of the Japanese cruisers, and he ordered his battle fleet to change formation to line abreast. Togo must arrive from the north, presumably in the normal battle formation of line ahead. When he did so, so must Rozhestvensky have reasoned, by ordering his ships either to port or starboard he would be in a position to 'cross the T' of the Japanese line, pouring all his broadsides into their leading ships. It was one of those over-clever plans which rarely succeed in war and worse, it postulated an unthinking enemy. As it turned out, it was not to be tested in practice, for it failed in its execution. The change in dispositions was still being carried out clumsily and sluggishly by his captains when the Japanese appeared again through the mist. So the element of surprise had gone. Worse still, the Russian fleet was still in the process of changing back on Rozhestvensky's order to its previous formation of line ahead, when at 1.40 p.m. the two battle fleets sighted each other at a distance of about 7 miles.

At that moment, as the two formations of massive ships steamed towards each other and the largest naval battle since Trafalgar began, the two fleets presented an impression which was in many ways to last throughout the action. The Russians, painted black save for their bright canary yellow funnels, made excellent targets as they moved and manoeuvred at a maximum of 11 knots into their final battle formation, the *Suvoroff* leading four battleships, to starboard of the fifth modern battleship the *Oslyabya*, leading the remaining seven armoured ships. Coming on at 14 knots on an almost parallel course were the dark grey, less well distinguished shapes of Togo's four principal ships, the *Mikasa, Shikishima, Fuji, Asaki*, followed by the *Kasuga* and *Nisshin* and then Kamimura's armoured cruisers, *Idzumi, Adzuma, Tokigawa, Yakumo, Asama* and *Iwate*. To the Russians they appeared to move with a superb precision keeping station 'as if chained together'.

At 1.55 Togo, no doubt recalling that other sea battle a century before and perhaps his training on H.M.S. *Worcester*, signalled by flag 'The Empire's fate depends on the result of this battle. Let every man do his utmost duty.' At the same time the great Rising Sun battle flags flapped out at the mastheads.

At first it seemed as if the two fleets would pass each other on opposite and parallel courses, but perhaps only as he came nearer could Togo really appreciate Rozhestvensky's curious two column disposition, so he decided on the dangerous course of turning about and steaming on a parallel course in the same direction as his enemy. The danger was to his own ships as they all turned on roughly the same sea area, masking each other's guns. The advantage was that if successful the faster ships with the better gunnery would be put in a position to inflict maximum damage for a much longer period than if the two fleets were steaming away from each other.

As the Japanese turned, inevitably the *Oslyabya* and the *Suvoroff*, followed by the other battleships, opened fire and raised columns of spray round the *Mikasa*. The two Russian lines were however still in confusion and Togo's daring paid off as six Japanese ships concentrated on the *Oslyabya* and four on the *Suvoroff*.

On board the flagship Commander Semenoff had never even imagined anything like it. As he was to recall, 'Shells seemed to be pouring upon us incessantly, one after another.' Raging fires broke out on the *Suvoroff* and on the *Alexander III*, next in line, while the *Oslyabya*, as well as being on fire, had her fore turret put out of action and a great hole blown in her bow at the water-line by two 12-inch shells which struck almost simultaneously. The Japanese had not however escaped the return fire, the *Mikasa* was struck repeatedly, and the *Asama* swung out of her line, holed and with her steering gear disabled.

The Japanese, having executed their turn to port of their enemy, were now curving round to starboard and ahead of the slow-moving Russians. At about 2.30 p.m. Rozhestvensky could have out-manoeuvred Togo by steering to port with twelve capital ships against eleven, passing astern of the Japanese and concentrating his fire on their rearmost ships.

However, he did not, and steering to starboard threw his gunners off target, and he allowed himself to be pushed round as it were by the faster fleet.

Once again the *Oslyabya* and the *Suvoroff* were the principal targets. The Russian line became bunched and confused as the Japanese described almost a semicircle ahead of them. At 2.25 the *Oslyabya* with fires raging was almost stationary and therefore an even easier target.

About five minutes later the Russian fleet was deprived of its Commander-in-Chief. A number of shells struck the *Suvoroff*'s bridge and a shower of splinters penetrated the conning tower, killing or wounding almost everyone inside it. Rozhestvensky was wounded in the head, back and legs. Still trying to exercise command he moved his position in the conning tower, only to be wounded again in the foot. Around him the deck of his flagship was a burning ruin and he began to lose consciousness. The *Suvoroff*, her helm jammed, swung more and more to starboard. Behind her the *Alexander III*, for minutes thinking her movements deliberate, followed in her wake. Inevitably the rest of the First Division following behind fell into confusion. The Second Division to port pressed ahead past the stationary *Oslyabya*. As they passed what was still thought by them to be Felkerzam's flagship the horrified crews saw the great ship capsize and after fifteen minutes, while frantic figures appeared on her upturned keel, disappear completely.

As a destroyer was despatched to inform Nebogatoff that the command of the fleet devolved upon him, Togo must have realised that the battle was his, and turning his First Division in two successive 90° turns, returned again to hammer the Russian line. At the same time Kamimura moved in to a range of a mere 3,000 yards to fire his light calibre guns at what was now the standing hulk of the *Suvoroff* and the blazing *Alexander III*.

By 3 p.m. there was no semblance of a Russian line of battle, just a collection of ships shrouded in dense clouds of brown smoke which the Japanese were able to pound almost at their leisure. The Russians had not given up the fight, and even on board the shattered *Suvoroff* gun crews were still firing the few remaining guns but each ship from now on operated as a separate unit vainly trying to fight off the collective fire of Japanese battleships or cruisers which were soon to be joined by destroyers and torpedo craft. The wounded and only intermittently conscious Rozhestvensky was transferred to the destroyer *Buiny* and Nebogatoff had received only an imperfect message that the fleet was to head for Vladivostock.

It was at this stage that both Togo and Kamimura in the smoke, confusion, mist and declining visibility virtually lost touch with the rapidly dispersing Russian fleet. The *Alexander III*, flames shooting up between her funnels, left what remained of the battle-line, her place being taken by the *Borodino*. The *Suvoroff* was now subjected to a torpedo attack but despite at least two hits she still remained obstinately afloat. Togo's division almost by chance came upon the *Ural* and sank her by gunfire and torpedoes.

The Japanese Commander-in-Chief did not really come upon another worthwhile target until nearly 6 p.m., and then it was the *Alexander III*, low in the water but with her fires now under control. Twice she was attacked and twice she fought back, trying to join the rear of the line headed by the *Borodino*. However, just after her second attempt she turned suddenly, hoisted the international distress signal and then slowly turned turtle and just as steadily sank below the waves, only four men of her complement of 830 saving themselves from the wreck.

The sun was now setting and the *Borodino* and *Orel* were leading a straggling line of lesser craft away to the west of the Japanese fleet, but still firing their guns at a range of 6,000 yards. At 7 p.m. as the Japanese turned to the north the *Fuji* fired probably the last salvo of the daytime battle, at the *Borodino*. They struck and detonated her magazine, there were two enormous explosions and then like her sister ship, the *Alexander III*, she capsized, floated bottom up for a matter of minutes and sank. From her crew there was just one survivor picked up by a Japanese fishing vessel hours later. At about the same time, after repeated attacks by Japanese torpedo boats, the *Suvoroff*, despite a fantastically courageous resistance maintained to the last by one 12-pounder gun, capsized and then, pointing her bow out of the water in a great cloud of ochre coloured smoke, sank to the bottom with all who remained on board.

As day turned into night the Russians had lost four battle-ships and three auxiliaries and considerable damage had been inflicted on the battleships *Orel*, *Navarin* and *Sissoi Veliki*. Almost every other ship had suffered damage, those least hit being in Nebogatoff's division to which the Japanese had given little attention as being of scant importance.

The rest of the battle, if it can be so called, was a retreat by the Russians, in some cases a retreat towards Vladivostock and in other cases simply an attempt to escape the Japanese. Notionally at least Nebogatoff was in command, and hoisting the signal 'Follow me' in the *Nikolai I*, he steered a course towards Vladivostock followed by the *Orel*, *Apraxin*, *Seniavin* and *Ushakoff*. At a fairly early stage he was deprived of the company and services of the next senior officer, Rear-Admiral Enkvist, who with the cruisers *Oleg*, *Aurora* and *Jemchung* disappeared to the south-west and was next heard of in Shang-hai, and then Manilla where all three ships were interned. During that night and the following day the remaining Russian ships were subjected to a constant attack by twenty-one Japanese destroyers and nearly forty torpedo boats.

In many ways the ordeals suffered by the Russian crews, trying to work damaged vessels through the night against considerable odds, were far worse than those endured during the day of battle which had just passed. During the night the two old battleships *Navarin* and *Sissoi Veliky* were sunk and the next morning the hopelessly damaged *Nakhimoff* and *Vladimir Monomahk* were scuttled by their crews. The Japanese lost three torpedo craft, two by gunfire and one in collision.

By the 28th, therefore, there was nothing left which might reasonably be described as a Russian fleet, save perhaps for those ships which had followed Nebogatoff. These were his flagship the *Nikolai I*, the damaged *Orel*, the *Apraxin* and *Seniavin*, both antiquated coastal defence vessels, and the fast cruiser *Izumrud*. They had moved by night without lights, something which Nebogatoff had trained his squadron to do on the journey to the East, but in the cold light of day they were sighted and Togo's battleship force and three divisions of cruisers hastened to intercept them. Soon Nebogatoff's command was ringed round by overwhelming force and while the *Izumrud*, taking advantage of her speed, escaped, the last active Russian admiral hoisted the surrender signal. Not without dignity he addressed the officers and crew of the *Nikolai I*, before being taken off to Togo's flagship:

I am only an old man of sixty, whose life is of trifling importance, but you are still young and charged with the duty of restoring the fame of the Russian navy. I accept the entire responsibility for this surrender.

The same day the *Ushakoff*, the last remaining ship of Rozhestvensky's line of battle, was sunk by two Japanese cruisers. Meanwhile, the unconscious Russian Commander-in-Chief with his staff had been transferred from the destroyer *Buiny* to the *Biedovy*, which somewhat ignominiously surrendered to two Japanese destroyers, unharmed and without firing a shot, while her sister ship, the *Grozny*, escaped.

The fates of the remaining ships were diverse: some went down firing their guns, others were run aground or scuttled or were interned in neutral ports, some simply surrendered. The *Izumrud*, which had escaped when Nebogatoff surrendered, ran on the rocks in Vladimir Bay, and became a total wreck, a stone's throw from Vladivostock. Only the cruiser *Almaz* and two destroyers the *Bravy* and the *Grozny* reached that port intact.

By one means or another the Russians had lost thirty-four warships against a Japanese loss of three torpedo boats. Of the sailors involved, 4,830 Russians had lost their lives, 5,917 (many of them wounded) were taken prisoner, and 1,862 were interned in neutral ports. The Japanese lost 110 killed, and suffered 590 wounded.

The appalling news of the result of the battle, the most signal naval defeat for a century, the enormous casualty roll, and the complete one-sidedness of the action, slowly filtered back to Russia. Rumours had abounded for a few days, even of a Russian victory. When the truth came it produced numbed despondency in St. Petersburg and Moscow, much more intense and final than any emotion aroused by any of the defeats on land.

The Tsar, who as a diarist was a master of bathos, recorded:

The terrible news about the destruction of almost the entire squadron in a two-day battle is now finally confirmed. Rozhestvensky himself taken prisoner, wounded! The weather has been wonderful, which made my grief still worse. . . .

Outside Russia, where the news of the long-awaited battle had been eagerly expected, nations and individuals reacted in their various ways. Paul Cambon, the French Ambassador in London, forgot the *entente cordiale* for a moment and described it as 'a disaster like Trafalgar'. The Kaiser, who at the time of the fall of Port Arthur had not failed to remind the Tsar that there were German firms which would willingly build him some new battleships, and who had recommended the despatch of the Baltic Fleet to the East, and the Black Sea Fleet as well, decided that a bit of plain speaking would do his cousin no harm. After some words of sympathy, he wrote, 'From the purely military, strategical point of view, the defeat in the Straits of Korea ends the chances for a decided turn of the scales in your favour.' Having predicted a Port Arthur-like fate for Vladivostock, Wilhelm then offered his services as a mediator, possibly in conjunction with President Roosevelt.

The German press predicted an early peace, but on occasions found difficulty in balancing some satisfaction at a defeat for Russia with the apprehension caused by the victory of an Oriental nation over a European one. In France there was no doubt that the Russians must now bring the war to an end. A number of journals made reference to the fact that in some Russian circles at least there would be satisfaction at the end of an unpopular policy, and a reverse inflicted on an autocratic government. In Britain, where a reduction in her own naval forces in the Far East could now be contemplated, James Walder, the author's father, then a schoolboy in Sussex, was given an extra day's holiday by a patriotic headmaster to celebrate the victory of his country's ally.

It was however in Russia itself that, naturally enough, the reaction to Tsushima was most marked. For the first time the upper classes had the effects of the war brought home to them. The 'colonial' war in Manchuria had not registered a great deal, the Imperial Guard had stayed in St. Petersburg. Now with the loss of the *Alexander III* officered by nobles, and the death of other naval officers of the 'Equipage of the Guard', a selfish but influential section of society was prepared to urge the ending of the war. On the stock exchanges of St. Petersburg and Moscow the prices of shares rose as did Russian stocks abroad in the cynical but confident expectation of peace.

TWENTY

'Asia advancing, Europe falling back'

GENERAL SIR IAN HAMILTON

To all intents and purposes, though armies still faced each other, the war was over, but it was not until June 8th that President Theodore Roosevelt, who had gone to the White House in 1901 on the death of President McKinley, and been triumphantly re-elected in 1904, was able to write to both the Japanese and Russian Governments. His letter was identical in terms to both and began:

The President feels that the time has come when, in the interests of all mankind, he must endeavour to see if it is not possible to bring to an end the terrible and lamentable conflict which is now being waged.

In fact it had been the Japanese who had secretly approached the President to use his good offices, as had the Kaiser, and Roosevelt had then sounded the Russians. Both sides were anxious to come to terms so that the President was assured beforehand of favourable replies.

As a result, in August the Russian and Japanese delegates came together at Portsmouth, New Hampshire. Baron Komura and Kogora Takahira, the former and present Ministers to the U.S.A., represented their country, but it was the Russians who captured the limelight. The Russian delegates were Baron Rosen, the Minister in Washington, who while Minister in Tokyo before the war had been a lone voice counselling caution, and, as his chief, Sergius Witte, recalled in an emergency from dignified impotence.

It was not until October 14th that the Tsar and the Emperor

of Japan put their signatures to the document which officially brought the war to an end. By its terms Russia formally accepted 'the paramount political, military and economic interests of Japan in Korea'. Russia ceded to Japan her lease on the Liaotung Peninsula, including Port Arthur and Dalny, plus the relevant section of the South Manchurian Railway and the southern half of the island of Sakhalin. At the same time all Russian property and rights in the ceded territory became Japanese. Both parties to the treaty agreed to evacuate their troops from Manchuria. During the negotiations the Japanese had argued for a war indemnity, but Witte, reinforced by St. Petersburg, had resisted. The cession of the southern half of Sakhalin, captured by the Japanese almost without effort after Tsushima, did however almost drive a wedge between the still bellicose Tsar and the more conciliatory Witte, and no doubt increased Nicholas' dislike of his most efficient servant.

That statesman had gone out of his way to influence American press and public opinion, as he later frankly admitted, by assuming at least on public occasions a bogus front of democratic affability. Yet it was not entirely the fact that he forced himself to shake hands with engine drivers that disposed his American hosts to modify their unfavourable view of the image of Tsarist autocracy. They, from the President down, were beginning to wonder where Japanese ambitions, fed by a victorious war, might lead next. Perhaps to confirm American apprehensions there were serious riots in Japan, which had to be put down by troops, when finally the peace terms were announced; many had expected more for their nation's expenditure of blood and treasure, and despite the fact that Japan had in the war almost reached her military and economic limits, their resentment a few months later forced the resignation of Prime Minister Katsura and his Cabinet.

The war which had just ended has been described as the last purely imperialist war ever fought, and in a sense it was true as both Russia and Japan had been fighting for control of Korea and for influence in an area extending far beyond their borders. However, the conflict was more than that, in both the short and the long-term effects, and the results direct and indirect which flowed from it.

In the purely military sense, many of its lessons went
unlearnt, despite the fact that it was closely reported by a
large number of newspaper correspondents and observed by
naval and military officers from all the principal states of
Europe and the U.S.A. Apart from aircraft and submarines, all
the ingredients of the 1914–18 War were present. Yet few of the
lessons of Manchuria and Port Arthur – the difficulty of con-
trolling large armies, the superiority bestowed on the defence
by modern weapons, the obsolescence, save in very special
circumstances, of cavalry – seem to have been absorbed.
Perhaps because the Russians were noticeably incompetent
and the Japanese suicidally courageous, British, German,
American and French military officers thought that generalities
derived from such sources would not apply in their own armies.
Tragically ten years later it was to be shown that neither
incompetence nor courage was the monopoly of any one nation
and that the nature of war itself had changed.

Tsushima had more effect than Port Arthur or Mukden, and
within a very short space of time. Even then, only one lesson
was learnt, and events were moving towards its acceptance even
if the Russian and Japanese fleets had never met. The comparative ineffectiveness of torpedoes was ignored, as was the complementary effectiveness of mines. What the admirals and naval
constructors did pick on was the fact that in all the naval engagements of the war the serious damage, the blows which
could send an armoured capital ship to the bottom with one
strike, was inflicted by the big guns. The secondary armament,
even if it had the opportunity of engaging at its shorter range,
could only inflict relatively trifling damage. Obviously, the
battleship of the future was the long-range, one-calibre, big-
gun type. So armed, its standard of gunnery, deriving from
training, techniques and new equipment, must be of the
highest, and certainly higher than that obtaining in most
navies in 1905.

At the same time successful experiments with turbine
engines were showing that the day of the reciprocating piston
engine was passing. It was the measure of the intelligence and
energy of Jacky Fisher, the British First Sea Lord, that he saw
that the two improvements might be combined in one new

warship. His hand-picked Committee on Design lost little time in choosing their favoured new model which had ten 12-inch guns, the secondary armament being mere 12-pounders to ward off torpedo boats, and steam-turbine engines developing 23,000 h.p. and producing a speed of 21 knots.

On October 2nd, 1905 Fisher's dream-ship was laid down at Portsmouth Dockyard, and a year and a day later sailed on her first trials. She was called H.M.S. *Dreadnought*, and with her appearance a new phase in naval warfare had begun. With the launching of a new heavily gunned fast battle cruiser, the *Inflexible*, a few years later, and the imitation of both designs by the principal navies of the world, a new naval race began and the ships which had engaged at Tsushima became museum pieces while the battle itself, the largest between Trafalgar in 1805 and Jutland in 1916, became in its isolation something of an historical curiosity.

On Russia itself the colossal and humiliating defeat she had sustained had three immediate and direct effects – on her internal situation, on the state of her own armed forces, and on her position in the world.

It has been seen already how participation in an unsuccessful war, though it had few direct causal connections with the demand for reform of the governmental system, was bound to provide at least ancillary arguments for the reformers, and also weaken the position of the Government. During 1905, after Tsushima, the position of the Tsar and his Government went from bad to worse. Unrest continued and increased in a familiar pattern: General Trepoff, the new assistant Minister of the Interior, put down disorders in St. Petersburg; in Moscow in February the Grand Duke Sergei, regarded rightly as the most autocratic of the grand ducal clique, was assassinated. On June 28th Count Shuvaloff, the Military Governor of Moscow, also died at the hands of a revolutionary. And on the same day the battleship *Potemkin* of the Black Sea Fleet, its crew in a state of mutiny, sailed into Odessa and provoked a minor revolution. On shore the disturbances were finally put down with considerable bloodshed by Cossacks, but for three weeks the *Potemkin* sailed about the Black Sea, joined temporarily by another mutinous battleship, while the Commander-in-Chief at Sebastopol realised that none of the other ships in his command, the crews in sympathy with the mutineers, would fire on them. Finally, the *Potemkin* was scuttled by its crew in the Roumanian port of Constanza.

By the time that Witte returned in September to Russia from the peace negotiations at Portsmouth, revolutionary unrest had mounted in nearly all the cities of the Russian Empire. In February, apparently much affected by the death of his uncle, the Grand Duke Sergei, the Tsar almost on his own initiative had proclaimed his future intention of summoning a State Duma. In August the universities had been given complete autonomy, an action which, if intended as a conciliatory gesture, failed in its object as immediately the flood gates were opened on anti-governmental agitation and not only from students. Henceforth the argument was as to what powers the Duma should possess. However, the vast volume of protest all over Russia went much further, often expressing a general but powerful disapproval of the Government and all its works.

In October a strike of printers and railwaymen in Moscow snowballed incredibly so that within weeks most of the Empire was in a state of general strike. In St. Petersburg there was the first emergence of a powerful revolutionary committee or Soviet. At the naval base at Sebastopol there was a mutiny on board the *Ochakoff*, and troops returning by the Trans-Siberian Railway from the Far East refused to obey their officers. On October 30th the Tsar proclaimed what was to be known as the October Manifesto, wherein the State Duma was born.

Although the Duma was to be elected on a franchise which deliberately gave more weight to the 'loyal' country than the revolutionary towns, and though its powers were more consultative than legislative, it was a beginning.

Two days later Witte, who had been created a Count for his performance as peace negotiator, became chairman of a council of Ministers which replaced the old committee of Ministers. Russia now had the shadow of a parliament with a Minister who exercised some of the powers of a conventional Prime Minister. It was her first, and as it turned out her last, chance of becoming a democracy under Nicholas II.

No doubt the Tsar was more interested in the reorganisation

of his army, the need for which had been made apparent in the late war. Under the control of the Grand Duke Nicholas Nicholaevich a State Defence Council was created in June 1905 which was the beginning of a number of attempts at reform and reorganisation, none of which, it must be admitted, had any great or lasting effect, so that the army which went into action against the Germans in 1914, though better equipped and better armed, was not in any important particular greatly different from its predecessor of ten years before.

In 1914 the Tsar's army, under the Grand Duke Nicholas, chivalrously invaded East Prussia to aid her ally France, hard pressed in the west by the operation of the dead von Schlieffen's master plan for the capture of Paris. The Russian 1st Army under General Rennenkampf and the 2nd Army under Samsonoff opposed the German VIII Army under von Prittwitz.

He was replaced by Hindenburg and Ludendorff but it was Colonel Max Hoffman on their staff who devised the plan which divided the two Russian armies. Among other factors he counted on the two Russians not co-operating, and was prepared, unlike his superiors, to credit the Russians with stupidity rather than duplicity, in sending their wireless messages not in code but 'in clear'.

In the resultant battle of Tannenberg both Russian armies were defeated, Samsonoff's being virtually destroyed. Samsonoff committed suicide during the retreat and Rennenkampf was disgraced.

Hoffman's insight into Russian military behaviour had been acquired as an observer in the Russo-Japanese war where among other things he had learnt of Generals Rennenkampf and Samsonoff boxing each other's ears on the platform of the railway station at Mukden.

Not untypically the Tsar and his advisers, seeking causes for their humiliating defeat in the Japanese war, looked more to personalities than to principles. There were a number of resignations of senior officers, including, not surprisingly, the Grand Duke Alexei from his post as head of the navy. There were enquiries and courts martial, the most important concentrating on the defeat at Tsushima, and the surrender at Port Arthur.

In the naval court martial Rozhestvensky, remaining something of an enigma to the last, apparently appeared at his own request as both accused and a witness.

Acquitted, as being obviously incapacitated by wounds, for any part he might have thought to have played in the final surrender of the *Biedovy*, he attempted to take full responsibility for the surrender by Clapier de Colongue and the others who had handed him over to the Japanese. Without success, for his Chief of Staff and a number of subordinate officers were all found guilty and sentenced to death.

At Nebogatoff's court martial, Rozhestvensky's testimony was decidedly unhelpful, leaving that officer without any excuse, save humanity, for his surrender. Nebogatoff was found guilty and sentenced to be shot but, as with the sentences on the other naval officers, the Tsar intervened, commuting them to short terms of imprisonment.

The Port Arthur courts martial did not take place until later, presumably because evidence of contraventions of the military code, in what was by any standards a complicated situation, was more difficult to obtain. Stoessel, Fock, Reis, by now a Major-General, and Smirnoff were all tried in 1907, on a number of counts, the principal accusation against the first three being that they had surrendered improperly and prematurely. Stoessel was also accused of sending false information to St. Petersburg on a number of occasions, and Fock of disseminating his defeatist 'notes'. Smirnoff, perhaps a little unfairly, was in reality blamed for not asserting himself and preventing Stoessel, Fock and Reis from behaving as they did. Smirnoff was acquitted as was Reis. Fock was found guilty, but in view of the lapse of time given no punishment. Stoessel was found guilty and sentenced to be shot. Again, however, the Tsar intervened and the sentence was reduced to ten years' imprisonment in a fortress.

For at least a year following the war Russia was in turmoil internally and powerless abroad. This situation was an obvious temptation to Germany and it was taken advantage of by the Kaiser and his advisers in two separate ways and with curious consequences.

The first opportunity occurred in Morocco where it will be

remembered France had been given a free hand by Britain. By the Madrid Convention of 1880 Germany, along with the other parties, was in fact entitled to equal rights in the area. When France began to increase her influence in Morocco a triumvirate of Bülow, Holstein and von Schlieffen, the Chief of the General Staff, decided to put pressure on France while her ally Russia was still weak. Their instrument was the Kaiser who landed on March 30th at Tangier and made a tactless and bombastic speech. The idea grew that Germany wanted a port on Morocco's Atlantic coast. Lord Lansdowne assured the French of British support. Delcassé, their Foreign Minister, therefore resisted the suggestion of a conference of all countries interested in Morocco. The Germans put pressure on Rouvier, the Prime Minister, and Delcassé was forced to resign. The Germans, seemingly winning all along the line, still insisted on a conference.

Meanwhile the Kaiser had been active on his own account, and in July met the Tsar, both monarchs being on their yachts off the island of Björko in the Gulf of Finland. There Wilhelm persuaded the gullible Nicholas to sign a treaty by which Germany and Russia pledged themselves to assist the other if attacked by another European power. The treaty was to operate after peace had been signed with Japan.

The treaty of course cut clean across Russia's alliance with France.

During the course of the Japanese war, especially at the time of the Dogger Bank incident, the Kaiser had tried to push the Tsar towards such an alliance, which he maintained the French would have to join, thus creating an anti-British coalition. He now thought for a brief moment that he had pulled off a master stroke of diplomacy, but he was too late and was considerably disappointed to find that Bülow was not enthusiastic. To the Tsar Lamsdorff, his Foreign Minister, explained that the agreement was an impossibility in view of the Franco-Russian alliance.

By the time that the Algeciras Conference was convened in January 1906 the result of all this rather spectacular German diplomacy was that France and Britain had drawn closer together and were supported by Russia, Witte wanting a substantial loan from France for which he was prepared to trade his support at the Conference. Germany gained nothing of any substance from the Conference, but through it France, Britain and Russia were brought together, a process which was to culminate in an Anglo-Russian Entente in 1907.

The French loan, of 2,250 million francs, was one of Witte's last acts. With the aid of the loan, the October Manifesto combined with firm repressive measures having put down extreme revolutionary activity, the Tsar was able to dissolve the Duma after only seventy-three days of existence. Witte, having served his turn, was dismissed and never held power again. Thus ended the Tsar's experiment with representative government, in which he did not believe, and the active career of the one Russian politician who might have saved the Romanoff dynasty. By then Father Gapon in exile had been murdered by revolutionaries under suspicion of being a police spy.

In order to maintain autocracy Russia had thus been drawn closer to France and thence to Britain. However, Russia, stronger internationally but deprived of her hopes of Empire and influence in the East, then resumed her interest in the West, in the Balkans. The Russian foreign policy pendulum swung back again for the last time under the Tsars. Russian involvement in the Balkans meant rivalry with Austria-Hungary and her German ally, a situation which was to be exploded by the assassination of Franz Ferdinand, heir to the Austro-Hungarian throne, in 1914, into a world war – and this again was to mean a familiar pattern for Russia, military defeat and this time a revolution which brought death to Nicholas II and an end to the Empire of the Romanoffs.

In that war Japan was Britain's active ally, the Anglo-Japanese agreement having been renewed and revised in 1905, the year in which Sir Claude MacDonald, once the hero of the besieged in Peking, became the first full Ambassador of any Western nation accredited to Japan. The alliance was again renewed for ten years in 1911, but in 1921 Britain, yielding to pressure from an increasingly apprehensive U.S.A., replaced a close alliance with the Washington Four Power Treaty which meant nothing, and Britain and Japan drifted apart.

After the Russian revolution in 1917 and the conclusion of

peace in 1918, Japanese troops were to stand alongside British and American in the ill-advised attempt to influence Russian internal affairs by military intervention. The Japanese in fact stayed in Russia long after the allies had gone home, only evacuating Eastern Siberia in 1922 and northern Sakhalin in 1925.

Way back in 1912 an era had ended with the death of the Meiji Emperor. In his enormous funeral procession there marched a detachment of Royal Marines from the British flagship in the Far East. The mood of national mourning was profound, but not even Japanese sentiment was prepared for the consequent suicide in the traditional manner of General Nogi and his wife. Reasons in explanation abounded. It was rumoured that the General had wished to end his life as an expiation of all the Japanese deaths at Port Arthur, but had held his hand at the Emperor's command; others took the view that the ceremonial suicide was of course the traditional gesture of respect, made because Nogi had wished to remind his countrymen again of the old Samurai virtues.

For Japan was changing even in the lifetime of the old Emperor. Ultra-nationalist societies were rising up, often with strong connections in the armed forces. Profiting from Japan's enormously enhanced prestige after her defeat of Russia, these began to have connections with Chinese, Indian, Annamese and Filippino dissidents. The phrase 'Asia for the Asians' began to be heard.

Yet at the same time Japan held firmly to her own absorption of Korea, which she was to use, although she had once looked benevolently on the Chinese revolution of 1911, as a base for her penetration into China in the 1920s and 1930s. Eventually, more and more in the grip of military cliques, she was to be at war with Chiang Kai Shek's China, was to leave the League of Nations and finally ally herself with Hitler's Germany and Mussolini's Italy.

In July of 1938 Japanese troops were again to find themselves fighting Russians on the borders of Manchukuo, Japan's puppet state of Manchuria. It was not however until the last days of the Second World War, on August 9th, 1945, a few days before the dropping of the atom bomb, that the two nations were to be formally at war again. This time the roles were reversed, for Stalin's divisions in a matter of weeks had occupied Harbin and Mukden. At the conclusion of that war Stalin could look back and regard the terms of the peace treaty by which a Russian and Chinese Commission, three Russian representatives to two Chinese, controlled Port Arthur and once again Russian interests were paramount at Dalny, as some revenge for Tsushima. The Russian triumph was however to be short-lived, as a Chinese Communist Government successfully resisted the new Russian imperialism. So Japan's hoped for dominance in South-East Asia was ultimately yielded to a new and revitalised China.

After forty years many wheels were to turn full circle, but perhaps the most spectacular example was to occur even later and within the lifetime of one man.

On April 11th, 1951, during another Korean war General of the Army Douglas MacArthur was dismissed from his supreme command by President Truman for seeking to extend that war into China. Immediately after 1945 MacArthur had been the virtual ruler of defeated and occupied Japan, but that was not his first acquaintance with the Japanese. Born in 1880, as a young lieutenant in October of 1904 he had been sent as an A.D.C. to join his father General Arthur MacArthur who was one of the American military observers with the Japanese army. MacArthur senior was later ordered to extend his observations to what his son, who accompanied him, called 'the colonial lands of the Orient, South-East Asia and India'.

For though it can easily be argued that Russia was not typically European and Japan not typically Asiatic, even during its course, for those who had eyes to see, the Russo-Japanese war had one overall significance. This was best expressed by General Sir Ian Hamilton, the senior British observer, who was himself a decade later to suffer defeat at the hands of the Turks at Gallipoli.

After the battle of Liaoyang he wrote:

'I have today seen the most stupendous spectacle it is possible for the mortal brain to conceive – Asia advancing, Europe falling back, the wall of mist and the writing thereon.'

PLACE NAMES AND THEIR MODERN EQUIVALENTS

Port Arthur	Lu-shun
Dalny (Dairen)	Lii-ta
Mukden	Shen-yang
Harbin	Ha-erh-pin
Chemulpo	Inchon
Pitzuwo	Hsin-chin
Kwantung Peninsula	Luta Peninsula
Chefoo	Yen-t'ai

The above is a list of places where the name has been completely changed. I have rendered them into the form most commonly found in current atlases which still, unlike the text of this work, retain the hyphen. There have been a number of minor variations since 1905 as for instance Seoul as Soul, Tieh-ling as T'ieh-ling, Kamranh Bay as Camranh, Kwantung as Kuan-Tung and the like. In many pre-1905 documents Korea is found as Corea. The names of the principal rivers have however remained constant. The one or two changes in European place names which have occurred since 1905 have been indicated in the text, save for St. Petersburg which was of course briefly Petrograd, during the course of the German war, and then became Leningrad.

A NOTE ON SPELLING

The names of places in the campaign of 1904 and 1905 were Korean, Manchurian, Chinese or Russian. Many of the two former were transliterated into Japanese.

Broadly speaking, at the time, Chinese place names were transliterated into English by the Wade system, which attempted an approximation of pronunciation and was then written with hyphens separating the syllables, e.g. Tai-tzu Ho – Emperor's Son River.

Korean names however tended to be written without hyphens, e.g. Chemulpo.

As a further complication a name such as Mukden which was in fact a Manchu form, though adopted by the Russians, was in Chinese either Feng-tien Fu or Shen-ching, all three versions meaning much the same thing, flourishing or prosperous city.

Modern practice however tends towards simplication and the avoidance of hyphens and this has been done, as far as possible, throughout the book, it being thought that there is little advantage to the eye or the understanding in rendering Kwantung as Kuang-tung. For similar reasons Russian forms such as Kharbin for Harbin have been avoided.

The most common suffixes in Chinese, Shan, Ling and Ho, mean respectively, hill, pass and river, and I thought it better to talk about the Sha river and the Liao river than the Sha-ho or the Liao-ho. However, some actions such as the Sha-ho or the Motien-ling, the battle of the passes, have become so enshrined in military commentaries by usage, even sometimes becoming 'the Sha-ho river', that where the battle itself is referred to and where unavoidable such forms have been allowed to survive.

Those place names which have been changed significantly since 1905 are the subject of a separate note.

The spelling of Russian names by way of transliteration from the Cyrillic presents problems all its own.

As examples, Admiral Vitgeft can be found as Withoft, Felkerzam as Fölkerzam and Stoessel as Stessel, Stossel and Stössel. Perhaps, however, the permutations of Alexieff as Alexieiv and Alexeev and

Aleksieff for instance, are, at least mathematically, the most variable.

Accordingly, it was thought that again the Wade system should be adhered to, as being closest to actual pronunciation, although Alexieff does look a little old-fashioned to the modern eye compared with Alexiev. On the principle of familiarity Nicholas is so spelt and not Nikolai, though technically to write Nicholas Nicholaevich (the Grand Duke) is to mix two systems.

With regard to the names of Russian warships, simplicity has been the aim so that the *Suvoroff* and the *Potemkin* are not rendered by their full names as *Kniaz* (Prince) *Suvoroff* and *Potemkin*. However, complete logic and uniformity is almost impossible so that the reader will encounter *Imperator Alexander III*, another usage which has been hallowed by time.

The Russian Emperor is referred to throughout, save in quotations, as the Tsar, partly because of usage, and also to distinguish him from the Emperor of Japan. Finally, however, on the subject of Russian spelling, perhaps the reader's sympathy will be engaged when he reflects that the English race meeting, the Cesarewitch, was so named as a compliment to the then heir to the Russian throne.

CONTEMPORARY NEWSPAPERS

The newspapers principally consulted have been *The Times, Morning Post* and the *Illustrated London News. Petit Parisien* and *Echo de Paris. Novoye Vremiya* when quoted is as reported in English or French newspapers. It may be pointed out that British and American diplomats reporting back on the state of public opinion made frequent reference to Russian and Japanese newspapers.

THE RUSSIAN CALENDAR

Until February 1918 the Russian Calendar was 'Old Style', as opposed to the Western European, 'New Style'. In consequence, in the nineteenth century Russian dates were 12 days behind Western European and in the twentieth century 13 days behind. Thus, for instance, the Bloody Sunday massacre in St. Petersburg took place according to the Russian Calendar on Sunday January 9th, but according to Western usage on January 22nd.

Throughout this book dates have been given according to the Western Calendar, although on occasions, e.g., when the Russians were celebrating Christmas, the Russian date has also been indicated. Times are on all occasions local, for instance the times of the various stages in the battle of Tsushima are according to Japanese local time.

NOTE ON SOURCES

My principal source throughout, so far as factual information is concerned, has been the monumental and detailed three volumes of the British Official History of the War, the first venture of the then newly formed Historical Section of the Imperial General Staff. In the preparation of their work the British authors had the advantage of consultation with and criticism from both the Russian and the Japanese General Staffs. In addition the Official History makes use of a number of eye-witness accounts such as *Vospominaniya* (Reminiscences) by Captain M. Bubnoff, *Pravda o Port Arturye* (The Truth about Port Arthur) by Nozhin, and Semenoff's *Rasplata* (The Reckoning).

Where necessary I have supplemented the Official History by reference to the reports of the British officers attached to both armies and the reports of the naval attachés. Like the separate account of the siege of Port Arthur also published, these were used in the compilation of the Official History, though not necessarily incorporated in their entirety. I have also used the German Official History, and the French translation of the Russian Official History. Quotations from documents in the text, for instance the Orders of the Day of both Kuropatkin and Oyama, are derived from the above-mentioned sources.

For descriptions of particular incidents, e.g. the action round Port Arthur or at Liaoyang, I have endeavoured to use as much as possible the accounts of actual eye-witnesses, particularly the large number of war correspondents who covered the war, many of whom later put their experiences into book form.

So far as the accounts by combatants themselves were concerned the material available is very variable in both quantity and quality. No Russian in the ranks of the army recorded his impressions of the conflict, the nearest approach was a few rather artificial interviews and allegedly genuine letters printed in Russian newspapers. The Japanese throughout the war published a popular weekly illustrated history in Tokyo which also had an English language version. It contained a number of comments by Japanese officers and men, but they too suffered from artificiality.

General speaking, officers of both nations, naturally enough in the circumstances of the time, produced more reminiscences than their men, and the navies would seem to have been more literate than the armies. Unfortunately, however, the Japanese accounts, at least in translation, are all much of a piece, full of courageous action and patriotic sentiments, while more or less every Russian tended to write an apologia. Plainly the most literate body of men, of whatever rank, either Russian or Japanese, were those of the Second Pacific Squadron. Consequently, there are a number of accounts of Rozhestvensky's voyage written by men who had considerable spare time and frequently an axe to grind as well. In J. M. Westwood's recent *Witnesses of Tsushima* there is an admirable analysis of the 'line' taken, for instance pro- or anti-Rozhestvensky, by each of the authors quoted.

Of the senior commanders involved, unfortunately only Kuropatkin, in his two-volume work, committed himself to substantial comment on the war. Many other Russians no doubt felt it better to keep silent. After the war there was a tendency in Russia to place blame for a national disaster on any shoulder but one's own. Consequently, Kuropatkin's account of the prelude to the war, just like Witte's, must be read with caution. Enough of Captain Klado's character has no doubt been already demonstrated in the text for his views to be treated very circumspectly indeed.

The reader will notice in the bibliography and list of official documents that I have paid particular attention to U.S. sources and commentators. This for a number of reasons, first, a great deal of work, more indeed than by any non-involved nation, has been done in the U.S.A. on the causes and developments of the war. Secondly, the U.S.A. can claim a greater degree of impartiality than say either Britain or France, who were allied to the two belligerents. Finally, because the shift of official opinion in the U.S.A. during the course of the war away from the Japanese was to be mirrored by many other nations later, as apprehension about ultimate Japanese ambitions increased.

In the bibliography I have attempted to give short explanations, where necessary, of the significance of particular works or authors.

Finally, I have to make an admission, part apology, part confession. I have a deep-rooted objection to footnotes which distract the eye and sometimes the mind. I object even more strongly to pages bespattered with asterisks and daggers or irritating little numbers. This is a work intended as much for the general reader as the specialist, so that I have attempted to make it 'self-contained'.

I must confess that I do not know if the ordinary reader on encountering one of those little numbers is expected immediately to suspend his reading and thumb his way forward to the often un-illuminating reference or else, after he has read the main text, to go through the source notes, referring back to the text.

Consequently, I have attempted to identify quotations on the spot by saying 'as Witte said in his memoirs', or 'as Rozhestvensky said in an interview with such and such a newspaper'. Sometimes in the case of the short quotation I have omitted the source both in the text or the source notes and bibliography, but I hope not inexcusably. For instance, Franz Josef's remark about the Boer War to the British Ambassador in Vienna, will in fact be found quoted in Edward Crankshaw's *Fall of the House of Hapsburg*, but that excellent work would, I feel, look somewhat out of place in a bibliography of the Russo-Japanese war.

On other occasions I have taken the view that the source is sufficiently obvious and that the reader seeking further illumination will find it where he might expect. For instance, the debates in the House of Lords and the House of Commons can be read in their full length and context in the relevant Hansard.

D. W.

OFFICIAL HISTORIES, DOCUMENTS
AND REPORTS

British Documents on the Origins of the World War 1898–1914. Vols.
I–IV. London 1926–38.

British Parliamentary Papers 1900–1905: China and the Far East
(Blue Books). London 1910.

Cabinet Papers 1904 and 1905. Public Record Office London.
(The three principal sets of papers are referenced as CAB 41/29
and 37/72 and ADM 116, 169 and 170.) Case 293, Vols I and II.

Committee of Imperial Defence Historical Section. *Official History,
Naval and Military, of the Russo-Japanese War.* Vols I–III.
London 1910.
(The last volume was completed in 1914 but not published until
1920.)

Correspondence relating to the North Sea Incident 1905. London 1905.
(Command Paper 2350.)

*Correspondence respecting Contraband of War in connection with
Hostilities between Russia and Japan.* H.M.S.O. London 1905.

*Dispatch from the British Agent forwarding the Report of the Com-
missioners of the International Committee of Inquiry on the North
Sea Incident.* London 1905.
(Command Paper 22382.)

Dispatches from the U.S. Consuls in Nagasaki 1860–1906. U.S.
National Archives.

Dispatches from the U.S. Ministers to Russia 1808–1906. U.S.
National Archives.

Foreign Relations of the United States, 1903, 1904, and 1905: Japan.
The Library of Congress.
(For the reports of the U.S. Consuls to the State Department.)

German General Staff Historical Section. *The Russo-Japanese War.*
Vols I–IX. London 1909.
(Translated by Karl von Donat.)

La Guerre Russo-Japonaise 1904–5. Vols. I–IV. Paris 1911.
(The French General Staff translation of the Russian Official
History.)

Official Reports of the Russo-Japanese War. Vols I and II. (Edited by M. Kinai.) London 1905.
These are the translations of the Japanese reports.

Passage of the Second Pacific Squadron. London 1904 (Naval Institute).
(Papers captured from the Russians by the Japanese and re-translated by G. V. Raymant.)

Reports from the British Officers attached to the Japanese and Russian Forces in the Field. Vols I–V. London 1908.

Reports of the British Naval Attachés. Vols I–V. London 1908.

Reports on the North Sea Incident by the Commissioners appointed by the Board of Trade. London 1905.
(Command Paper 2451.)

The Official Report (Hansard) of the House of Lords and the House of Commons. 1904 and 1905.

U.S.A. Office of Naval Intelligence 1904–5. Register No. 169. U.S. National Archives.

War Department U.S. Army. Reports of the Military Observers attached to the Armies in Manchuria. Washington 1906.

LETTERS AND DIARIES

The Kaiser's Letters to the Tsar. (Edited N. F. Grant.) London 1920. This, the 'Willy-Nicky Correspondence,' began in 1894 and continued until early 1914.

The Letters and Friendships of Sir Cecil Spring Rice. (Edited S. Gwynn.) Vols. I and II. London 1929. Spring Rice was in the British Embassy in Washington from 1886–95 when be became a friend of Theodore Roosevelt. From 1903–6 he was Secretary of the Embassy at St. Petersburg and from 1913–18 he was Ambassador to the U.S.A.

The Diary of Emperor Nicholas II (Dnevnik Imperatora Nikolaya II), *1890–1906.* Berlin 1923; also *Nicholas II, Journal Intime* (Translated A. Pierre). Paris 1925.

The Secret Letters of the Last Tsar (to and from his mother, the Dowager Empress Marie Feodorovna). (Edited J. E. Bing.) London 1937.

The Letters of Theodore Roosevelt. (Edited Elting E. Morison.) Vols II, III and IV. Harvard 1951–4.

Selections from the Correspondence of Theodore Roosevelt and Henry Cabot Lodge, 1884–1918. Vol. II. New York 1925.

SELECT BIBLIOGRAPHY

(This does not include all works, especially those of a general nature, consulted by the author, but is an attempt where possible to give a representative selection of eye-witness and contemporary reports as well as later commentaries.)

ALEXANDER, GRAND DUKE. *Once a Grand Duke.* New York 1933.

ANDREW, C. *Theophile Delcassé and the Making of the Entente Cordiale.* London 1968.

ASAKAWA, K. *The Russo-Japanese Conflict: Its causes and issues.* London 1904. (This was the first Japanese 'version' and was published simultaneously in Britain, the U.S.A. and Japan.)

BALFOUR, M. *The Kaiser and his Times.* London 1964.

BARING, M. (Correspondent of the *Morning Post.*) *With the Russians in Manchuria.* London 1905.

BARR, P. *The Coming of the Barbarians. The Story of the Western Settlement in Japan.* London 1967.

BARTLETT, ASHMEAD, E. (Correspondent of *The Times.*) *Port Arthur: The Siege and Capitulation.* London 1906.

BECKMANN, G. M. *The Modernisation of China and Japan.* New York 1962.

BIRD, LT-COL. W. D. *Lectures on the Strategy of the Russo-Japanese War.* London 1911.

BODLEY, R. V. C. *Admiral Togo.* (The Official biography.) London 1935.

BOMPARD, M. *Mon Ambassade en Russie 1903–1908.* Paris, 1937.

BROOKE, LORD. (Reuter's Correspondent.) *An Eye Witness in Manchuria.* London 1905.

VON BÜLOW, PRINCE. *Memoirs 1903–1909,* Vol. II. New York 1931.

BURLEIGH, B. (Correspondent of the *Daily Telegraph.*) *Empire of the East.* London 1905.

CHARQUES, R. *The Twilight of Imperial Russia.* London 1958.

CORDONNIER, COLONEL E. L. V. *The Japanese in Manchuria,* Vols I and II. (Translated by C. F. Atkinson.) London 1912 and 1914.

COWEN, T. (Correspondent of the *Daily Chronicle.*) *The Russo-Japanese War.* London 1904.

CURZON, HON. G. (later Lord Curzon). *Russia in Central Asia.* London 1889. (The product of his tour of the area, part travelogue, part reflections.)

CUSTANCE, ADMIRAL SIR R. *The Ship of the Line in Battle.* London 1912.

DALLIN, D. J. *The Rise of Russia in Asia.* New York 1950.

DARRIEUS, CAPTAIN G. *War on the Sea.* (Translated by P. R. Alger.) U.S. Navy Institute, Annopolis 1908. (The French and Anglophobe view of the Japanese victories.)

DILLON, E. J. *The Eclipse of Russia.* New York 1918.

DUA, R. *The Impact of the Russo-Japanese War on Indian Politics.* Delhi 1966.

ESTHUS, R. A. *Theodore Roosevelt and Japan.* Washington 1967.

EUBANK, K. *Paul Cambon.* Oklahoma, 1960. (French Ambassador in London during the war.)

DE GRANDPREY, GENERAL C. *Le Siège de Port Arthur.* Paris 1906.

GURKO, V. I. *Features and Figures from the Past. Government and Opinion in the Reign of Nicholas II.* Stamford 1939. (Gurko was a member of the Imperial Chancellery until 1906, serving for a period as assistant to Plehve.)

HACKETT, R. F. *Yamagata Aritomo and the Rise of Modern Japan 1838–1922.* Harvard 1971.

HAMILTON, LT-GEN. SIR I. *A Staff Officer's Scrap Book during the Russo-Japanese War,* Vols I and II. London 1905, 1907. (This is the journal of the senior British observer and is written almost entirely from the Japanese point of view.)

HARCAVE, S. *First Blood, The Russian Revolution of 1905.* London 1964.

HARGREAVES, R. *Red Sun Rising. The Siege of Port Arthur.* London 1962.

HOUGH, R. *The Fleet that had to die.* London 1958.

HOUGH, R. *The Potemkin Mutiny.* London 1960.

HOWLAND, COLONEL C. R. Lectures to the U.S. Command and General Staff College 1921. (Unpublished, made available to the author by the U.S. War College, Carlisle, Pa.)

JAMES, D. (Correspondent of the *Daily Telegraph.*) *The Siege of Port Arthur.* London 1905.

JANE, F. T. *The Imperial Russian Navy.* London 1904.

JANE, F. T. *The Imperial Japanese Navy.* London 1904. (Factual details of both fleets.)

KLADO, CAPTAIN H. *The Battle of the Sea of Japan*. London 1906.

KLADO, CAPTAIN H. *The Russian Navy in the Russo-Japanese War*. London 1905.

KOKOVSTOFF, V. N. *Out of my Past*. Stamford, 1935. (Kokovtsoff was' Finance Minister from 1906–11 being dismissed, like Witte, after he had obtained a French loan.)

KUROPATKIN, GENERAL A. N. *The Russian Army and the Japanese War*, Vols I and II. (Translated by A. B. Lindsay.) London 1909. (Very much a tactful apologia by the Russian C.-in-C.)

LANGER, W. L. *The Diplomacy of Imperialism*. New York, 1951.

LANGER, W. L. *The Franco-Russian Alliance 1890–1894*. Cambridge, Mass. 1929.

VON LAUE, T. H. *Sergei Witte and the Industrialisation of Russia*. London 1963.

LEDERER, I. J. (Editor.) *Russian Foreign Policy* (especially Part III, 8, and Part IV, 16). Yale 1962.

LUVAAS, J. *The Education of an Army*. London 1965. (For 'The Voice of the Thunderer' on Lt.-Col. Repington.)

MACINTYRE, CAPTAIN D. *The Thunder of the Guns*. London 1959. (For naval battles of the Russo-Japanese war.)

McKENZIE, F. A. *From Tokyo to Tiflis*. London 1905. (Uncensored letters from the Correspondent of the *Daily Mail*.)

MAGNUS, P. *King Edward VII*. London 1959.

MAHAN, CAPTAIN A. T. *Naval Strategy*. London 1911. (Comments on Port Arthur and the naval battles.)

MALAZEMOFF, A. *Russian Far Eastern Policy 1881–1904*. Berkeley, California 1958. (Perhaps the only, and certainly the best, presentation of the Russian viewpoint in English.)

MARDER, A. J. *From the Dreadnought to Scapa Flow*. London 1961.

MASON, R. H. P. *Japan's First General Election 1890*. Cambridge 1969.

MAXWELL, W. (Correspondent of the *Standard*.) *From the Yalu to Port Arthur*. London 1964.

MIRSKY, D. S. *Russia, a Social History*. London 1931.

DE NEGRIER, GENERAL F. O. *Lessons of the Russo-Japanese War*. London 1906.

NEWTON, LORD. *Lord Lansdowne*. London 1929.

NORREGAARD, B. W. *The Great Siege*. London 1906.

NOZHIN, E. K. *The Truth about Port Arthur*. New York, 1908.

NISH, H. *The Anglo-Japanese Alliance: The Diplomacy of the two Island Empires 1894–1907*. London 1966.

NOVIKOV-PRIBOY, A. S. *Tsushima*. Moscow 1958.

OKAMOTO, S. *The Japanese Oligarchy and the Russo-Japanese War.* Columbia 1970.

PALMER, F. *John J. Pershing, General of the Armies.* Harrisburg 1948. (Early chapters only. Pershing was a U.S. observer with the Japanese at Mukden, but his comments do not appear with those of the other U.S. military observers.)

PARES, B. *The Fall of the Russian Monarchy.* New York 1939.

PAYNE, R. *The Fortress.* London 1967. (Not Port Arthur, but St. Peter and St. Paul, being a study of the Russian revolutionaries in the nineteenth century.)

POLITOVSKY, E. *From Libau to Tsushima.* London 1907.

POOLEY, A. M. (Editor). *The Secret Memoirs of Count Tadasu Hayashi.* London 1915.

ROOSEVELT, THEODORE. *An Autobiography.* London 1913. (By no means as revealing as his letters.)

ROSEN, BARON R. R. *Forty Years of Diplomacy,* Vols I and II. New York 1922. (Written after his escape from Russia, without his papers, and therefore, as he admits, somewhat hazy on dates and details.)

SAKURAI, LIEUT. T. *Human Bullets.* Boston 1907.

SEMENOFF, CAPTAIN V. *The Battle of Tsushima.* (Translated Captain Lendery.) London 1906.

SEMENOFF, CAPTAIN V. *Rasplata* (The Reckoning). (Translated 'L.A.B.') London 1909.

SETON-WATSON, H. *The Decline of Imperial Russia 1055–1914.* London 1952.

SIMPSON, B. L. *The Re-shaping of the Far East.* London 1911.

SMITH, R. W. (Associated Press Correspondent.) *The Siege and Fall of Port Arthur.* London 1905.

TAKEUCHI, T. *Wars and Diplomacy in the Japanese Empire.* London 1936.

TOGO, CAPTAIN. *Naval Battles of the Russo-Japanese War.* Tokyo 1907. (This Togo was a nephew of the Admiral and also a participant in the actions.)

THE TIMES. *The War in the Far East.* London 1905. (This is in essence a collection of the dispatches of the principal War Correspondent, Colonel Repington.)

TRETYAKOFF, LT. GENERAL N. A. *My Experiences at Nanshan and Port Arthur.* London 1911.

WESTWOOD, J. M. *Witnesses of Tsushima.* Tokyo 1970. (Selected extracts from the accounts of eye-witnesses such as Semenoff,

Novikov-Priboy and Politovsky before, during and after the battle with informed linking commentary.)

WHITE, J. A. *The Diplomacy of the Russo-Japanese War*. Princeton 1964.

WILSON, H. W. *Battleships in Action*, Vol. I. London 1926.

WITTE, COUNT S. I. *Reminiscences*, Vols. I, II and III. London 1922. (Translated and edited by A. Yarmolinsky and published after Witte's death in 1915.)

YOUNG, K. *Balfour*. London 1963.

INDEX

Index 319